RAISING LAZARUS
INTEGRAL HEALING IN
ORTHODOX CHRISTIANITY

What an amazing book! Drawing on the integration of science and the magnificent depths of Orthodox Christian faith and practice, I believe that *Raising Lazarus* will help psychotherapists, physicians, nurses and priests of any faith who are called to help others find the Way to spiritual wellbeing. Persons who are in counseling as well as healing professionals themselves, on their own spiritual journeys, will be helped to find in their souls "the place where God and man come to meet each other in greatest intimacy and greatest creativity".

Dimitrios G. Oreopoulos

Raising Lazarus takes an adventuresome approach to the fundamental practical issue raised by the Christian faith: how are we to live the union of divine and human life that is offered to us by Christ? The book's clear reply is: Certainly not by a 'spiritual' manner of living, if that means ignoring the psychological and bodily aspects of our being. In their different ways the contributors invite us to use the insights of the Fathers as well as those of contemporary depth psychology in our search for wholeness in Christ, thereby confirming that the Tradition of the Church is quite capable of facing the challenges of the new century in a lively and constructive manner.

Bishop Basil of Sergievo

"*Raising Lazarus* invites the reader to enter into a conversation with Orthodox thinkers about how and why the two thousand year old theological, liturgical, and spiritual traditions of Orthodox Christianity engage with the contemporary world. Read this book for a unique and wholesome perspective."

Fr. Stanley S. Harakas

Integral Healing, at least according to Orthodox Christian theological teaching and spiritual practice, involves more than mere correction and improvement of various aspects of mind and soul. It includes the death and resurrection of the entire human person. The papers in this volume underline precisely that. Such is the legacy of the early ascetic tradition and the emphasis of contemporary therapy. Anyone who has even remotely tasted such a death recognizes and rejoices in this truth.

Fr. John Chryssavigis

RAISING LAZARUS

INTEGRAL HEALING IN
ORTHODOX CHRISTIANITY

Edited
by
Stephen Muse

HOLY CROSS ORTHODOX PRESS
Brookline, Massachusetts

© Copyright 2004 Holy Cross Orthodox Press
Published by Holy Cross Orthodox Press
50 Goddard Avenue
Brookline, Massachusetts 02445

ISBN 1-885652-79-8

LIBRARY OF CONGRESS CATALOGING–IN–PUBLICATION DATA

Raising Lazarus : integral healing in orthodox Christianity / edited by Stephen Muse.
    p. ; cm.
 Includes bibliographical references.
 ISBN 1-885652-79-8 (softcover : alk. paper)
 1. Spiritual healing. 2. Lazarus, of Bethany, Saint. 3. Orthodox Eastern Church--Doctrines.
 [DNLM: 1. Eastern Orthodoxy. 2. Religion and Medicine. 3. Religion and Psychology. 4. Spiritual Therapies. 5. Spirituality. W 61 R159 2004] I. Muse, Stephen.
 BT732.5.R35 2004   261.5'61--dc22
                                2004025957

This volume is dedicated to

John T. Chirban

the "founding father" of OCAMPR, who has provided over a decade of creative, tenacious and generous leadership among a small, but growing group of Orthodox Christian priests and healing professionals in the United States and abroad, who are committed to the dialogue and integration between religion and science in service of the Church and our aching world.

Thank you John.

CONTENTS

Preface   1
Fr. Nicholas C. Triantafilou

Introduction: Physicians for this World and the Next   3
Stephen Muse

Healing the Bodymind

Historical Precedents for Synergia: Combining Medicine,
   Diakonia and Sacrament in Byzantine Times   15
John G. Demakis

Regenerating the Heart: A Holistic Perspective   25
Peter Bistolarides

From Neurobiology to Uncreated Light   41
Paul Kymissis

Healing the Suffering Person

The Complexities of a Person   53
Stephen Muse

Psychiatric Considerations   61
Jeff Rediger

Theological Considerations   85
Fr. Stephen Plumlee

Pastoral Psychological Response:
   An Orthodox Expression of Pastoral Counseling   95
Demetra Jaquet

The Journey Continues: Postscript on "Ted"   113
Stephen Muse

Christian Asceticism and Cognitive
   Behavioral Psychology   119
Fr. George Morelli

Healing the Healers

Pollution of the Soul:
   The Dangers of Literalism and Psychologism   131
John Perkins

Spiritual War: The Relevance to Modern Therapy
   of the Ancient Eastern Orthodox Christian
   Path of Ascetical Practice   145
Jamie Moran

Healing in Community

The Spiritual Life and How to be Married in It   215
Philip Mamalakis

Ekklesia, the Relational Heart of Community   229
Fr. Niko Graff

Response to Fr. Niko Graff   247
George Christakis

Response to Fr. Niko Graff   255
Fr. George Morelli

Contributors   259

Preface

Looking at his spiritual daughter or son, our late and beloved Bishop Gerasimos of Abydos would often place a finger on his own lips and lovingly gesture that she/he not speak but listen – listen prayerfully. Early into my privileged reading of this wonderfully edited text by Dr. Stephen Muse, I vividly pictured our wise confessor and mentor beckoning me to be a prayerful reader of a most timely and needed writing.

Question: Which color of the fall foliage is distinctively more attractive than the others?

Question: Which writing in Raising Lazarus is distinctively more penetrating than the others?

The answer to both questions might be the same. Without all the colors, the fall foliage would lack degrees of grandeur. Without all the articles, Raising Lazarus would lack degrees of visionary impact.

Each pilgrim seeks personal dimensions of healing. Each human has empty space waiting to be filled by God's understanding presence. In each offering, readers will find particular insights that will answer questions, inspire contemplation and evoke challenges. Raising Lazarus can be helpful for class discussion, for personal study and for topical paper assignments. Throughout the book, authors present factual data with wise commentary as they invite the reader to reflect upon personal experiences.

1

While healing is certainly multidimensional, God's gift of grace remains the essence of all medical practices and counseling venues. The contributing authors reveal the intimacy of healing within a world threatening to become tragically impersonal. Each address represents a door opening to special research and study meeting the needs of searching believers. The recognition of divine presence is wonderfully coupled with a humility of professional expertise. Quotations from ascetic giants and historic church fathers are woven into this tapestry of authentic Christian Orthodox intercessory appeal for God's revelations toward healing. We who prayerfully read Raising Lazarus undoubtedly will experience God's restoring grace.

Rev. Nicholas C. Triantafilou

Introduction

PHYSICIANS FOR THIS
WORLD AND THE NEXT

STEPHEN MUSE

Use your health, even to the point of wearing it out.
That is what it is for.
Spend all you have before you die;
do not outlive yourself.
– George Bernard Shaw

My prayer is that I am fully alive when I die.
D.W. Winnicott

In the twenty-first century, as in the first, we do not wage war against flesh and blood, but against "powers and principalities in the heavens" (Eph 6:12), who increasingly would have us believe we are merely flesh and blood and therefore must cling to this life alone as the only one we will ever have, infected by fear of death and all the other associated afflictive passions that cripple the heart's capacity for embracing the cross and risking the love which is manifest in Christ who is the Way, the Truth and the Life of humanity. It is precisely our attachment to these blinding and heart-deadening illusions which is the real sickness in our lives.

An increasing interest in "spirituality" has arisen in American culture in recent years – particularly the relationship between spirituality and health. "Spiritual" has become a lucrative word that adds thousands of dollars in sales if included in a book's title or on a conference's agenda. Perhaps it is because it reminds us of a great need that is going unmet in our wildly affluent (for some), self indulgent and increasingly materialistic time. Yet it is a highly ambiguous term and ill-defined word, though wrapped in the unquestioned warmth of generally positive associations with it.

The U.S. Government spent $28 billion dollars on health research and training in 2003, an amount in excess of the combined totals of all nations in the rest of the world (1). We have a health care technology that is the best the world has ever known. Yet for most of recorded history, medicine and religion developed together, but perhaps with the advent of antibiotics and other modern methods that often bring quick and dramatic physical or mental results, healing has become increasingly the province of physicians (and to some extent psychotherapists). Over the course of the last century, until quite recently, religion slowly faded from the medical scene. Persons first became "patients" and then, as both the healers and those seeking relief were managed and defined by forces that regulated our lives not according to wholeness, ecological harmony, depth and meaning in the light of Christ, but rather according to numerical efficiency and cost, "patient" has given way to "customer" or merely *consumer*. This is certainly *not* "spiritual" progress, whatever face may be put upon it.

Orthodox Christianity provides an important counterweight to these culturally defining forces inundating us through increasingly sophisticated advertising and market pressures that shape and in many ways distort and defame human value by inflaming appetites that fuel a voracious economic machine whose success appears to be dependent on accepting a lower view of human potential than that proclaimed by the reality of the Christian Gospel. As the contributors to this volume reveal, Orthodox Christianity provides a lucid critique of the aims and quality of modern therapeutic practices as well as an integral context for healing which involves a "synergy" between human and divine, locating both healer and healed as co-pilgrims traversing the same Divinely-given common ground, which has been a hallmark of Christian faith from its inception.

As early as the fourth century, the Cappadocian fathers articulated a spiritual anthropology of *personhood* rooted in the Orthodox Christian understanding of the Incarnation and the Holy Trinity which linked healing science with the Sacramental Theology and compassionate ethos of Christian faith. It was an unprecedented historical advance, yet some 1700 years later, the twentieth-first century marks a rapidly deteriorating trajectory that is depersonalizing and undoing what was begun in those early centuries and protected in subsequent ones by those few who "gave blood in order to receive Spirit."

Orthodox Christians do not see themselves as citizens of this world only, but of a greater kingdom than Caesar's whose bounds are not time and space, but the infinite pure Body and Precious Blood of Jesus Christ in whom we place our hope to one day live in the fullness and eternal joy of the Holy Trinity. For Orthodox Christians, life is primarily an arena of struggle to respond with body, mind, soul and heart, to the Uncreated Grace of God which is "in all places and fills all things, the treasury of blessings" which transfigures us so that we are born, "not of the flesh or of the will of man, but of God" (Jn 1:13). It is an effort and a wakefulness that is made together in harmony with the created world and the fellowship of the whole human race. Nor is this deep healing of body, mind, soul and heart for the "patient" alone, but is needed by all who seek to alleviate the ills of others. This is true whatever our calling, whether to medicine, psycho-therapy or the priesthood, for all are called to *personhood*.

Though simply put and gratefully acknowledged, the synergy of religion and science is not easily embraced in practice. It involves not merely (or necessarily) a technical or academic education, but, as Jan Perkins and Jamie Moran point out, it is an intentional and lifelong engagement in *spiritual struggle* with forces that impede the aim and obscure the intention of coming to full repentance and free obedient response to God in and through the Passion of Christ, on behalf of all life that renders us existentially *real*. This is the great medicine Christianity offers the world. Apart from it, humankind, though made in the image of God, cannot achieve God's *likeness* and in so doing, in the words of St. Anthony, *become ourselves* or be in harmony with the created order. Orthodox Christianity is not a religion but a love relationship. If God is not *person*, then we cannot be either.

Lazarus was brought back to life physically, but physical healing and life extension are not equivalent to spiritual well-being. Even if Lazarus had managed to live another hundred or even a thousand years in perfect physical health, as modern technology increasingly aims for, death would eventually have overtaken him. The more important question for Lazarus and for each of us, whether we are given a few years or many to live, with physical or mental infirmity or with vitality, is whether we receive it from the hand of God in peace and through prayerful responsiveness become *persons* in the fullest sense of the word, *with and for others* as Christ is for each of us. For as St. Irenaeus observed, "The glory of God is a human being fully alive."

Neither is physical or mental vitality a necessary sign of spiritual health, as the lives of the saints reveal. In our own times the celebrated Athonite, Brother Joseph the Hesychast, had a bacterial infection from a boil that he almost died from because he would not get it medically treated. His way in life, as for so many who have gone before him, was to accept whatever happened without protest as being from God's hand. Fortunately for those who benefited from his life and counsel, Brother Joseph responded to the entreaties of his spiritual children to seek medical help and survived to continue as spiritual leader to many who then went on to provide light for thousands of spiritual children on Mt. Athos and around the world.

Another modern spiritual elder, Porphyrios, beloved of thousands of spiritual children around the world, suffered shingles "like hot scalding oil" on his face, along with several other serious, painful and debilitating maladies throughout much of his life and though his prayers healed others, he would not pray for his own healing because he said the sickness helped his repentance. He even worked as chaplain in the Polyclinic hospital in modern Athens, where he was consulted by physicians on difficult medical problems, even though he himself was not academically trained. Through his faithfulness and ascesis, the Grace of God enabled the Elder early in his life to "see" the type and position of tumors in the body, correctly diagnose illnesses and his holy prayers healed many. He frequently offered physicians guidance as to how to perform their own interventions of healing for which they were scientifically trained. The Elder even began to read medical journals, amazed at the partnership that had arisen between God, himself and the hospital. Indeed it was a wondrous partnership here in our own time, as miraculous as the stories from the first-century Gospel accounts, yet nevertheless there remains a certain tension. Does one become a *physician* by academic learning and/or by ascesis? To what extent does one seek healing for oneself along the way or does it interfere with one's repentance? Surely these are personal and individual questions requiring discernment, pastoral care and guidance, yet they are also questions that evoke interest in the relationship between Grace and technology, being and becoming, human will and divine will in co-creative synergy. The tension inherent in these examples provokes important questions regarding ministry to suffering persons as well as implications for how we train priests, physicians and psychotherapists in terms of both science, ascesis and the sacramental life..

Elder Zacharias of the Community of St. John the Baptist in Essex, England, founded by Archimandrite Sophrony, tells of a woman who sought him out with a diagnosis of cancer. Her physician had given her a life expectancy of six months, based on his medical knowledge. When she asked the elder's counsel, he responded in an unusual way: "Wonderful. You have six months to prepare for the most important encounter of your life…"

With his counsel and prayers and the woman's fervent response, she used those six months to pray continuously in her hospital room in the midst of the comings and goings of physicians, nurses and hospital personnel. On the elder's third and last visit with her, he reports that her body was eaten up with cancer and only her face seemed alive. She was weeping (as her lips said the prayer continually according to his counsel) and he asked her what was wrong.

"Elder, I do not feel that I am worthy of the Grace of having this illness!"

Can you imagine such humility! The elder reports that after her death he found himself weeping openly even in the midst of his brother monks at the monastery, something that one tries to hide out of humility. The oldest monk, Fr. Symeon, noticed his unusual state and asked him what was wrong. Elder Zacharias told him that he was experiencing something rare that had happened only twice before in his life. In his heart he was hearing over and over the words, "She is saved. She is saved." It was a wondrous consolation for him and we are fortunate that he shared it as an example of the power of repentance and prayer to open a way for grace in our lives, even in seemingly the worst possible conditions.

Such are the mysteries of Christian faith and the incredibly wide range of "healing" partnerships that are involved according to the mystery of God. Some are healed without ever being cured physically, because healing is deeper than the flesh itself. In other cases, perfect health and/or beauty attained through the means of liposuction, breast implants and other forms of "extreme makeovers" do not affect and may even damage the growing soul in the same way that wealth, beauty, intelligence and other potential gifts can be sources of curse rather than blessings, according to the disposition of the soul and the intentions of the heart.

One of the tensions that evoke many questions regarding the relationship between academic learning, technical training and ascesis is that God-bearing elders like Brother Joseph, Elder Porphyrios and other physicians of soul and body tend to be trained, like St. Anthony, in the "university of the desert." Asceticism, worship, fasting, prayer, repentance and obedience are the courses they take to become physicians of soul and body and such courses last a lifetime. Furthermore, they never work alone, apart from the oversight of their Supervisor, the Physician of our souls and bodies. This is a key element of Orthodox Christian healing, for as Peter Bistolarides points out in his reflections on medicine, not all "spirituality" is Orthodox. And not all psychological theories are equally useful in understanding and ministering to suffering persons as is shown in the case of "Ted," examined from theological, psychiatric and psychological perspectives. Yet the value of seeing from many perspectives is undoubtedly useful, for as Einstein observed, "It is theory which shows us what we can observe."

In a time when, as Jamie Moran points out, "superman" is preferred over Christ and the self-divinizing Promethean path to God re-emerges in the form of technological attempts to understand and usurp the power of God apart from humble personal relationship with the Creator, it is not surprising that the production of alpha waves, acquisition of supernormal powers, physical vitality, beauty and material prosperity are held to be the signs of divine blessing, in contrast to the more invisible fruits of the Spirit, which remain the same as always, such as charity, faithfulness, humility, poverty of spirit, kindness, gentleness and compassion.

Apart from the fullness of the divine life, there will always be something incomplete in us, a kind of longing that cannot be satisfied in this world, but only in the next, and never alone, but only in relationship with God and others. Therefore we desperately need healers who treat us not only for ills in this world, but offer guidance and care for achieving health and citizenship in the Other; healers who rely not on technology derived from humanly devised research protocols alone, but who themselves are struggling to enter into the fullness of relationship with God and the beloved community and so bring to the healing partnership humility, a loving awareness of the presence of God and the sanctity and mystery of every life.

All of the contributors to this volume take this challenge seriously and with their contributions invite the reader to consider how our approaches to illness and health exist within a much larger context than the ones we generally respond from. If the aim of life is to find out how to love and bear our crosses along with Christ for the redemption of all Creation, then achieving physical or psychological comfort and well-being in and of themselves may not be the most vital necessity.

Synergy between God and humankind involves a tension that remains worthy of exploration personally and professionally. This is one of the *raisons d'etre* for OCAMPR (the other being fellowship among members) and it is evidenced by the perspectives of contributors to this volume, adapted from presentations in the 12th and 13th annual national conferences of the Orthodox Christian Association of Medicine,

Psychology and Religion held at Hellenic College/Holy Cross Greek Orthodox School of Theology in 2002 and 2003 on the weekends of the feast day of the Patron Saints of OCAMPR, Sts. Cosmas and Damian, the Unmercenary Physicians. By their prayers we offer this volume to the glory of God and in praise of the Incarnation and Passion of our Lord Jesus Christ who shows us the depth and eternal love of our Father in Heaven and in thanksgiving for our Lord's Resurrection and the eternal procession of the Holy Spirit who is our Comforter and Guide, by the prayers of the Holy Theotokos and all the Saints.

Notes

1. G. Weissmann, "American Medicine and Mozart Quartets." (in *Science & Spirit*. Nov/Dec. 2003), p38.

References

Archimandrite Zacharias Zakharou, *Ascetical and Pastoral Theology of St. Silouan the Athonite and Archimandrite Sophrony,* (Springdale, Arkansas: Orthodox Christian Cassettes), 2003.
Elder Joseph, *Elder Joseph the Hesychast,* (Mt Athos, Greece: Holy Monastery of Vatopaidi), 1999.
Constantine Yiannitsiotis, *With Elder Porphyrios: A Spiritual Child Remembers,* (Athens: Holy Convent of the Transfiguration of the Savior), 2001.

The body is the unconscious mind.

Mind doesn't dominate body, it becomes body – body and mind are one.

What Descartes once thought of separately as body and mind are seen now as different expressions of the same information carried by chemical transmitters. These neurotransmitters are what make it possible for a mental perception coded electrically in the brain to be translated into chemicals that influence hormonal secretions which change the body which in turn sends other messages to the brain through the nerves in a constant feedback loop.

For Freud and Jung, the unconscious was still a hypothetical construct. For us, the unconscious more definitely means psychobiological levels of functioning below consciousness. Deep, deep unconscious processes are expressed at all physiological levels, down to individual organs such as the heart, lungs, or pancreas. Our work is demonstrating that all the cells of the nervous system and endocrine system are functionally integrated by networks of peptides and their receptors.

– Candace Pert

It is natural for a sick man to rejoice when he sees the physician, even though, perhaps, he receives nothing from him. Therefore acquire, O wondrous man, plasters, potions, razors, eye-salves, sponges, instruments for bloodletting and cauterization, ointments, sleeping draughts, a knife, bandages. If we do not have these things, how can our science be manifested?

– St. John Climacus

All evil begins in the mind, when it is interested only in science. Scientists don't find their inner peace and their balance then. However, when their minds are attached to God, scientists use their science to cultivate their inner world and to help the world, for their minds are sanctified.

– Elder Paisios of Mt. Athos

Chapter 1

HISTORICAL PRECEDENTS FOR SYNERGIA: COMBINING MEDICINE, DIAKONIA AND SACRAMENT IN BYZANTINE TIMES

JOHN G. DEMAKIS

Background

Today we hear much about the relationship between medicine and religion and/or spirituality. Books and papers have been written, and courses are now available in medical schools to teach physicians how to approach religion and spirituality with their patients. New research has stressed the interrelationship between the body and mind. The Heritage Foundation recently sponsored a symposium entitled "Is Prayer Good for Your Health?" One of the proponents was Harold Koenig, M.D., who has reviewed the literature as well as done original research and published extensively on the topic. This type of discussion and these courses would have been unthinkable 15-20 years ago. In fact, throughout the twentieth century, religion, prayer and spirituality were considered to have no place in the treatment of patients. Physicians were taught to stay away from these topics or at most to refer patients to their priests, ministers or rabbis.

Some consider this movement a totally new phenomenon. Yet, for those familiar with the Byzantine Empire and the Orthodox Christian Church of medieval times, they will immediately see the similarities with what was practiced then. In this paper, I would like to relate to you how medicine, religion and spirituality were integrated in the Byzantine

15

Empire from the fourth century to its fall in 1453 to the
Ottoman Turks. As we learn more about how the Byzantines
approached this, we may learn much that could be useful
today. I will discuss first the role of society in philanthropy
and then specific role models that we might use today.

Philanthropy In Byzantium

Early Christians were divided on the use of physicians and
medicines. Some believed that faith in Christ was all that
should be necessary for a Christian. They were especially
suspicious because so much of medical theory and practice depended on pagan Greek physicians. However, by the
fourth century, as Christianity was no longer persecuted and
became the dominant religion in the empire, Eastern theolo-
gians forged an enduring alliance between Christianity and
classic culture including secular medicine. Greek philosophy and Greek learning were accepted in the East.

From the earliest times, the Church understood the relationship between physical and mental health and illness because
they understood how man was created. The Greek Fathers
of the Church led the way. St. Gregory of Nyssa said "medicine is an example of what God allows men to do when they
work in harmony with Him and with one another"(1). Basil
of Caesarea maintained, "God's grace is as evident in the
healing power of medicine and its practitioners as it is in miraculous cures"(2). And St. John Chrysostom said "because
God gave them (physicians) a special talent to save others
from pain and sometimes death, they have an urgent responsibility to share their talents"(3). ".. the fourth-century fathers emphasized the image of medical practice as the most
suitable example of love in action-philanthropia, as Clement
of Alexandria had called it. Medicine and its practice thus
came to symbolize the central Christian virtue for Greek
Christians. The learned theologian Gregory of Nyssa told his
friend the doctor Eustathios that the highest Christian virtue

of charity belonged especially to the physicians. Because of this, Gregory judged their profession superior to all the others"(4). This acceptance of secular medicine by the great Fathers of the Eastern Church paved the way for the flowering of medical science and the development of institutions of medical care in the East.

By the latter half of the fourth century and into the fifth century, philanthropic institutions supported primarily by the Church flourished in the East. There were homes for the poor (*ptochotropheia*), homes for orphans (*orphanotrophia*), homes for the aged (gerokomeia) and hospitals (*nosokomeia* and *xenones*)(5). These philanthropic institutions thrived because the Church took seriously its role in relieving suffering (Matt 25). Rival Christian factions often vied with each other in who would do more good works. In those days it was the Arians versus the Orthodox Christians. Wouldn't it be wonderful if we had such contests today? Who could do more to relieve the suffering of their fellow man?

Role Of The Orthodox Church

These philanthropic institutions were often associated with monasteries, with the monks themselves providing the necessary medical and nursing care. St. Basil of Caesarea (370-379), whose monastic rules all Orthodox monasteries still follow today, established a City of Charity (*ptocheion*) outside of Caesarea where his monks were expected to go and minister to the poor and sick of the city. St. Basil himself, who had been trained in medicine in Athens, often was seen working with his monks and caring for the sick and infirm. It is interesting to note that St. Basil did not expect his monks to stay cloistered in their cells and pray all day, but rather should balance their prayerful life (*theoria*) with good deeds for their fellow man (*philanthropia*).

When St. John Chrysostom became Patriarch of Constantinople in 390, he led the way by establishing many philanthropic institutions, including hospitals. In fact, St. John spent much of the Church's accumulated wealth on such institutions. This was one of the main reasons that he was so loved by his flock. By the sixth century, the philanthropic institutions had grown so rapidly that the state became the main source of the funding. However, the Church remained active, often running the now state-supported hospitals and other institutions. Justinian (527-565), one of the greatest of the Byzantine emperors, moved the *archiatroi* (main doctors of the city – a holdover from ancient times) into the hospitals. With the best physicians of the state now working out of the hospitals, the care and reputation of hospitals improved significantly. Soon, every major city in the empire had several hospitals. It became a source of pride. Monasteries remained active in these institutions, but there was much debate over the centuries of the proper role of monks in these institutions – a debate that has never been resolved.

Although the existence of some of these institutions was known, the exact running and administration of these institutions were not well understood. However, in 1896 the Typikon (Founding Charter) of the Pantokrator Monastery of Constantinople was published in Russian and in 1974 in French. The monastery was established and endowed by the Byzantine Emperor John II Komnenos in 1136. This Typikon is one of the few that has been found in its entirety. It is the only one in which a Byzantine hospital is described in great detail. In 1989 Timothy Miller published "*The Birth of the Hospital in the Byzantine Empire*," in which he describes medical care in the early Christian era and outlines in great detail the Typikon of the Pantokrator Monastery (6). The Typikon is so specific that it gives us a rare opportunity to see and understand how medical care was organized and administered in Byzantium and especially the role of the Church. The entire Typikon can be downloaded from the Internet (7).

Typikon Of The Pantocrator Monastery

The Typikon called for several institutions. This included the monastery, three churches and two philanthropic institutions: the xenon or hospital and a gerokomeion or old-age home. Xenon was the common term for hospital in the Byzantine Empire. Nosokomeio was another common term. The main church of the monastery still stands in Istanbul today and is known as the Zeired-kilisse-tzami (a mosque). The hospital building is no longer standing.

We are all so familiar with hospitals today that it is easy to think we have had them from antiquity. However, as Miller points out, there were no hospitals in antiquity and it was not until the seventeenth or eighteenth centuries that hospitals as we would know them became common in Western Europe. What served as hospitals in Western Europe during the Middle Ages were little more than hospices. It was where the poor and homeless went to die. There were no physicians to be found in these institutions. However, the concept of a hospital as we would understand it developed in the Byzantine Empire in the 4-5th centuries during this great outpouring of philanthropic activities mention above.

Many of the characteristics of a Byzantine hospital we would recognize today as expectations of our modern hospitals:

1. RESTORING HEALTH: It is clear that the goal of a Byzantine hospital was to restore health. This is an immediate distinction from hospitals in Western Europe during the middle ages, which were little more then hospices – places to go to die. The Typikon makes several provisions that make this clear.

2. MODERN FACILITIES: The Typikon provided for modern, well-kept facilities. Five wards were specified with approximately ten beds per ward. The wards were divided by specialties: surgical, gastrointestinal, etc. A separate ward was provided for women – with a provision that it be staffed

by female physicians! It specified one patient per bed (an important distinction – in Western Europe patients were often forced to sleep several in one bed). Provisions were made for mattresses, sheets, pillows, and extra covers in the winter. Provisions for replacement of worn bedding was also specified. Six beds were provided for bedridden patients – they had perforated mattresses. The Typikon also provided for two latrines (a men's and a women's). Patients were to be bathed twice a week. And three hearths were provided strategically for the colder months.

3. MEDICAL STAFF: The Typikon specified a full staff of physicians, including physicians in training – what we would consider today as residents and interns. The best physicians of the city were required to attend on the wards of Byzantine hospitals. They would be on service every other month. During their months on service they could not see their private patients. This is a clear distinction with medieval hospitals of Western Europe where there were no physicians present. Physicians of Western Europe saw patients in their clinics or in the patient's homes but not in hospitals. It was considered beneath their dignity. This was usually because these institutions were poorly kept. In Byzantium, it was considered an honor to be chosen to serve in the city hospitals, since only the best were chosen. This undoubtedly made it easier for them to get private patients during their months off.

The Typikon specifically banned physicians from taking tips for the care they delivered at the hospital. The physicians received a modest stipend, but in addition they received training and the opportunity for a better private practice.

The physicians were to make rounds once a day in the winter and twice a day from May through September. The Typikon then says that "after singing a psalm they will examine the sick carefully and scrutinize each person's illness in accurate detail, treating each person with appropriate remedies, making suitable arrangements for all, and showing great devotion and careful concern for all as they are going to render an account of these actions to the Pantokrator"(8)! How is that for a charge to the physicians!

4. ANCILLARY STAFF: The Typikon provided for a number of ancillary staff including nurses, pharmacists and dietary staffs. It even specified how much food and what kind the patients would receive each day.

5. QUALITY ASSURANCE AND UTILIZATION REVIEW: The Typikon antedated these concepts with careful thought and attention. Two chief physicians (Chiefs of Staff?) were to be hired that would oversee the entire medical care. They were to make daily rounds and "ask each of the patients how he is being treated and whether he is being tended by those appointed to this task with proper care and attention, and he will actively correct what is not right, reprove the negligent, and firmly put an end to anything being done improperly." "He will watch over everything with care and will properly attend to straighten out each matter"(9).

6. MEDICAL EDUCATION: The Typikon also provided for medical education at the hospital. A respected academic physician would be full-time at the hospital to teach medical students as well as the younger residents and interns. This physician would be the highest-paid physician on staff. A medical library was also provided for.

From the above description, we would recognize the essentials of a modern hospital. However, the Typikon goes further in emphasizing that the spiritual needs of the patients were also to be addressed. Two chapels were provided for (one for men and another for women). Each chapel would have a full-time priest and lector. Divine Liturgy was celebrated in each chapel four times a week: Wednesdays, Fridays, Saturdays and Sundays. At least one priest was always to be available to hear confession. The concept of holistic care (physical and spiritual) was key to the Byzantines' understanding of health and healing.

The Emperor then gave an exhortation to the entire hospital staff in the Typikon:

> "We give this instruction to all, to the doctors, the supervisors, assistants and the rest, that they all turn their gaze on him, the Pantokrator, and not neglect their careful examination of the sick, knowing what a great reward this work has when it is properly carried out and again what danger it brings when it is neglected and falls short of what is fitting. For Our Master accepts as his own what is done for each of the least of our brothers (Matt 25: 40) and measures out rewards in proportion to our good deeds. So then with regard to these our brothers we will all behave as people unable to escape the unsleeping eye of God and view with apprehension and great fear the time when we shall fall into his hands." What a fitting way to end the Typikon (10) .

Physician Saints

As we meet today on the feast day of our patron Sts. Cosmas and Damian, what can we learn to make ourselves better physicians, psychotherapists, or health care workers in general? When confronted with questions and challenges, I also like to look to the saints of our church to see how they handled similar problems and concerns. Fortunately, we have many Orthodox Christian physicians that are numbered among the saints. These men and women can serve as excellent role models for today's health care workers. An excellent book by Georgia Hronos outlines the lives of several such Orthodox saints that were physicians (11). When we think of physician saints, the names of Sts. Cosmas, Damian and Panteleimon easily come to mind. And well they should. However, I would encourage you to read the lives of other physician saints as well, such as Sts. Sampson, Thalleleos, Tryphon and many more. Physician saints are not just limited to medieval times. Especially inspiring is the life of St. Luke the surgeon of Simferopol in the USSR. His love and care for his patients and his sufferings are very poignant (12). There are several traits that are common to all of these physician saints, traits that I believe we should try to emulate:

1. They were all pious Orthodox Christians before they became physicians.

2. They lived an exemplary Christian life – they were conscientious in their prayer life, meditation and fasting. They regularly prayed for their patients. How often do we do this for our patients?

3. They were excellent physicians, often ending up first in their medical school class. For me this was most interesting. These early Christian physicians were not only priests or monks who learned just enough medicine to be helpful. They took their science seriously. They studied intensely and were renowned for their knowledge – an important lesson for all of us.

4. They had a deep and abiding love for their fellow man, often working long hours, forgoing pay (thus unmercenary) often. They often turned their own homes into early hospitals and fed and cared for their patients personally. They saw the image of Christ in each of their patients.

5. They believed that their skills to heal were God-given and therefore there was no arrogance about them – they were humble (how often do we hear that about physicians today?). There is the beautiful story of St. Sampson who always prayed for his patients to be healed. However, he also gave them medicines so that the patients would not know that they were miraculously healed by his prayers and not by his medicines!

As Orthodox Christian health care workers we have a rich tradition of holistic health and healing from which we can learn, both personally from our physician saints and from Byzantine Orthodox society and how they organized their medical services. The Byzantine Christians considered philanthropy as "love in action" and their philanthropic institutions the manifestation of this love. We should ask ourselves: Where are the manifestations of our love today? Where are our Orthodox hospitals, nursing homes, orphanages and homes for the poor, for the homeless, etc. today?

Although the Byzantine Empire came to an end over five hundred years ago, our Orthodox Church's commitment to philanthropy must never come to an end. As Orthodox health care workers, let us work with our Church to be sure our love for our fellow man turns into action. It is a great challenge and a wonderful opportunity. And we have great models to follow.

Notes

1. Greg. Nys. *Pauperibus* p.12.

2. Basil, *Regulae fusius tractatae interogatio* 55, PG, 31:1048.

3. Chrysostom, *De perfecta caritate* PG, 56:279-280.

4. Timothy S. Miller, *The Birth of the Hospital in the Byzantine Empire*, (Baltimore, MD: Johns Hopkins University Press, 1985), p.56.

5. Demetrios J. Constantelos, *Byzantine Philanthropy and Social Welfare*, (New Jersey: Rutgers University Press, 1968).

6. Timothy S. Miller, *The Birth of the Hospital in the Byzantine Empire*, (Baltimore, MD: Johns Hopkins University Press, 1985).

7. http://www.stmaryofegypt.org/typika/typ038.html.

8. *Typikon of the Pantokrator Monastery,* p. 34.

9. Ibid.

10. Ibid.

11. Georgia Hronos, *The Holy Unmercenary Doctors: The Saints Anargyroi, Physicians and Healers of the Orthodox Church,* (XXX, MN: Light and Life Publishers, 1999).

12. Vasily Marushchak, *The Blessed Surgeon: The Life of St. Luke of Simferopol,* (Point Reyes Station, CA: Divine Ascent Press, 2002).

Chapter 2

REGENERATING THE HEART: A WHOLISTIC PERSPECTIVE

PETER BISTOLARIDES

> Developing the heart means developing within it a taste
> for things holy, divine, and spiritual, so that when it finds
> itself amidst such things it would feel as though it were
> in its element. Finding them sweet and blessed, it would
> be indifferent to all else, with no taste for anything else;
> and even more – it would find anything else revolting.
> – St. Theophan the Recluse, *Three Powers of the Soul
> and Their Curative Exercises*

We are flesh and spirit seamlessly wed. What are the peculiar stresses of our culture and period of history and how
do advances in medicine complement the holy wisdom of
Orthodoxy in growing, preserving and regenerating the deep
heart of personhood that is the basis of true well being? This
paper takes a brief look at the traditional roots of medicine
and healing and the natural link with the divine, considers
some of the forces which have tended to split this link, re-
views the Orthodox theology of the person and illness, and
finally, attempts to reconnect Orthodox practitioners in the
helping profession with the divine mission given them, and

focusing on the "heart" of that mission: the therapeutic relationship with the patient.

A Historical Perspective

  History shows that medicine and religion have roots which are deep and co-mingled. In the Old Testament, Ecclesiasticus (Sirach) 38:1-15 is a testimonial in which five main points are made: a) The Lord gave us physicians and others that heal. b) Their power of healing comes from Him. c) God gave skill to human beings that he might be glorified. d) Prayer to the Lord when ill cleanses one's heart from all sin so that healing may occur. e) Give the physician his place. The latter two points can be viewed as parts of one, or as two separate points – prayer and appeal to God in times of illness and the intervention of the physician can be seen as part of a unified whole or as two solitudes which at least will complement each other.

  As noted, those who are engaged in the art and/or science of healing can take heart in a long and honorable tradition. Ambroise Pare, a French surgeon of the sixteenth century, considered the father of military surgery, summed up the belief found throughout Scripture: "Je le pansay et Dieu le guerit" – "I treated him, God healed him". In writing reminiscent of Ecclesiasticus, we find strong support among the Church Fathers for the role of secular medicine (1, 2).

  In the Byzantine Empire, the church played an active role in advancing and delivering medical care over the years, through the building of hospitals, hiring of medical staff, organizing and systematizing care, with benefits accruing to the population as a whole, and to the indigent and infirm in particular. Under the direction of the Emperor and through the active assistance of the church, the hospital was set up primarily as a therapeutic center designed to heal, rather than provide just palliative comfort for the dying. By appearances, this model of cooperation between secular medicine, the church and the government was the apex. The writings of Constantelos and Miller elaborate further on this period in history (3, 4).

Thus there is certainly no lack of example of the intersection between the divine and the practice of secular medicine, at least not historically. Tensions between the two have been present almost as long. Back in the fifth century B.C. the natural orientation of the Hippocratic School (which was the underpinning of the Galenic model of medicine which guided medical practice especially during the first millenium) looked for physical explanations for disease, rejecting divine causes for illness. In his treatise on *The Sacred Disease*, as epilepsy was called, Hippocrates declares: "It is not, in my opinion, any more divine or more sacred than other diseases, but has a natural course, and its supposed divine origin is due to men's inexperience, and to their wonder at its peculiar character," further expounding that men continue to believe in its divine origin "because they are at a loss to understand it" (5). With time, and the advance of the medical knowledge (which even superseded the Hippocratic teaching on illnesses), there are few diseases or conditions which can be classed as being divine as to physical etiology. Those which have no apparent explanation, and they do exist in this day and age, are termed idiopathic – at least, until their ultimate cause is elucidated.

The Great Divide

The connections between religion and medicine managed to maintain themselves over the centuries, but the gulf between the two gradually increased. In the latter part of the nineteenth century, the pace of new medical knowledge accelerated. Improvements in life expectancy, mortality rates, treatment and therapy began to take hold especially in the late nineteenth century. In the public eye, and in the eyes of the medical profession, these improvements came through the advances in science and rational medicine, and religion was seen to play little or no role in helping achieve these societal improvements. Science became the religion of society and its practitioners the new high priests. In 1910, the leading physician of his day, Sir William Osler, was asked to editorialize on the role of spirituality in medicine (6). Though expressing interest and desire to see real work done in this area, he privately held the notion that society as a whole benefited more from the advances in secular medicine and, although not hostile to religion, it was not the central theme in his life (7, 8). Though there was always room for the personal expression of faith by individual practitioners, medicine itself was more concerned with treating the body – the mind and soul would benefit as a result, if anyone cared to think about them.

The Human Person "Redux"

The twentieth century also saw the increasing specialization of medicine – certainly a natural outgrowth of the burgeoning knowledge in medical science (9). This added another confounding factor to the religion – medicine dichotomy: the deconstruction of the human person into constituent body systems. The mind was accorded space in this schema, but soul and spirit were relegated to the periphery. The benefits in advancing knowledge and developing expertise, certainly for the benefit of the patient, through specialization, are not in dispute. The unintended consequence was and is that of new barriers to communication (as each physician retreats into what is familiar and focuses on that which he or she has chosen to develop an expertise in), the human person is reduced to parts of a whole. To the difference in language and thought between secular medicine and religion is added a gulf between various medical practitioners who, it would seem, should be speaking the same language. Yet often that communication fails to occur, with occasionally tragic results.

The advancement of medical science and technology has continued at a fast clip. In the last twenty-five years alone, we have seen the normalization of the use of organ transplants, and advances in understanding of human genetics, cell biology, imaging, pharmaceuticals and other areas. In surgery alone, the advent of "minimally-invasive" surgery and robotic surgery has incorporated technology in which the machine is an extension of the surgeon – and more disturbingly, vice versa.

While technology and knowledge have kept pace, the ability to deliver health care in the United States has not. New jargon entered the health care arena – "managed care," "preferred providers," "covered lives," "gatekeeper," "risk management." Furthermore, the economics of health care has introduced business models into the delivery of health care at all levels. The "patient" has now become a "customer." Although this has brought some benefits in delivery and efficiency, on a global basis, the health care system has not solved its most fundamental problems, and has created new ones. Pressures on providers to "process" customers, spin-off of certain specialties into hospitals all their own, resources devoted to "boutique" or "concierge" services rather than to clinical services, do little to address the alienation being felt by patients and providers in the system. The "customer," or his employer, who has money to spend on health care, is the main focus of the new "business model" of medicine. The "customer" who is uninsured or unable to pay is, to put it mildly, simply out of luck.

Not surprisingly, the physician-patient relationship has gradually become a mechanistic, contractual relationship. The relationship has become a "transaction." Where the Hippocratic Oath once governed this relationship, we now have myriad rules, regulations and laws. Third party pay-ers and other entities enter into the relationship; where once the Hippocratic Oath gave privilege to the physician-patient relationship and protected patients from violation of their privacy, we now look to government and secular law as the protection. The documented abuses and excesses by entities outside the therapeutic relationship are now governed by (but not eliminated by) the privacy provisions of HIPAA (Health Insurance Portability and Accountability Act).

"Spirituality" in Health Care – The Return of God (sort of)

The dynamics and issues described above seem to have taken their toll, not only on the physician-patient relationship, but on those individuals in the helping professions themselves. Though one cannot generalize, there are many in the helping professions who are disillusioned, defeated, and some are even despondent. The meaning, the "soul," of what is being done is gone, or more likely, submerged under the ways of the world which are totally at odds with the divine intent of helping the sick.

Interestingly, however, the last quarter of a century has seen another phenomenon – the increase in attention given to the role of "spirituality" in health care. A number of articles have appeared in the medical literature, even in journals not normally considered "friendly ground," ranging from those devoted to surgery to those devoted to medical management. Much has been written about the beneficial effects on outcome in patients who held deep religious or spiritual beliefs. Even neurobiology has seen active research, with studies looking at changes in the brain occurring with subjects in deep meditation or prayer, and a burgeoning field of "neurotheology," which advances the notion that we believe in God because our brains are programmed to do so (10). Aside from some cynical use of spirituality to create a "competitive advantage" in getting customers, its potential role in health care is focused on providing "whole" care for the patient.

Most of the spirituality issues have been addressed to "end of life" care and the terminally ill. Significantly, the health of providers and their spiritual needs is of a lesser concern.

While it is encouraging that attention is being paid to an aspect of the patient which has not received it for some time, the cause for celebration is premature. Spirituality is not synonymous with religion, let alone Orthodox Christianity. Generic "spirituality" in the current usage rather uncritically incorporates any and all religions, faiths, practices and philosophies as if there were no ontological distinction among them. In our multi-cultural, politically correct environment, this appears to be the only safe recourse; however, it limits the role of spirituality in health care to the gathering of information and merely acknowledging the "awareness" of man as a "spiritual being."

Another problem is that most spiritual modalities see the soul as a separate entity from the mind and body, just like any other body system. And, there are those spiritual practices whose sole aim is to "elevate consciousness" or some other lofty aim, purely through the mind and body, without addressing the soul and without moving closer to God. For the Orthodox practitioner (and for the Orthodox faithful), an effort must be made to understand the Orthodox Christian viewpoint in health care, as there is the pitfall of syncretism and a confusion in the Orthodox Christian practitioner's mind of what is and is not valid. In order to do this, one must begin with an understanding of the person and of illness according to Orthodox Christian theology.

The Human Person and Illness in the Orthodox Christian Tradition

The separation of the human person into body, mind and soul is a logical mode of thinking. However, herein lies the fault with most views of the human person – each of these is an entity, but there is emphasis on the separation of these, which is an artificial one, and which is not as clear-cut as it might seem. Unfortunately, most approaches to therapy maintain this construct. The question arises: Is a human being a body with a soul, or a soul with a body? The way one answers this question goes a long way in determining how the therapeutic interaction should take place. Furthermore, in considering the treatment of illness, how is illness viewed from an Orthodox Christian perspective? This is a rich and complex area of discussion beyond the scope of this paper, but it is important to briefly articulate some of this thought in considering caring for the ill person from an Orthodox perspective.

In the Orthodox Christian tradition, the human person is looked at as body, soul, heart and *nous* (mind), but these are seen as inextricably woven together, inseparable. Some even reduce this to a unity of body and soul. St. Gregory Palamas states: "The word Man is not applied to either soul or body separately, but to both together, since they have been created in the image of God" (11). Created in the image of God, Orthodox theology views the person as primarily a divine creature, understood by the Fathers as a theological being, being the image or icon of the archetype, within which man finds his ontological meaning (12). Archimandrite Sophrony describes the "persona," the "hidden man of the heart…the most precious kernel of man's whole being…*manifested in his talent for cognition not only of the created world, but also of the divine world*" (italics mine – quoted in (13)). Zizioulas gives us man as two modes of existence: the hypostasis (person) of biological existence, and the hypostasis of ecclesial existence. In other words, the human person is not merely a philosophical or humanistic construct; the concept of the person in Orthodox Christian understanding "is indissolubly bound up with theology" (14, p. 46). A key element is, as Vladimir Lossky states, that personal existence supposes a relation to the other; one person exists "to" or "towards" the other (15, p. 106). Thus, one of the hallmarks of personhood as understood in the Orthodox tradition is that of relationship with and for others.

Illness, and man's susceptibility to it, is likewise bound up in theology. Humankind's weakness and susceptibility to illness and mortality, its deficiency, if you will, is traced to the fall of Adam. Yet careful distinction is made between our propensity for illness and ultimate bodily mortality based on inheriting the human nature of Adam, and illness caused by personal sin. Naturally, there are potential consequences arising from personal sin (which includes not only the corporeal ones such as gluttony, but also pride, avarice, lust, and others), but as Larchet notes "..several passages of Scripture demonstrate that there exists no *a priori* link between a person's illness or infirmity and any specific sin or sins which that person or his or her immediate ancestors might have committed" (16). Illness of the body has been seen by various Fathers as purifying (St. John Climacus), perfecting (St. John Chrysostom), a means in attaining the virtue of patience (again, St. John Chrysostom), and as a source of humility (St. John Chrysostom). Certainly, from a theological standpoint, illness (like so many other things) can also be transfiguring and transcendent. In a pastoral situation, though, it is difficult to focus the one who is suffering on this aspect of illness in the acute situation.

Jesus Christ as the True Physician

Throughout the Gospel, Christ is found encountering people with ailments of both body and soul, recognizing their real human need. He is found to heal both by word and by touch; interestingly, those ailments of a spiritual/mental/neurological nature are addressed by Jesus more by word than by touch (for example, in Luke 9:37-43, the boy with a "demon" – reminiscent of Hippocrates' "Sacred Disease," or epilepsy – is cured when Jesus "rebukes" the unclean spirit; in

Matt 9:2-7, the paralytic is healed by the command to "rise, take up your bed, and go home"; in John 5:2-18, the healing of the man paralyzed for thirty-eight years, through a command similar to the one given to the paralytic in Matt 9; Matt 8:14-17 describes the many who were possessed with demons, and "he cast out the spirits with a word"). Illnesses with more physical manifestations tended to be healed by touch – occasionally using matter such as the mud or clay he used to cure the blind man in John 9:6. Besides the aforementioned, we also have Matt 8:14-17, which mentions the cure of those possessed by demons, where he cures Peter's mother-in-law with a touch, we also have Luke 13:10-17 and the healing of the woman unable to stand up straight for eighteen years – described as one "who Satan has bound"; Matt 9:27-31, and the healing of the two blind men by touching of their eyes. Of special note are the cures of physical ailments effected even without visiting the person, purely by intercession in faith by some intermediary (in John 4:46-54, the healing of the official's son in Galilee, and in Matt 8:5-13, the healing of the centurion's servant). There is also the account in Matt 14:34-36 of the healing of the sick in Gennesaret, who "begged him that they might touch even the fringe of his cloak, and all who touched it were healed." In all of these accounts, we are witness to true healing from the true source of healing, God Himself incarnated in the human form as Jesus Christ.

When we examine the Gospel accounts of Jesus' healing miracles, there are some important characteristics: Jesus addressed the immediate human need to be relieved of suffering, He did this without any qualification (independent of age, gender, social status), and it was done for the glory of God the Father (John 9:3 – Jesus answered, "Neither this man nor his parents sinned; he was born blind so that God's works might be revealed in him"). One must also add that the healing was done in humility; Christ never used the occasion to boast about His healing, but to direct those who were healed towards God the Father not only in gratitude, but in joy as well. Christ performed these miracles so that the Kingdom of Heaven could be proclaimed on earth; some he healed already had faith in Him, others were healed, and then experienced the revelation of their deliverer as the Son of God. However, there were others who apparently didn't experience this revelation, but were healed nonetheless (Luke 17:12-17 and the account of the healing of the ten lepers is a prime example for this). Jesus Christ sets the example for the Orthodox Christian practitioner, and leaves us to consider what the practitioner needs to do to imitate Christ's healing ministry, the "heart" of the helping professions. This forms the basis for countering the trends extant in modern health care.

Therapeutic Relationship from an Orthodox Viewpoint – A Divine-Human Encounter

Based on the Orthodox theology of the person described earlier, the divine element is not limited to the patient, but is also important in the practitioner. Those in the helping professions enter into a therapeutic relationship with another human being, irrespective of the beliefs or faith of either party, yet the point is made here that it is crucial to recognize the divine element in the relationship. Any practitioner, of course, can minister to persons in a spirit of dignity, respect and professionalism that come with the practice of the healing arts. Yet in the deconstructed milieu of health care today, it is not enough to treat persons as merely "patients" or worse, "customers" who are simply sentient, autonomous psycho-biological entities, but to go even deeper. Healing requires recognition of the patient as a human person who is a creation of God's love and made in the divine image and potential likeness. For the Orthodox Christian practitioner, this means approaching the relationship and understanding it beyond the finite limits of science and cognition. It also involves a clearer relationship with God for the practitioner, what C.S. Lewis described as "losing yourself in your relationship with the Creator" (17, p. 115) or as Metropolitan Anthony of Sourozh describes it, being like an open and empty purse "and an intelligence completely open to the unknown and the unexpected" (18, p. 145).

Thus, we consider an Orthodox Christian therapeutic approach to the care of persons as being faithful to four principles: the Incarnational, the Trinitarian, the Sacramental and the Mystagogical. The Incarnational aspect is, as described, the recognition of the divine element in every human being dwelling together with the human nature. This is equally true of the practitioner. It is important that we recognize our talents and skills for what they are: though humanly acquired they are divinely inspired for a divine purpose. But, we must not confuse this with being divine; our human natures limit our skills and knowledge, and are vulnerable to the physical and mental, as well as spiritual demands of caring for others. The source of healing is God; we are, at most, intermediaries of that healing.

The human person is body, mind and spirit, as identifiable entities, but like the Holy Trinity, seamlessly united. The health of one can affect the others, as has been noted. The implications for patient care are obvious. The care of the patient needs to be oriented in this manner, not only to address the non-physical manifestations of physical illness, but also to diagnose patients in a complete and accurate manner. The Orthodox practitioner must be acutely aware of his or her own personhood being in the image of the Trinity, and engage in care of his or her own body, mind and spirit. Nurturing of the soul is especially important, and requires a life rooted in the Orthodox Christian faith, embodied as full participation in the liturgical and sacramental life of the Church. Experienced spiritual guidance is especially important, as one's life needs to be examined and re-examined on an ongoing basis, in order to continue the journey towards God.

Given the current forces arrayed against the physician-patient relationship, its devaluation and mechanization, viewing the therapeutic relationship as having a sacramental dimension is important in reorienting us in the conduct and performance of our respective disciplines. It should be made clear that this is not equating the therapeutic relationship with the Holy Mysteries or Sacraments of the Church. However, as a therapeutic relationship does involve people, in whom we have acknowledged a divine element, viewing of this interaction as sacramental is valid and allows us to reinforce the sanctity of this relationship in the face of the increasing dehumanization rampant in our society today. It is interesting to draw parallels between the practice of medicine and the Church. Medicine has its "dogma," its rubrics, its procedures and practices, and its hierarchy. As the Church is involved in its mission of salvation of the whole person, medicine uses the same dynamics in its quest for salvation of the physical being of the human person.

Finally, there is consideration of the mystery. At its core, the mystery involves our understanding, or more accurately, our limited understanding of the human person from a physical and mental standpoint. The mystery of the human person, which makes him or her absolutely unique and irreplaceable, cannot be grasped in a rational concept and defined in words (15, p. 107). The mystery further deepens in our consideration of how patients recover from their illnesses, and in some cases don't. Medicine, as has been pointed out often, is still an art with a strong component of science. Medical research extends the limits of our knowledge of the human body, the human mind, and gives this new technology for diagnosis and treatment. Though we have advanced tremendously in understanding the human body, disease, and even mental illness, we have an incomplete understanding of how these interact, and particularly how they interact with the human soul. When we even stop to consider how the human body is structured, has been given the means of preparing itself, healing, fighting infection, and countless other functions, one has to be in awe of God as Creator of our human nature. That these mechanisms sometimes break down or fail us is a reflection of the weakness of our human nature which we inherited through Adam. Furthermore, with each new advance in medical knowledge come new questions which need to be answered. The seemingly inexhaustible questions which arise even in trying to understand ourselves as part of the profound mystery of the Holy Trinity.

In our rich tradition of Orthodoxy, the mystagogical is also manifested in our sacraments, particularly Holy Unction and Holy Communion, and by our intercessory prayers for the sick and the active intervention of the saints of our Church. Secular medicine and Orthodoxy has had many meeting points among its faithful, as evidenced by the numerous physician-saints, physician-priests, and in the works of certain ascetics and monastics over the years who, being particularly gifted with the Holy Spirit, have manifested healing of physical illness but more often acted in concert with physicians in helping diagnose ailments in certain cases which have evaded diagnosis by conventional means. Nor is this a historical phenomenon of days long gone – such individuals have been manifested to us even in modern times. Though most of us have had little personal experience with this extraordinary grace of Orthodoxy, these events have been witnessed and documented (19).

Conclusion

What does this all mean for the Orthodox practitioner in our society today? Regardless of the roles each of us plays in treating the ill, and despite the array of negative forces in the world which seek to alienate us not only from our patients, but from our divinely inspired mission, Orthodox practitioners have a rich armamentarium to draw on in order to strengthen themselves spiritually and equip them to deal with whatever the outcome will be in their interaction with the patient. It is important to draw on that armamentarium from the outset of any therapeutic relationship, and not just in times of difficulty or crisis. Fundamentally, it calls on the faithful Orthodox Christian practitioner to relinquish ultimate control to God the Father, God the Word, and God the Holy Spirit who created us, knows us intimately, and is the source of all healing. It leaves us with the awesome task of making ourselves worthy to act as God's intermediaries and be tangible human evidence of God's love for humankind. Through this, we not only help to treat our patients and perhaps even give some the opportunity to experience the divine grace in their healing, but for us, it regenerates not only our hearts but our entire being and dedicates it to God, to Whom belong all glory, honor, and worship.

Notes

1. Jean-Claude Larchet, *The Theology of Illness,* (Crestwood, NY: St. Vladimir's Seminary Press, 2002), p. 131.
2. Stanley S. Harakas, *Health and Medicine in the Eastern Orthodox Tradition:Faith, Liturgy and Wholeness*, (in Health/Medicine and the Faith Traditions, ed. J.P. Wind, New York: Crossroad), p. 190.
3. Demetrios J. Constantelos, *Medicine and Social Welfare in the Byzantine Empire*, (in Medicine nei Secoli, Arte e Scienza, 11(2), 1999), p. 337-355.
4. Timothy J. Miller, *The Birth of the Hospital in the Byzantine Empire*, (Baltimore, MD: Johns Hopkins University Press, 1985), p. 287.
5. Hippocrates, *The Sacred Disease*, (in *Hippocrates II - Loeb Classical Library*, Cambridge, MA: Harvard University Press).
6. John Tarpley and Margaret Tarpley, *Spirituality in Surgical Practice,* (in Journal of the American College of Surgeons, 194(5), 2002), p. 642-647.

7. Michael Bliss, *William Osler: A Life in Medicine*, (Toronto, Canada: University of Toronto Press, 1999).

8. Osler's most famous work is *Aequanimitas*, his farewell lecture to the University of Pennsylvania on his departure for the professorship at Johns Hopkins; it is a study on how the physician must conduct himself with equanimity in all situations. Too often, however, this has been misinterpreted as meaning that the physician should act with emotional detachment from the patient.

9. Specialization in medicine is not a recent phenomenon, but it has become highly developed over the past century

10. Andrew Newberg, Eugene G. D'Aquili and Vince Rause, *Why God Won't Go Away*, (New York: Ballantine Press, 2002), p. 240.

11. George C. Papademetriou, *An Orthodox Christian View of Man,* (Athens: Theologia, 1985), p. 22.

12. Panayotis Nellas, *Deification in Christ,* (Crestwood, NY: St. Vladimir's Seminary Press, 1987), p. 254.

13. Metropolitan Hierotheos Vlahos, *The Person in the Orthodox Tradition*, (Levadia, Greece: Birth of the Theotokos Monastery, 1999), p. 349.

14. John D. Zizioulas, *Being as Communion*, (Crestwood, NY: St. Vladimir's Seminary Press, 1985), p. 269.

15. Vladimir Lossky, *In the Image and Likeness of God*, (Crestwood, NY: St. Vladimir's Seminary Press, 1974), p. 227.

16. See John 9:1-3: "Master, who sinned, this man or his parents, that he should have been born blind..."

17. Armand M. Nicholi Jr., *The Question of God: C.S. Lewis and Sigmund Freud Debate God, Love, Sex, and The Meaning of Life,* (New York: Free Press, 2002), p. 295.

18. Anthony Bloom, *The Essence of Prayer,* (London: Darton, Longman and Todd, 1986), p. 452.

19. Two modern examples include St. Luke, Archbishop of Simferopol, the surgeon-saint, who was a noted university professor during the Soviet era, and endured persecution under Stalin (see *The Blessed Surgeon: The Life of St. Luke of Simferopol* by Archdeacon Vasiliy Maruschak, Divine Ascent Press, 2002). Also, there is the remarkable Elder Porphyrios (Bairaktaris), who reposed in 1991 (see *Elder Porphyrios: Testimonies and Experiences by Klitos Ioannidis*, published by the Holy Convent of the Transfiguration, Athens 1997).

Chapter 3

FROM NEUROBIOLOGY
TO UNCREATED LIGHT

Paul Kymissis, MD

The late Professor John Meyendorff, a friend of OCAMPR, saw the organization as a catalyst for dialogue between behavioral scientists, physicians and the Church, a dialogue which is desperately needed in our time. One of the areas where this is increasingly evident is in the new developments in the field of neuroscience and their relationship with Orthodox Christian spirituality.

Once when I was a psychiatric resident, I met with Dr. Kaufman, a visiting Professor and the former chairman of Psychiatry at Mt. Sinai School of Medicine, and asked him to summarize the current mode of thinking in psychiatry. He replied that the older he became the more he realized the importance of genetics in understanding human behavior. Indeed, genetic research has contributed enormously throughout the past few decades to our understanding of psychiatric syndromes.

The first director of Child Psychiatry at New York Medical College, Dr. Stella Chess, studied three hundred children from birth up to thirty years of age. She discovered that the early behavioral characteristics she was able to observe in a person in the first few weeks and months of life were in

41

fact the dominant characteristics of that person throughout the thirty years of the study. These characteristics, which she labels the 'temperament', seem to be closely related to the genetic endowment of each person. There is much evidence for this in studies of identical twins reared apart. The similarities are sometimes striking, down to the level of identical twins giving their dogs the same name or choosing the same brand of toothpaste.

During the last half of the nineteenth century, psychiatry, with leaders like Kraeplin, Werwicke, Lombroso and others, placed most emphasis on the biological basis of mental illness. In the first half of the twentieth century, with the introduction of psychoanalytic theory by Freud, there was much emphasis placed on the psychology of the individual. During the last thirty years, with the new discoveries from the field of neuroscience, a new interactive model has been emerging. Biological and psychological factors both play important roles in the etiology of mental illness. In certain conditions like bipolar disorder or schizophrenia, biology plays a major role, whereas in other conditions like depression, psychological factors are more prominent.

The discovery of certain neurotransmitters and their role in human behavior opened new avenues of thinking about many psychiatric disorders. Neurotransmitters are the chemicals used to communicate across synapses (the junctions between brain cells). These communications are related to several brain functions like perception, memory, emotions and thinking. So now we can study the mind, not only through observable behavior, but by looking at parallel and simultaneous neuropsychological functions.

There are specific synapses that participate in the formation of memory, coordination and numerous other functions. Obsessive-compulsive disorder, for example, seems to be related to a neurotransmitter called serotonin. The use of medication that selectively inhibits serotonin reuptake (SSRIs), such as fluoxetine, has resulted in a dramatic improvement in many patients with this disorder. Another example is that genetics has been found to play an important role in some persons suffering from alcoholism. Epidemiological studies have shown that the risk of alcoholism is almost seven times greater in persons with a first-degree alcoholic relative than those without such familial associations. In addition to the genetic factors, there are a number of environmental factors that play an important role, such as parental modeling, cultural patterns of alcohol use, and stressful events of life.

Findings from the field of neuroscience have also demonstrated the importance of biological factors in many psychiatric syndromes. It is well documented that dopamine receptors in the brain play an important role in schizophrenia. These patients may also present with hypofrontality and a host of other neuroanatomical abnormalities. Further, young children at risk of schizophrenia have a lower degree of neuronal migration to the periphery of the brain's cortex. Head and brain trauma has often resulted in personality changes, including oppressive and violent behaviors. Other syndromes like depression, panic disorder, post-traumatic stress disorder and personality disorders may also have biological correlates.

A fascinating discovery in the quest to understand the connection between the mind and the brain has come from using the latest brain-imaging technology. New studies have demonstrated that the neuropsychological milieu of the brain is influenced by psychological interventions, not only chemical ones. These physiological changes were detected using SPECT (single photon emission tomography), PET (positron emission tomography), MRI (magnetic resonance imaging), and three-dimensional PET/MRI scanning. Using this equipment, the studies could detect functional changes in the brain, in addition to the already known structural changes. Patients with obsessive-compulsive disorder (OCD) were discovered to have an elevated level of activity in the frontal lobe and caudate nucleus using PET. The over-activity in these segments of the brain could be overcome using medication or through a psychotherapeutic intervention (in this case, cognitive-behavioral therapy).

One should not underestimate the capacity of psychotherapy to restore 'normal' brain functioning. Depressed patients who were randomized to treatment with either psychotherapy or antidepressant medication in a number of studies were shown to have largely the same outcome success. Paroxetine, an antidepressant, was found to produce identical functional changes in the brain as interpersonal therapy in a recent study by Dr. A. Brody from UCLA. Dr. Eric Kandel, a Nobel Prize-winning psychiatrist and neurobiologist proved that the process of learning in fact changes the structure and function of the brain.

Cognitive therapies and learning have become popular in modern psychotherapy. Many people have said that their lives had changed after they read a book, heard a lecture, or were made to think of alternatives they had never considered. Other popular therapeutic methods include the utilization of relaxation and exercise to enhance the emotional state of a person. There is some evidence that physical exercise could be an effective method of treating depression. Another important factor which could have an important influence on the psycho-biological system is suggestion. Many of the so-called 'treatments' of the past (of the pre-scientific era of psychiatry) have been forms of suggestion.

Jerome Frank, in his book *Persuasion and Healing*, describes the power of the placebo effect in psychobiological processes. One study involved randomizing anxiety patients to either a placebo or anti-anxiety medication group. The first experiment of the study used a young, unconvincing and apparently inexperienced therapist. In this experiment the patients on medication fared better than those on placebo. When the experiment was repeated with a more mature, convincing and apparently experienced doctor, the group on placebo fared better than the group on anti-anxiety medication.

Suggestion plays a major role in the doctor-patient relationship, but also in many other phenomena of life. Suggestion and hypnosis can induce anaesthesia, paresthesias, and even olfactory hallucinations. How are these findings, and the great wealth of other research data not presented here, connected with the healing process and our understanding of Orthodox Christian spirituality? The phenomena observed in the above-mentioned studies extend the frontier of our understanding of the natural realm. It is our Christian duty to offer to our brothers and sisters the medical treatments developed using modern scientific discoveries. This capacity to learn more about the natural order of the universe is given to us by God. According to the *Wisdom of Sirach*, "God gave science." Further, it says that one ought to "give honor to the physician, because God created him," and in fact that "medication was created by God." Surely it is ridiculous to demand miracles from God if we do not use the medical means available to us to tackle a medical problem.

It is the temptation of "charismatics" to expect miracles, where God has provided a means of resolving a medical problem. It would be absurd for a person to demand that God heal his tooth instead of going to the dentist. In a similar way, where there is a clear genetic and biological component to a psychiatric disease, then the available medical and pharmacological interventions are indicated.

However, there are a number of conditions where cognitive changes, a healthy lifestyle and alternative complementary non-medical interventions could play a role. The cognitive and belief structure of a person has a direct relationship with his or her emotional and affective state. The way a person perceives him or herself, others and the world may generate feelings of hope, contentment, frustration or despair. In the Bible there are a number of references to temptation and despair. In Acts 14 and 22 it is written that we must go through many tribulations to enter the kingdom of God. Paul writes to the Corinthians (2 Cor 4:8) that "we are hard pressed on every side, yet not crushed" and that we are "perplexed, but not in despair" (απορουμενοι αλ ουχ εξαπορουμενοι). Freud, in his work on mourning and melancholia, described how the usual process of mourning may end up in the stage of despair he called melancholia.

There are conditions where the boundaries between biological and psychological factors are blurred, and hence require not only medical and pharmacological interventions, but a spiritual process, for true healing to come about. This especially applies when the stressors include: sin, guilt, an irrational fear, hate, and holding a grudge. A recent study demonstrated the power of forgiveness, that is, being able to forgive, in bringing about personal healing.

When we talk of Orthodox Christian "spirituality" we should be sure of what we are speaking about. Orthodox Christian spirituality is not the result of some suggestive experience; nor is it the end result of an artificial state of well-being achieved through the process of relaxation and meditation; nor is it related to the excitement and enthusiasm created by inspirational speakers of so-called "charismatic" groups; nor is it guided by manmade means like art, music and other human devices. St. Seraphim of Sarov said that the purpose of life was the acquisition of the Holy Spirit. St. Silouan of Mt. Athos exclaims that he "asked for forgiveness and (he got) not only forgiveness but the grace of the Holy Spirit, and then (he) knew God." Our desire for communion with God cannot be filled with manmade artificial substitutes.

During the fourteenth century there was a major debate in the Church about the ability of man to experience God.

Barlaam, a western philosopher, insisted that what the "hesychasts" were experiencing was a product of their imagination. He mockingly labeled them as 'ομφαλοσκοποι' (men with their "soul in the navel"). To their defense came St. Gregory Palamas, who suggested that a distinction should be made between the essence and energies of God. Both are uncreated. While the essence of God cannot be communicated, humans can experience God as He is revealed through His divine uncreated energies. Prayer is not a movement of the spirit only, but also of the body. St. Gregory Palamas writes: "What pain or joy or movement of the body is there which is not shared by the soul and the body?" He affirms that in spiritual men the grace of the Spirit is transmitted to the body through the soul as an intermediary. The Spirit gives to the body an experience of divine things; it grants it the capacity to feel the same passion as the soul. In this way Palamas rejected Barlaam's dualistic mysticism, which has continued to define Western approaches where the body and soul are seen as separate from one another. St. Gregory suggested that the experience of the uncreated Light by the body was not the product of a suggestion, but the action of the uncreated energies of God. The divine energies cannot be examined scientifically, because they are beyond the laws of physics or nature.

Therefore there should be a clear distinction between what is natural and subject to the laws of nature, and what is supernatural; a distinction between what can be achieved through human effort and research, and what is revealed or given as a gift. The Greek word for gift is "charisma." Charisma is not the product of human effort, but by definition is a gift, which is given at the discretion of the giver. Palamas' contribution to our understanding of the divine substance and energies, is pertinent to understanding the role of psychiatry as a scientific method, as distinguished from the pursuit of spirituality, which is to participate in Christ's life.

It is important to keep this distinction in mind when addressing psychopathological phenomena, particularly phenomena which are evidently subject to the laws of nature, and can be alleviated by human intervention. Whenever God gives us the knowledge to understand and treat a disorder, we have the responsibility to use this knowledge to treat the suffering person.

It is also true that stress is a major factor in precipitating psychiatric symptoms like anxiety, panic, depression, etc. In treating persons with mental disorders it is also important to address such factors as sin, guilt, shame, narcissism, a preoccupation with oneself (selfishness), and an inability to delay gratification or control sexual and aggressive impulses.

St. Mark the Ascetic said that there are two major reasons for a man's unhappiness: love for himself and a love for pleasure. People who have been suffering from anxiety are able to find comfort when they understand the meaning of life. Anxiety is defined as the fear of something going wrong. Hope is the opposing emotion to fear. Therefore St. Paul writes that through hope you will find peace. An existential vacuum is another potential source of anxiety. This is where an individual who is created in the image of God fails to understand himself because he doesn't know God. Orthodox Christian spirituality can be a major source of healing for many of these people.

In and of itself, "spirituality" is one of the most abused and ambiguous words of our time. "Spirituality" without God has become the new religion of our day. In the name of religious pluralism, tolerance and cultural sensitivity, people are willing to talk about spirituality without even mentioning the Holy Spirit. "Spirituality," emptied of its power, is taught at college, presented in workshops at conferences, and becomes a new dimension of psychological care. These "spiritual" pursuits are in fact anthropocentric. They begin and end with man. "Man is the measure of everything," as one Greek philosopher wrote. Orthodox Christian spirituality, by contrast, is summed up in St. Silouan's statement, "I asked for forgiveness, and I was given not only forgiveness, but also the gift of the Holy Spirit, and then I knew God." Furthermore, for St. Silouan, the fruit of such knowledge was not merely self-aggrandizing, but manifested itself relationally as a "love for one's enemies." This kind of experience of God is called by St. Gregory "θεοπτια" (a vision of God). Such is the immense difference between talking about God and being with God.

This charisma – 'χαρισμα' – is not an experience produced by suggestion, art, music, or powerful oratory, but by the presence of God, a divine visitation, a response to the request for forgiveness, as St. Silouan had put it. Psychotherapy is a scientific method of healing the whole human being. It is based on what is known and understood at any given moment in history.

Orthodox Christian spirituality ultimately transcends scientific barriers. It cannot be manipulated by human effort or scientific research because it is primarily the work of God. It is a gift, a charisma, which represents God's response to a humble and contrite heart.

HEALING THE SUFFERING PERSON

(With regard to clinical outcomes)…*techniques seemed to matter less than the therapist's personal qualities. I felt that Albert Schweitzer's idea of reverence for life captured the distinction I was struggling with. Some therapists, regardless of their theoretical orientation, length of experience, professional affiliation, etc., appeared to have this quality, and I came to surmise (although I could not prove it) that they were better therapists. Others appeared to be notably deficient in this regard. They seemed to be technicians who plied a trade; they might have shrewd insights into the patient's dynamics; they might be clever in confronting the patient with his conflicts and neurotic patterns, but they lacked a human quality I came to regard as the supreme qualification of the good psychotherapist.... Perhaps the principal ingredient is compassion. It is the deeply felt understanding of another human being's suffering, coupled with gentleness and tenderness. It is empathic in the sense of understanding another person's inner world – notably his loneliness, anguish, suffering, and basic helplessness.*

– Hans Strupp

Chapter 4

THE COMPLEXITIES OF A PERSON

STEPHEN MUSE

Theodore, "Ted," is a sixty-six-year-old American-born Caucasian man who has never married. He was engaged once earlier in his life and recently lived with a female companion for a number of years, but without sexual engagement. He has felt the most intense emotional longing in his life for males, but as a Christian, he has always felt much shame about this. He has been "secretive" and reclusive for some forty years, fearing that if he got close to men he might desire them sexually, and with women, he just couldn't quite make a commitment to any of those he dated, feeling he needed a kind of distance at times from being "smothered" by them.

About thirty years ago, Ted began a long-term psychotherapy relationship with a female therapist who tried to kiss him during one of his sessions. He eventually stopped therapy with her after she denied responsibility for her behavior in a group therapy setting in which he was a participant, immediately following her boundary violation. With this denial, Ted felt further violated. He tried again a few years later and found a psychologist whom he saw on a regular basis for a decade. This man told him, as had others he'd spoken with, "It doesn't matter what you fantasize about in your mind as long as you don't act on it." Ted eventually consulted with

53

another therapist, a pastoral counselor. Ted told the counselor that his former therapist (of ten years) had been having a social conversation with him, but he felt he hadn't accomplished anything.

Presented now with an Orthodox Christian view of the mental life, the role of passions, the importance of guarding the fantasy life, etc. Ted came to tears feeling "for the first time someone has described what I felt in my heart to be true, but no one ever said." He told of a couple of miraculous healings he'd had of serious illnesses in his life during times of prayer while watching a television preacher and felt God did this for him. Though not Orthodox, Ted's Christian faith was sincere and very deeply rooted in him.

In the realm of his intimate life, Ted has suffered tremendous loneliness to the point that he began to disclose, for the first time in all his years of therapy, that he began some thirty or forty years ago, to fantasize in his mind around sadomasochistic sexual themes and gradually it had gotten to the point that he could induce the imagined characters to come alive within him and speak for themselves. He had a certain set of cups in his kitchen with faces of celebrities on them and he could get them to actually change shapes as their mouths moved to speak to him.

Now he began to be afraid because the characters were commenting to him within himself beyond what he was "creating" and causing him not to be able to sleep. These were not audiovisual hallucinations of a schizophrenic nature, but more on the order of voices of dissociative disorder, although even this was not totally clear. Ted would insist "I am creating them," while at the same time saying, "They talk to me and get angry and comment on what I'm doing." He noted that he is bothered most by the "voices" during periods when he has self-administered diet pills.

As an adolescent, Ted said he'd been seduced and fondled by an older man on one occasion. He remembered no other sexual abuse, though he had a memory which moved him to tears, of being a baby and remembering the smell of his father's sweaty crotch after he'd come home from work and lay on the porch with him resting between his legs. This memory troubled him.

He stated that his mother dressed him in girl's clothing sometimes as a child and his brothers made fun of him. This memory is one upon which Ted's doubts about his masculinity have been hung in terms of the narrative he's told about himself to himself over the years.

Ted's younger brother was overweight and got picked on growing up and Ted protected him. When the boy thinned out and became strong, he repaid Ted's kindness by constantly criticizing him and questioning him, apparently projecting onto him the weakness he himself was trying to avoid. This wounded Ted, but he remained loyal until eventually the brother attempted to hoodwink him out of a family inheritance. Ted, with much grief, got a lawyer and protected himself, but his brother would no longer speak to him as a result.

In sessions, Ted is outwardly jovial, intellectual, with moments of sadness springing up which he initially moved away from quickly as he'd learned to do all his life. He both yearns for closeness as well as fears it. He is an engaging interlocutor and it is easy to see how he could have "entertained" and been entertained by his former therapist, as well as had fantasies about him in his mind that he never spoke about with the therapist.

As Ted began to disclose the nature of the voices to his new therapist, he began to experience some increased anxiety. On one occasion, the "voice" in his head told him not to tell the therapist about him when Ted was disturbed by it. The therapist talked with him about cutting off the thoughts according to patristic counsel of recognizing *logismoi* and the process of formation of the passions through linkage with the attention. He read material on the Jesus prayer suggested by the therapist, who gave Ted an icon of Christ at some point in the therapy. Ted related one day that the voice had been 'converted' and was now saying the Jesus prayer and on a couple of occasions appeared to do this from the icon when he looked at it.

Later the voice stopped saying the Jesus prayer and began to be angry again. Ted was referred to a psychiatrist to get a low dose of Risperdal, which he did, and this helped him so that he was not troubled by the "voices" though they still remained in the background and he still fantasized on occasion.

Along with these symptoms, Ted suffers from cancer, currently in remission. He is making friends with people in the apartment where he lives, is financially independent, reads and has plans to redecorate a house he owns for investment purposes. He has some social contacts with extended family and is as developing a close friendship with a male who has good boundaries, good communication skills and is clear he doesn't want a sexual relationship with Ted.

Currently, Ted has no other symptoms than the vestiges of chronic loneliness he's lived with much of his life and a mild depression at times evidenced by some difficulty sleeping and questions about periodic pangs of doubt in his self-worth. He also has a latent anger that attacks him from within at times, though the Risperidal appears to have quieted this. He has achieved a degree of interpersonal honesty with his therapist which dispels some of his loneliness. Along the way, Ted has disclosed fears and fantasies about this therapist and experienced subsequent relief that he could "talk freely about the messiest things in my life and it won't hurt you and you won't turn away."

Ted identifies with the Christian faith and explored various Protestant denominations, until he finally found a Protestant congregation where he feels cared for by some of the people with whom he has made friends.

Diagnostic Impressions:
Axis I: Dissociative Disorder NOS; Identity disorder; dysthymia – mild, chronic; r/o amphetamine abuse (diet pills)
Axis II: none
Axis III: Cancer
Axis IV: Stressors: interpersonal loneliness; cancer; family conflict with brother; psychosexual conflict stressing social relationships, faith and identity
Axis V: CGAF: 70 HGAFPY tentatively 80
Rx:Risperidal; Zoloft

Discernment Impressions:
Demon of Fornication: Co-opting the unmetabolized rage and longing that are part of the dyscommunion between self/other and God, creating a stronghold for the passion of lust appearing in sadomasochistic forms and arresting further development of mature emotional expression in interpersonal relationship.

Demon of Despair: Attacking his sense of belovedness to God and hope of ever having a fulfilling intimate relationship in which he is "chosen" and cared for, for who he is. This tempts him with further self-hatred and unrequited love for God and human companionship and alienates him interpersonally.

Questions for Discussion:
• In addition to standard psychological understanding patristic psychology includes concepts of sin, redemption, salvation and cosmology of "demons," temptations, passions and the devil to address human growth and development. In light of this cosmology and anthropology, what are the treat-

ment options in terms of prayer rule, application of canon law, access to Holy Communion, almsgiving, etc. that could complement psychological and medical standards of care?

• How do we best integrate Orthodox Christian patristic teaching on spiritual illness with modern advances in understanding and treatment of mental/emotional disorders and avoid spiritualizing, medicalizing or secularizing the *human* and uniquely *personal*?

• What method do you use to make a differential *discernment*? Some authors use "demons" and "passions" in similar ways as semi-autonomous entities that "possess" and enslave the heart, fragmenting the "I." What Bureau of Standards informs your methods, similar to DSM-IV in the psychological arena?

• What is the value of bringing the psychotherapeutic and religious domains together in the service of helping heal Ted's suffering?

• What kinds of anthropological and scientific assumptions provide the context for the following "diagnoses" and what are the associated developmental norms that guide treatment from these perspectives? Which are most useful and why?

In what way is Ted "sick"?

In what way is Ted "developmentally arrested"?

In what way is Ted "traumatized"?

In what way is Ted "addicted"?

In what way is Ted "possessed by demons?"

In what way is Ted suffering from prelest or spiritual deception?

In what way is Ted cut off from the therapeutic aids of the Church? What would these be?

In what way do Ted's symptoms indicate unrealized longings and blocked eros?

•What was the effect on Ted of his previous therapist's failure to offer him an Orthodox Christian patristic viewpoint regarding entertaining fantasies in the inner world and use of attention, etc.?

•What Bureau of Standard Observers determines the "reality" and worldview for therapeutic disciplines and assumptions out of which Orthodox Christian psychotherapists and physicians practice?

•What is our obligation as Orthodox Christian healers to be critical of all these assumptions and raise them up for consideration with those who seek relief from their suffering by consulting with us?

•What are the ingredients that are making it possible for Ted to find greater communion with himself, others and God and healing him from the division at war within him?

PSYCHIATRIC CONSIDERATIONS

JEFF REDIGER

And in the last days it shall be, God declares,
that I will pour out my Spirit upon all flesh,
and your sons and your daughters shall prophesy,
and your young men shall see visions,
and your old men shall dream dreams;
yea, and on my menservants and my maidservants in those
days, I will pour out my Spirit; and they shall prophesy.
– Acts 2:17-18

Our normal waking consciousness, rational conscious-
ness as we call it, is but one special type of consciousness,
whilst all about it, parted from it by the filmiest of screens,
there lie potential forms of consciousness entirely different .
– William James

The above case study is an excellent choice because it illustrates with unusual clarity the kinds of issues that exist at the heart of the dialogue between materialist and more open or traditional assumptions (1) about the nature of the world in which we live. One would wish we could say that Ted's experience raises questions that go to the heart of the dialogue between psychology and theology; unfortunately, however, much of Western theology itself is a child of its age and has been perhaps unduly influenced by the materialist lens through which we have come to filter so much of our daily experience.

Ted's symptoms and clinical response raise questions that bring into sharp focus a conflict between two different ways of perceiving the world: either the world is primarily and fundamentally a material world that is known through the evidence of the five senses and depends in a decisive way on a clear, inviolable distinction between the knower and the known, or it is also a spiritual world, where sensory data are only part of the story, and a rigid distinction between subject and object, or knower and known, is helpful but also in part illusory and misguided.

In what follows, we will look more closely at Ted's experience as he reported it, and consider the evidence and clinical implications for a worldview informed by traditional Orthodox Christian theology. Orthodox theology, we should note, has a particularly significant role to play in the dialogue between psychology and theology and deserves a broader, more midwifery role as our world labors to give birth to a new and different consciousness, inasmuch as historical events have sheltered it from some of the cultural ascendancies of Western culture and its powerful but one-sided epistemological assumptions.

Psychiatric Symptoms from the Standpoint of Two Different Forms of Consciousness

Passages from the Holy Scriptures such as the one at the beginning of this article were deeply perplexing to me as a child and then as a young adult, simply because they seemed to be at such complete odds with the assumptions I was being taught in school. All the way through elementary and high school, college, medical school, residency and even seminary, I was schooled into a world that emphasized the priority of sensory data in the quest for knowledge and truth. With the tool of skepticism, one's goal was to reach a residue of certain, unassailable knowledge, and this was thought to arise from a close examination of all available sensory data. Although my seminary training was rigorous and a great deal of emphasis was given to understanding the kind of problem this creates for the spiritual life, solutions were generally attempted from "within the problem" in such a way that transcendent ideas or theological concepts were rendered abstract rather than grounded in a way of knowing that was practical and experiential.

Some of the details that Ted gave to his therapist would be quickly interpreted by most therapists and psychiatrists as symptoms of psychotic or dissociative behavior. The question is whether there is ever a clinical reason to slow down and consider more carefully. In the case study, Ted told his therapist that, after thirty or fourty years of fantasizing, he could induce the characters in his fantasies to actually come alive within himself and speak for themselves. For example:

> He had a certain set of cups in his kitchen with faces of celebrities on them and he could get them to actually change shapes as their mouths moved to speak to him. Now he began to be afraid because the characters were commenting to him within himself beyond what he was 'creating' and causing him not to be able to sleep. These were not audio-visual hallucinations of a schizophrenic nature, but more on the order of voices of dissociative disorder, although even this was not totally clear. Ted would insist "I am creating them" while at the same time saying "They talk to me and get angry and comment on what I'm doing." He notes that he tends to be bothered most by the 'voices' during periods when he has self-administered diet pills.

A great deal is packed into this short narrative, and in what follows I will attempt a sort of "thought-experiment" that renders Ted's account more intelligible. If Ted's symptoms are best accounted for by traditional psychiatric criteria for psychotic processes, then that pathway should be pursued. If Ted's symptoms are best accounted for by what is known about the manifold presentations and effects of dissociative processes, then the treatment lies in that direction. What we have to consider, however, is the possibility that from within certain modes of consciousness – such as the mystical consciousness described by saints and increasingly reported by many people today – some of the normal rules of everyday reality are relativized by a higher order, and that this is not just a disease process but can have beneficial results as well. If this is the case, then the experience must be understood on its own terms and not pathologized by the categories of traditional psychiatric nomenclature. Otherwise new possibilities for self-transcendence will be lost and the person will lose the opportunity to integrate potential sources of power and life into his or her daily living.

Clues to whether this latter understanding should be considered involve the congruence of Ted's affect when he describes these experiences, whether he is known to be an honest and reliable reporter of his experience, whether any secondary gain is present (e.g., for attention) and whether some of the experiences that he reports have borne clear and tangible fruit in his life. The author of this case study did not comment on either Ted's affect-congruence or his reliability, but did take his reports seriously enough to raise them for our discussion. No secondary gain is apparent from the report as written. There are, however, some indications of possible beneficial effects that should be considered. Ted did find significant help from the pastoral counselor who understood that the fantasy life is directly connected with what one then experiences in the outer world, and Ted did report some miraculous healings in the past. Lab tests or radiological reports, from before and after the healings, and consultation with intimate acquaintances can be helpful in unearthing the truth in these situations.

When a clinician decides that psychotic or dissociative symptoms are present, an entire worldview is typically implied. Auditory and visual hallucinations are *ipso facto* thought to reflect the hearing of sounds or the seeing of sights that do not really exist. They may reflect, for example, the disordered neurochemistry of dopaminergic neurons in the ventral tegmental region of the mesolimbic-mesocortical tract, but no more. Consciousness is thought to be only the result of neuronal functioning and in fact it is considered axiomatic that consciousness cannot exist without the firing of neurons.

The point of treatment, according to this view of the world, is to obtain, either through psychopharmacology or psychotherapy, the alleviation of the voices or the cessation of the disturbing visions. As the materialist paradigm has had the time and resources supplied to extend itself further, biological psychiatry has become more and more the focus, and today's medicines play an increasingly pivotal and often helpful role in the management of psychotic and dissociative symptoms. The question is whether this view of reality, where the material world is thought to be in a final and absolute way the ultimate arbiter of reality, sufficiently accounts for all of the evidence.

A few years ago, when I was a resident in psychiatry, a young man began to see me shortly after becoming clean and sober for the first time. As I began to get to know him, I was surprised by how dedicated he was to sobriety and to obtaining a college degree. He had one of the most violent histories that I had ever seen, with cruel blody beatings, until his alcoholic father left left forever, and often huddled in a corner while his mother sold her body for heroin. His stepmother pulled a shotgun on him at one point and at other times cheered on his father in their fistfights. He eventually ran away from home and spent the next ten years as a drug dealer and gang member.

I knew that he had had years of involvement with the mental health system and that he also had a history of difficult relationships with the psychiatrists and clinicians who had been assigned to his care. So I asked him why things were different now, and what had helped him attain sobriety and begin such clear efforts for a new life. What he said surprised me.

He told me that he gave up the drugs and alcohol after his dead Native American grandmother, who herself had been alcoholic, appeared to him one night, sat down on the edge of his bed, and told him to give up the alcohol. He had been particularly struck by what he took to be her surprise at his tattoos, which he had not had during the years when she had been alive.

Shortly after that experience, he became clean and sober for the first time and began making plans for college. That experience, which he believes was with his grandmother, did more for him in five minutes than ten years of regular contact with psychiatrists and therapists. And, with a few setbacks, the progress persisted, in spite of the fact that he continued to live in a slum with his mother and four veterans with substance-abuse problems. He continued to see me for both low-dose medication and psychotherapy, but something essential had shifted and I was not so much treating an illness as I was helping him get to where he wanted to go. Accepting his experience as somehow important seemed to melt the resistances that had characterized many of his prior clinical relationships and allowed us to really get to work.

To understand his experience as being simply the reflection of psychotic or dissociative processes implies a pathologization of his experience and symptoms that was deeply aversive to him. What traditional psychiatry views as symptoms to be removed, he viewed as the clarion call to a new life.

Since then, I have listened to other patients or people involved in our research at the Institute report experiences that I am not sure can be adequately accounted for within the framework of traditional psychiatric or medical assumptions. And there are stories in the history of Christian spirituality that also highlight questions about how different can be the maps of reality and consciousness created by the great founders of psychiatry which over time have received the blessing of the church. Jean-Martin de Charcot, for example, director of the famous Salpetrière mental hospital for women in Paris, photographed the women he was treating for hysteria in poses labeled "Ecstatic State" and "Beatitude" and concluded that such women were across the board suffering from delusions. And Sigmund Freud's colleague, Josef Breuer, dubbed St. Teresa of Avila the "patron saint of hysteria," though he did admit that she was "a woman of genius with great practical capacity."(2) It is for the reader to decide whether such descriptions as the following, which St. Teresa believed sharply increased her capacity to receive God's love and love others, reflect thought content that is strictly delusional and misguided:

> It pleased our Lord that I should sometimes see this vision. Very close to me, on my left, an angel appeared in human form, which is not how I usually perceive them – though I do once in a while. Even though angels often appear to me, I don't actually see them, except in the way I mentioned earlier. But our Lord willed that I should see this vision in the following way: He was not tall but short, and very beautiful, and his face was so aflame that he seemed to be one of those superior angels who look like they are completely on fire. They must be the ones called cherubim – they don't tell me their names – but I am very aware that in heaven there is such a difference between some angels and others, and between these and still others, that I would not know how to explain it. In his hands I saw a large golden spear, and at its iron tip there seemed to be a point of fire. I felt as if he plunged this into my heart several times, so that it

penetrated all the way to my entrails. When he drew it out,
he seemed to draw them out with it, and left me totally inflamed with a great love for God. The pain was so severe, it
made me moan several times. The sweetness of this intense
pain is so extreme, there is no wanting it to end, and the
soul isn't satisfied with anything less than God. This pain is
not physical, but spiritual, even though the body has a share
in it – in fact, a large share. So delicate is this exchange between God and the soul that I pray God, in his goodness, to
give a taste of it to anyone who thinks I am lying.(3)

Delusional or not, St. Teresa's *Vida*, filled with passages
like this, has inspired a wide variety of responses, such as
from George Eliot, who made her the genius loci of her novel
Middlemarch, and Gian Lorenzo Bernini, who immortalized
her in his *The Ecstasy of St. Teresa* in the Cornaro Chapel
of Santa Maria della Vittoria, Rome. It is worth examining
whether some mystical experiences actually do have a beneficial impact on the recipient, and increase his or her capacities to give and receive love.

Orthodox *Logismoi* and Materialism vs. Mysticism

Now, what does Orthodox theology offer in regards to the
symptoms that Ted reported? According to the above quote,
Ted reported that years of fantasy had brought him to the
point where characters could actually come alive within him
and speak for themselves, and even the faces of celebrities
on his coffee cups would move their mouths to speak to him.
A former psychologist, consistent with a materialist vision
of the world, had told Ted that it didn't matter what he fantasized about as long he did not act on it.

The mystical vision that permeates Orthodox theology
teaches that the world of our everyday existence is characterized by polarities and sharply competing dualisms – for
example, up and down, cold and hot, night and day, positive and negative, good and evil, male and female, individual

and community, mind and body, etc. We have been given the opportunity to live within these polarities in order to learn and grow towards theosis; i.e., towards that stage where we become conscious of the actual presence of God within ourselves. According to this vision of the world, these polarities, and the pain and suffering that are often connected with them, are phenomenal and not realities in and of themselves. Things are not as they seem.

In order to be adequately Aristotelian, or give due credit to both sensory and spiritual realities, perhaps it is more accurate to say that material reality is real from one perspective but, from another vantage point, it becomes relative and conditioned by a larger perspective, much in the same way that, for a young child, the moon appears to move along with the car but, from a more mature developmental perspective, the same sensory data are relocated into a larger context and the adult recognizes that the moon's movement with the car is not what it appears to be.

This can be understood in a partial way by examining the familiar gestelt pictures which can be seen in distinctively different ways. For example, while looking at the picture, some people will see an old hag. Others will see a young maiden. This demonstrates that, even when people have the same data, they can see completely different things. And, significantly, try as one might, one cannot see the old woman and the maiden at the same time, though facility at flipping back and forth between the two views can be developed.

This illustrates in a partial way how two visions of the world can both be true within their proper spheres. However, the mystical vision goes beyond this because, whereas the pictures of the old woman and young maiden are comprised of data from within the same frame of reference and depend exclusively on which details the knower pulls out of the picture and integrates into a picture, the mystical form of consciousness is of a different order than that of ordinary consciousness. The relation of the mystical consciousness to ordinary consciousness is akin to that of an adult's view of the moon moving along with the car, in spite of the child's perception.

Although most of us live each day within the confines of ordinary consciousness, there are enough people – and past saints – who report experiences consistent with a mystical frame of consciousness that it is worthy of serious consideration. It does seem to bleed through – in some people more clearly than in others – too frequently to be ignored.

Ted's pastoral counselor proceeded with the treatment by helping Ted recognize destructive *logismoi* and replace them with the Jesus Prayer and an icon of Christ. What are *logismoi*? Etymologically speaking, *logismoi* has to do with "thoughts," with the thoughts that one has. According to St. Maximus, some thoughts are simple and others are composite.(4) Thoughts which are not linked with strong emotion or passion are considered to be "simple." Composite thoughts, however, are those conceptual images which are passion-charged, or combined with strong feeling or passion.

At the heart of the mystical consciousness is the understanding that phenomenal reality is not as it seems. A truly mystical consciousness, therefore, will see the fantasy life as not only contributory to what one experiences in the outer world, but even as in some way decisive, in the long run. Because what we see and experience is in part related to what we really believe to be true about the world.

A way of thinking that may help us understand *logismoi* from the perspective of the mystical consciousness has to do with elementals.(5) Elementals are thought forms. They are the energies that we project outward as we generate ideas and feelings. As Kyriacos Markides describes, elementals have shape, form and energy. When we think of the ocean, we construct the form of the ocean in our mind. If we have a desire to visit the ocean, we inject the idea of the ocean (the form) with desire (the energy). The greater the desire, the greater the energy that is injected into the form. The strength of the elemental depends on the amount of energy as desire or passion that is injected into it.

It is worth wondering whether thoughts carry with them a form of energy that can be detected. I work with a number of extraordinarily sensitive individuals at the Institute, and the kinds of experiences that they both report and that I observe when with them certainly does lend itself to the idea that there is a sort of subtle energy emitted by thoughts that can be detected by some people.

What these individuals tell me is that we all have such capacities, but that they tend to lie latent within most of us. These capacities can be developed, but they seem to involve developing aspects of ourselves that we tend not pay to a lot of attention to in this culture. These persons seem to be extraordinarily intuitive – even meta-intuitive – and sometimes can catch the thought of what someone is about to say before it is actually said. Even though mistakes certainly do occur, I have also seen individuals hear the name of someone who I know they have never met, and proceed to tell me all kinds of things about that stranger at a level of detail that is truly astonishing. It's almost like they have antennae attuned to a particular frequency, much like radio waves. Sometimes meeting a stranger face-to-face actually blurs the amount and clarity of information that the intuitive receives, almost as if appearances can get in the way of what is even more real but invisible.

One way that I have begun thinking about all of this is to consider that left-brained, analytical reason has given us tremendous resources; however, it has left many intuitive, more gestalt-oriented people – especially women, who are more naturally inclined to the intuitive – a bit cold and feeling that something essential has been omitted. And it does seem that those who have made great discoveries – e.g. Kekule's discovery of the structure of the benzene ring after dreaming about a snake eating its tail, Francis and Crick reaching after the structure of DNA by looking for the most beautiful structure, Einstein imagining himself riding on a beam of light, etc. – often moved towards discovery by relying on subtle cues that seem more akin to intuition and even mysticism than to just analytical logic, strictly defined.

Thomas Merton once described Western culture as a great one-eyed giant, stumbling around causing both great benefit and great destruction. What we need is to develop our second eye, he said, meaning by that our eye of intuition, wholeness and wisdom.

If thoughts fused with feelings create elementals, the question is how far the implications extend. One question has to do with the kind of invisible connection that exists between all of us. At the very center of philosophy has always been the debate about being – whether there are many beings, or just one Being, and the nature of the connection between all beings. For the past three hundred years, our culture has emphasized the discrete, isolated nature of all beings. However, in recent years many in the West are turning to the East and its mysticism as they begin to suspect that such emphasis has been one-sided and not adequately sensitive to the ways in which we are all interconnected with and need each other. Perhaps it is more accurate to say that while ordinary consiousness depends on cause-and-effect, rational analysis and the evidence of the five senses; another, more spiritual form of consciousness relocates tangible reality into a larger context in a way that does not invalidate the findings of a more materialistic version of the world as much as reformulate them on the basis of new information.

Another question has to do with whether our materialist vision of the world has been true to a point but far more limited than we can easily see. Perhaps we are not bodies with souls at all. Perhaps the truth is far more radical. Perhaps it is more true to say that we are souls first: souls who take on the envelope of the body in order to use the polarities of temporal existence in order to move towards theosis. This way of thinking places a lot more emphasis on the invisible world that surrounds us, and suggests that perhaps the visible world is a manifestation of the even more real but less tangible invisible world.

Our desire forms elementals and continues to keep them alive by infusing them with energy. They continue to have life until the desire has been satisfied or the person has abandoned it for a different desire. As long as a particular elemental exists, it seeks to move in the direction of fulfillment. Perhaps this is why spiritual teachings instruct that what you desire you shall eventually have. The elementals you construct eventually catch up with you, and the outer world begins to match the inner world that you have created.

Another way of saying this is to say that what we project outward in the form of thoughts and feelings eventually returns to us as the world that we have created, good or bad. We draw towards ourselves the elementals corresponding to the elementals produced in our minds, and are in turn influenced by the elementals we attract. In this sense, one could say that two people can sit next to each other but be living in quite different worlds. In other words, we punish or reward ourselves through the thought forms that we create. When we harm someone with our thoughts or feelings, we actually are doing the harm to ourselves. When we love or perform an act of kindness for someone, we are doing that to ourselves.

What is possible, and consistent with this line of thinking, is that at some point these projected thoughts and feelings take on a life of their own and an independent existence. They become "things" in the same way that electricity, magnetism and light are things. And the elementals that we project onto the world also draw towards them similar elementals that have been created by others. I and others have had the ex-

perience of occasionally feeling in an almost physical way
the thought that someone else is having, even if the other
person is on the other side of the room. At the Institute where
I work, some of the unusually sensitive individuals report
that, at times, they even see thoughts (usually best typified as
"colors."). This of course raises the question about whether,
with the proper instruments, it will eventually be possible to
detect or even weigh thoughts and feelings.

If *logismoi* take on, at some level, objective properties, then
we would expect that, when we break our connection with
that elemental, it will still be out there in the environment
for a certain amount of time, even as stoking a fire leaves
an afterglow. The stronger the fire, the longer the afterglow
will last. This line of thinking does have some explanatory
power for Ted's report about the nature of the voices: "Ted
would insist 'I am creating them' while at the same time saying 'They talk to me and get angry and comment on what
I'm doing.'"

Given the fact that, at the time of this writing, the United
States has just entered Iraq in pursuit of Saddam Hussein,
one should probably consider the possibility of collective elementals. Perhaps groups of people can also create elementals that are relatively high and pure or less so. And these
collective elementals can have more or less power depending on how much energy has been infused into them. We all
exist within a web of interacting elementals, and continually
influence each other's subconscious through our elementals.
It is worth asking about our deepest intentions and desires
as we enter this war. And to remember that we are deeply
interconnected to the past and the future of the Iraqi people
in ways that we do not readily see.

There still remains a particularly difficult problem to resolve. How is one to think about Ted's report that the faces
of celebrities on the coffee mugs spoke to him? Although
this goes beyond my personal experience, one thing to con-

sider, perhaps, is the report by some spiritual teachers and healers that there is an energy field that surrounds all of us, including likenesses of us. These teachers and healers report that when they see the photograph of an individual, what they see is the energy field surrounding that individual at that moment in time. It is not the energy field present at the time the photograph was taken, but the energy field at that moment. This, they say, is how they know details about the health of the individual at that moment. These kinds of reports, to the degree that they can be taken seriously (and one must move carefully in this regard) imply that all of reality is far more interconnected and multilayered than we readily see from the standpoint of ordinary consciousness.

Returning to the neurochemistry that was mentioned earlier, it is now known that the abstract concepts of quantum mechanics and atomic theory also have direct relevance for understanding the chemistry that underlies brain function. For example, all students of chemistry are familiar with the periodic table of elements, which are built up by successively adding protons and neutrons to the nucleus of the lightest atom (hydrogen) and a corresponding number of electrons to its atomic "shell." The number of electrons in the atoms of an element determine each element's chemical properties, and the interactions between the atoms give rise to the various chemical processes. So chemistry is essentially one extension of atomic physics.(6)

If the foregoing hypothesis is true, that there is a type of invisible energy associated with our thoughts and feelings, then one might hypothesize that the atomic structure underlying neurochemistry in some way participates in this. This, however, reaches far beyond the confines of the current article. It is worth mentioning, however, that quantum mechanics also is quite provocative in its claims about the nature of the relationship between subject and object and about the related nature of particles at a distance from each other. Returning to Ted's report about the medicines that he took, it was Ted's belief that the "voices" were worse when he self-administered diet pills, and that the Risperdal diminished or muffled the voices. Perhaps when the neurochemistry is aligned in certain ways and in a certain context, dimensions of reality less available to ordinary consciousness become more accessible, almost as if a portal has been opened. Certainly there are centuries-old writings that imply this sort of relationship between the mystical consciousness and the use of herbs or drugs. Perhaps the Risperdal provided a sort of insulation for Ted from the negative *logismoi* so that he could begin developing a life that participated in new and healthier elementals.

Recovery from Trauma
as the Healing of Destructive Logismoi

This leads us to a consideration of the process of healing from destructive *logismoi*. If a person harbors thoughts of fear, malice or hatred for a length of time, then one will be flooded by more malice and hatred than one ever expected. One eventually can become a center for such thoughts. If this way of thinking becomes a habit, then the person will begin attracting circumstances and actions that provide opportunities to manifest the thoughts.

Ted was exposed at a young age to *logismoi* that clearly were of a relatively low-level and dark character. His mother dressed him in girl's clothing and his brothers made fun of him to the extent that a deep fear and doubt about his masculinity was born within him. This was extended when, as an adolescent, an older man fondled him. The fantasies that Ted developed over the course of the next forty years, of course, were related to these events and the elementals with which they were associated.

Perhaps lower-level elementals tend to be comprised of

ideas that are subordinate to desires. These relatively low-level elementals are comprised not only of animal passions and appetites, but also of the passions related to insults and trauma. Higher-level elementals, on the other hand, may tend to be comprised of desires that are subordinate to the higher and more noble ideas/ideals. One of the great and terrible sphinxes that one must face in recovering from sexual abuse is fear – fear that as a child one somehow attracted the abuse and is therefore somehow faulty or bad. Since the truest things are self-evident and can only be known by an open heart, fear renders the world opaque. It is, one could say, the great epistemological blinder. It is also a magnet for lower-level elementals.

Ted's therapist wanted to help Ted develop mastery over his thoughts and emotions and, in so doing, generate elementals of thought and feeling that are higher and purer than the elementals that grew out of the abuse and suffering. Ted's therapist seemed to be working from a premise that, as one gains mastery over one's thoughts, fears, desires and egotism, then the old and less constructive elementals become de-energized and replaced by higher-level elementals. If one cultivates the habit of thinking the highest and best possible thoughts, then one is eventually drawn into conditions that are harmonious with those thoughts. And that person will draw to him or herself people with similar thoughts. We make our surroundings and company by our thoughts of yesterday and today.

The elementals we create either attune us to ourselves, others and God, or induce fragmentation. Ted's therapist counseled him to cut off the thoughts according to the Orthodox Christian patristic teachings in regards to the elementals, or *logismoi*. Ted then began reading material on the Jesus prayer. "The therapist gave Ted an icon of Christ at some point in the therapy and Ted related one day that the voice had been 'converted' and was now saying the Jesus prayer and on a couple of occasions appeared to do this from the icon when he looked at it." This did not last, and the Risperdal played a role in moving the voices into the background. It is possible that the old elementals, which had developed their power over the course of several decades of being actively "fed" by Ted's fantasy life, were powerful enough that it was going to take some hard work to snap the strings and replace them with lasting elementals of a different quality.

Healing from trauma involves coming to see oneself and the world differently, and knowing better how to safely negotiate a world that is full of both peril and wonder. In the higher stages, the world begins to appear as it does in the reports of poets and great mystics. As the poet Gerard Manley Hopkins said: "The world is charged with the grandeur of God. It will shine out like shining from shook foil." As one moves towards theosis, one becomes free from fear, and truly likes what one sees in the mirror. This seems consistent with how Metropolitan Hierotheos Vlachos understands patristic teaching:

> Certainly aside from evil thoughts there are good thoughts, those coming from God. How can we distinguish these thoughts? Those of us who are beginners in the spiritual life should ask experienced spiritual fathers, and especially those who have the gift of distinguishing spirits. In any case, one general teaching is that when a thought suggests something to us and joy comes, it is a sign that the thought is from God. The thoughts of the devil are full of disturbance and dejection. St. Barsanuphios teaches: "When a thought suggests to you to do something according to the will of God, and you find in this matter joy, and at the same time sorrow which fights against it, know that this thought is from God...The thoughts which come from the devil are filled with disturbance and themselves in sheepskins, that is, they instill thoughts which in appearance are right, but within are "ravening wolves." It must be noted that a thought is capable of evoking a joy which, however, comes

from vanity and a self-indulgent heart. Therefore thoughts can be distinguished only by one who has tasted the grace of the Holy Spirit and has been cleansed from the passions which are found in the soul. Those who lack this experience should consult experienced spiritual fathers…(7)

There are always a few spiritual souls who are so advanced that even the worst trauma and violence result only in beneficial influence on their souls:

When the Communists took over Tibet, they imprisoned many monks, nuns, and lamas…Some were imprisoned in Chinese labor camps for twenty or thirty years and are only now being released. A while back, I met a monk who had been imprisoned for twenty-five years. He had been tortured and treated badly, and his body was pretty much a wreck. But his mind! When you looked into his eyes, far from seeing bitterness, brokenness, or hatred in them, you could see that they were glowing. He looked as if he had just spent twenty-five years on retreat! All he talked about was his gratitude to the Chinese. They had really helped him develop overwhelming love and compassion towards those who caused him harm. He said, 'Without them I would just have continued mouthing platitudes.' But because of his imprisonment, he had to draw on his inner strength. In such circumstances, you either go under or you surmount. When he emerged from prison, he felt nothing but love and understanding towards his captors.(8)

Although the good clinician always pays attention to denial and wishful thinking when it exists, it is a truly remarkable thing to observe self-transcendence and genuine resilience where it does exist.

Spirits and Possession

The above discussion understandably raises questions about whether spirits and spirit possession exist. There are many ways to go astray in this kind of discussion. Certainly

specters like the Salem witch trials and the subsequent murder of over twenty individuals helped create a strong desire
on the part of sane and healthy people for a rational culture which protects innocent people from mass hysteria, the
projection of unconscious fears onto others, egoism and the
misuse of ecclesiastical power.

Because of this and the ways in which demon possession
and exorcisms are often portrayed, it is probably important
to note that some spiritual teachers teach that all humans
tend to attach themselves to a variety of helpful and less-
than-helpful spirits, much in the same way that we tend to
attach ourselves to a variety of elementals. This is why they
make a distinction between attachment and possession and
say that most of human life deals with attachments rather
than possession as it is popularly portrayed.

Whatever aspects of human and spiritual life are denied or
repressed in a culture will tend to manifest in distorted and
sometimes destructive ways. So it makes sense that, since we
live in a culture that *ipso facto* regards voices as having only
a materialistic or biological basis, discussions about spiritual
attachment will be easily misunderstood and misapplied.

With that said, the Holy Scriptures depict a world where
we are surrounded by a cloud of invisible witnesses. As a
child raised in a Protestant home, I grew up confused by the
ontological differences between the world as revealed in the
Bible and the apparently uniplanar world around me. If the
reports by Ted and other patients have some validity, then
there is a lot going on outside the narrow band of reality
taught even in some seminaries.

The issues raised by the present case study raise the possibility that there is something to the biblical view of the world
that, though not easily reconciled with our modern maps of
the world, still hints at something true. Perhaps both science and the Bible are right in their spheres, though it does
seem to me that one must allow oneself to be drawn into

the biblical stories through a mystical doorway, and be open to believing that the world may appear very different from the standpoint of different forms of consciousness. There are groups of Christians who believe that the devil exists; unfortunately, however, for some of these groups the devil seems omnipresent and it is clear that this omnipresence grows out of a deep fear and mistrust of the world.

Holy Scripture and the Church have always supported the belief that, behind all the polarities and difficulties of all that is apparent, it is a truly glorious world, where God is real and love connects everything and everyone. We are all children of God and the Kingdom of Heaven is available to all who desire to enter. Imperfect spirits may exist, but they are inferior in both power and knowledge to the higher spirits who dwell more nearly to God's pure light and goodness. Reality is a marvelous and complicated affair and one must develop a great deal of savvy to pass the tests that will arise, but it is still, in the best and highest sense, good.

Conclusion

The above case study was well-chosen for the kinds of issues that it raises. Popular culture seems to be witnessing a return of the repressed in regards to a new and burgeoning interest in the spiritual life. In contrast to Nietszche's famous adage that "God is dead," the number of best-selling books and movies exploring overtly spiritual themes suggest that it may be more accurate to say instead that "Nietszche is dead." As our culture becomes more open to spiritual realities, psychiatry and medicine will continue to undergo great, unanticipated changes. We need to improve our capacities for recognizing and distinguishing true human advances in self-transcendence from false subjectivities and false claims. To the degree that we do not learn to do this well, we will continue to see more of the kinds of atrocities fostered in

Inquisitions and witch hunts.

We now live in a culture that has made unparalleled prog-ress in the understanding of external objective reality. But let us not allow this consciousness to make us prisoners of its own effects. The present case report raises the possibility that the frontier before us has to do with mapping the ob-jective laws of robust inner development. As Ralph Waldo Emerson intoned, "What lies behind us and what lies before us are tiny matters compared to what lies within us." We will need a different kind of science for some of this quest, with a new understanding of the relationship that pertains between subject and object, and new criteria for objectivity. We will do well to look to some of the great saints for guidance. We may find that the world of the Holy Scriptures is not as for-eign as one might expect.

Before Galileo's work was accepted, people accepted the apparent movement of the sun and moon across the horizon as common-sense evidence for the earth's existence at the center of the universe. Unfortunately, the Roman Catholic hierarchy did not treat Galileo or other scientists well who challenged their view of the world, and this gave rise to a deep schism between science and the church. It is a great and important irony that we are now in a position where we can fairly invoke Galileo's name as a reminder that all hu-man systems of thought – even the ideas underlying science as it typically understands itself – must be held with humil-ity. What are held as dearly beloved "facts" from one level of analysis appear very different when viewed from another perspective.

All epistemological maps, whether of science or faith, are limited in their capacity and, at some level, conceal the very reality they seek to reveal. It is a deeply human tendency to take our representations of reality for the real thing, and for-get that they are only symbols that point towards the greater reality, which is beyond words and symbols. A finger can help locate the moon, but it is of course a great error to think that the finger is somehow the moon. So we must proceed with humility.

Notes

1. By "traditional assumptions," I mean to indicate not the traditional assumptions of recent western culture, but the traditional assumptions that are more common in other cultures and time periods, where spiritual beliefs have been much more accepted. Western culture is a relatively recent and brief blip on the timeline of history.

2. Cathleen Medwick, *Teresa of Avila: The Progress of a Soul,* (New York: Alfred A. Knopf, 1999), p. xv.

3. Ibid, p. 57.

4. Metropolitan Hierotheos of Nafpaktos, *Orthodox Psychotherapy: The Science of the Fathers*, trans. by Esther Williams, (Levadia, Greece: Birth of the Theotokos Monastery, 1994), p. 394.

5. See Kyriacos Markides, *The Mountain of Silence: A Search for Orthodox Spirituality,* (New York: Doubleday Press, 2001), p. 64f.; and *Riding with the Lion,* (New York: Penguin Books Ltd), p. 47f.

6. Fritjof Capra, *The Tao of Physics,* (New York: Bantam Books, 1984), p. 54.

7. *Orthodox Psychotherapy*, p. 416.

8. Ani Tenson Palmo, *Reflections on a Mountain Lake: Teachings on Practical Buddhism*, quoted in "*Spirituality and Health*," vol. 6, no. 1, April, 2003, p. 76.

THEOLOGICAL CONSIDERATIONS

Fr. Stephen Plumlee

The case of "Ted" presents numerous pastoral and clinical questions. As a clinician I am stimulated with questions about his psychology and therapy. There are also numerous ways one could go about approaching a theological perspective on this vignette. I would like to propose one that I think is productive and then look at Ted's situation within that framework.

The core of Orthodox Christian experience of God is the Holy Trinity. We understand, of course, that our experience is of God's energies, not the essence of God, which is beyond the order of human reason and comprehension. The energies of God present themselves to us as three Persons or Hypostases, and indeed Orthodox declare that they know God only in the hypostasized energies. We do not know God in God's beingness as such, but in the interactive components of the Divine life that are revealed to us.

Furthermore, we understand that the relationship among the three Hypostases is about the life of God, not just an "invariant organizing principle" of human psychology, to use Stolorow's language. God as we know God is a dynamic internal interaction of cooperation, love, and mutual support in the actions of the three toward creation. The characters of these three are usually described in terms of their modes of being: the Father is the uncreated source of the others, the Son is uncreated but begotten by the Father, and the Holy Spirit is uncreated but proceeds from the Father. However,

85

there are other characteristics of the three hypostases that profoundly affect their relationship with each other and with us, their creatures. The will of the Father and his loving and chastising behavior towards us when we are true to or deviant from the path of life he gives us has led to our creation and re-creation. The Second Person, revealed as the Word in the Prologue to the Gospel of St. John, is known as the agent of order and structure in creation, and the Holy Spirit is the activating, energizing source. Within the Godhead the desire of the three for united connection with each other is what moves us the most.

This brief and superficial overview serves primarily to focus our attention on the created, human side of the equation. In the description of Creation that occurs in Genesis 1:26 and 27 there are two aspects of the human person that reflect the Godhead. God says, "Let us make man in our image, after our likeness . . . So God created man in His own image, in the image of God He created him." The first aspect that is declared here, and one we are all familiar with, is that of image and likeness. Orthodox Christians understand that we are first of all created with godlike creativity, that from the beginning of our being we have the capacity to be loving, creative and cooperative, first in response to God but also to all others in creation. As we exercise those creative behaviors we grow more deeply into an ever-developing likeness to the hypostases of God.

Secondly, when God talks to Himself and says "Let Us make man in our image," he reveals that He is a God of internal relationship and communication, that God is a Trinity. In making his triadic quality known God also declares that human persons, made in the divine image to grow into God's likeness, are also Trinitarian in their created nature. Since God is a relationship of three within Himself and we are modeled to be like Him, then each of us is also a relationship of three within ourselves. If God is intra-active in love, cooperation and mutually dynamic support, then it follows that each of us is to be such also; that we are to deal within ourselves with care, support and cooperation.

The great gift of libidinal love, that desire and yearning the hypostases of God have for each other, is the source and model of our own internal dynamic encounter. The part of me that is yearning for connectedness is to be supported and encouraged by the part of me that seeks to maintain a healthy separateness. The two of them are to be mutually cared for and nurtured by the element of myself that mediates the relationship of the whole with the external environment.

The triadic paradigm for the human person is simply, but beautifully, illustrated by the Borromean Knot: it is a diagram designed by its inventor to illustrate the essential relationship of the Trinity. Each of three rings is attached in such a way that if one is removed the other two come apart also; only within the systemic whole can each have a place, and unless each is in its place, the whole cannot be.

The same eloquent model can be used to describe the human person made by God in "our image and likeness." As is true of the internal life of the divine creator, so also for His creature. Each of the three elements of our own hypostasis must also have a place in the whole person, and the whole person cannot exist unless each ring is in its connected place.

The Case

Let us turn our attention now to Ted. Ted's libidinal aspect, his yearning for connection both in the form of interactive attachment and of desire for an affiliation group, seems to be highly energized. This appears clearly in the second sentence of the "The Complexities of a Person." He "has felt the most intense emotional longing in his life for males." In that longing Ted demonstrates the basic motivation of the human person. He desires to be united with the other, to have an interactive attachment in the joy of oneness with his fellow creatures. Furthermore, as is always the thrust of libido, he desires to unite himself with an affiliation group (or, in fact, groups), to have an energic connectedness with a set of others to whom he belongs. In this case that is a gender group, males.

Ted's longing troubles him because he experiences that yearning as sexual. He has appropriately learned that the desire for sexual connectedness belongs toward the opposite sex, that the "right" object for his desire is woman. He knows that the focus of sexual libido in his affiliation group is normatively toward women, that if he desires men he is in some degree outside the identity connection, and that makes him anxious. Ted needs a strong component within himself as a person to help keep him from being absorbed into personal oblivion within his affinity group, that of males.

In expectable development we could look for another essential circle to occur, linked with the one of libidinal identity but distinct from it. That is a component of the person that perceives the self as differentiated, distinct and separate from the other members of the affinity group. In some terminology that part of the person is known as the "I," in others as the "counter-libidinal self." Whatever the term, it performs the necessary function of restraining the impulse to connect into merger, loss of self, with the rest of creation. Its purpose is not to crush or kill libidinal energy, but to direct it.

In Ted this aspect seems to be overly developed, for although one would expect Ted's libidinal energy to be directed away from total assimilation into male connection toward connectedness with females, something quite different occurs. Ted's anxious fear of merger and disappearance impedes his ability to connect libidinally with a woman, for by his own declaration he is unable to "commit" and must keep a distance to avoid being "smothered" by woman. His "hypostatic" differentiation and separation of self works overtime and does not allow him to connect genuinely with others; he is anxious that he will be absorbed. He lived with a woman for some years but without a sexual liaison and his sexual fantasies tend to involve men, causing him to fear intimate contact with them as well. So in effect, Ted is unable to function in a truly libidinal way with any other person of either gender. That is, his capacity to fulfill his yearning for deep connection with others is crushed by his separating energies.

Thus it appears that the third essential hypostatic aspect of Ted's self, a central one which would regulate the balance between his libidinal and counter-libidinal parts and between the two of them and the outside world, is only superficially developed. We know little about his life pattern of work, but at age sixty-six he is financially independent and active in making real estate investments. We might conclude that his capacities to interact effectively with his environment are sufficiently developed for him to have been able to maintain his own physical needs. We are told that he is beginning to develop a non-genital connection with another man. In this project he appears to be relying on the other man's counter-libidinal strengths to keep him from merging into a homosexual liaison.

Since this is a theological overview of the case, we might now turn our attention to Ted's relationship with God. It appears that his spiritual life also suffers from hypostatic developmental arrest or suppression. He declares himself to be drawn to Christianity, but there is little sense of an intimate experience of God. When he is introduced to the Jesus Prayer he seems initially to find respite in it from the conflict of judgmental voices within him. Eventually, however, the voices take up again their angry criticism of him. Whether these voices are Ted's creation, ways his insufficiently developed and linked triad of aspects talk to each other, or are diabolical spirits who have taken advantage of his weak formation of personhood, is unclear. Whatever may be the case, this part of the case presentation reveals a restricted, partial relationship to the Holy Trinity.

It seems that Ted's attraction to Christianity is of a moralizing nature. That is, the primary impetus may be not connection or communion with the Holy Trinity, the Living God. His hope may be that the moral teachings of the Christian tradition offer him an external source of control and limitation on his libidinal energy. In that frame of mind Christian ethics are a restraint on his yearning for connection that he fears will lead him to sexual behavior and subsequently loss of self through merger with the other. From an Orthodox theological perspective, on the other hand, the developmental goal is not conformity to an abstract absolute of behavior, but participation in Christian morality via relationship, as the framework that protects and shapes the progress of the person in his or her developed communion with the Holy Trinity. This means, of course, a trinitarian communion with the body of fellow travelers and the increasingly solid integration of the tri-unity of the person. Each of these "communions" successfully, and progressively negotiated, nourishes the others in a continuous growth from glory to glory. "We are all, with unveiled face, beholding as in a mirror the glory of the Lord, are being transformed into the same image from glory to glory, just as by the Spirit of the Lord" (2 Cor 3:18).

Ted's fears of merger and absorption seriously constrain his capacity to nurture the maturation of his three parts. Apparently his memory of the experience in his infancy of resting against his father's warm, pungent crotch triggers his anxiety about erotic pleasure in connecting with males. His reaction to his mother's using him as a doll to dress up as a girl has led to further continuous fear, in this case of losing his membership in the club of males and being absorbed into a pool of femaleness. The result appears to be a libidinal paralysis of almost seven decades: Ted is frightened of exercising erotic energy in relationship to others or relationally within himself. His development – spiritually and psychologically – was inverted: that is, he learned to suppress and control his erotic love impulses before he could experience the flowering of them. In normative personal development the joy and power of eros (i.e., the libidinal energy of love) emerges in infancy and later in puberty; then the second aspect of shaping and redirecting that energy, the ascetic processes, can appear (the counter-libidinal self). Simultaneously the central self emerges to mediate these two aspects. This process has been inverted in Ted, and the result is suppression of the image of God within him and the stultification of the growth of the likeness within him.

This does not make Ted a hopeless case. Each of us, whatever the stage of our personal development "from glory to glory," is struggling to cooperate with the grace of the Holy Spirit. In this way each enacts the will of the Father in our lives, with the result that the salvific acts of the Son can reshape our own distortions of person. In doing so each becomes an explicator of the theology of the Church, that is, of the experience of the revealed Trinity, in the process of becoming an increasingly healthy triune relationship within the self.

Suggestions For Treatment

I have a few suggestions for the psychotherapeutic process. One interaction that I have often found effective is to correspond with the aspect of the self that is active at the moment in the session. That is, when Ted talks about his fear that he will have genital contact with other males, I might mirror his statements to him in paraphrases, one by one. I might also accompany those verbal reflections with a mirroring of his physical postures and gestures. I have found that when I do that with someone whose thought processes are as highly developed as are Ted's, another of the two triadic aspects of the self almost always emerges strongly to declare its point of view. That movement often takes the form of an "on-the-other-hand" and a major shift in posture and gesture. The result is that the client develops a conscious awareness of the strength of his other, modulating self-aspects and produces a stronger sense of his own mature capacity to allow all elements of himself to be active without overwhelming the others.

I might also want to encourage Ted to describe his most dreaded fantasies in word, gesture, and perhaps in some simple form of art. This has to be done very carefully and on the steady foundation of the moralizing restraints of Ted's faith. Any inference he might make of approval for acting them out could lead to a crisis for him personally and for his therapy. However, when people talk out their fantasies in detail they often are recognized as but symbolic expressions of yearning for power or connection and they then lose their capacity to terrorize or paralyze those who have them. Although discussion of abstract concepts is not necessarily a facet of psychotherapy, I might also consider introducing the Borromean Knot to Ted as a simple but clear demonstration of the need for well-developed libidinal, counter-libidinal, and central organizing aspects for him to have a full self. If he can grasp that concept he may be less frightened of being overwhelmed by any one part of himself.

I think I would also encourage Ted to participate with other males in activities such as sports or physical projects. Group affiliation with other males is extraordinarily important in the development of secure masculine identity, particularly during adolescence, a stage at which Ted seems to be arrested. The more solidly connected Ted experiences himself with other males, the more securely he is likely to perceive himself distinctly as a man and the less he will fear being absorbed and consumed by women. The development of firmer masculine identity might allow him to experience more safe-ty in libidinal energy directed towards females.

Finally, if the therapeutic setting allows for it, I would want to give Ted room for the development of a conscious relationship with the Holy Trinity. Given his commitment to the Christian faith this encouragement could take the form of exploring with him the attributes of the three persons of the God he already feels connected to, perhaps offering him biblical passages that reveal the distinctive but cooperative functioning of the Three. If he seems disposed to explore further, introducing him to an icon of the Holy Trinity to analyze together or some passages of Trinitarian theology might be appropriate. These latter actions must also be taken with extreme care and observing Ted's response at each step. It would be destructive to him personally and to the therapy if he began to perceive the actions of his therapist as prosely-tizing rather than psychotherapy.

References

(1) Robert D. Stolorow and George E. Atwood, *Contexts of Being: The Intersubjective Foundations of Psychological Life,* (Hillsdale, NJ: The Analytic Press, 1992), p. 97.

(2) As described (and utilized differently) by Jacques Lacan, "The Real, the Symbolic and the Imaginary," (*Ornicat*, Nos. 2-5, 1974-75).

PASTORAL PSYCHOLOGICAL RESPONSE: AN ORTHODOX EXPRESSION OF PASTORAL COUNSELING

DEMETRA JAQUET

In this case it is clear that Ted has finally met a therapist with good boundaries who is willing to talk about the fantasies Ted is having, not dismiss them as delusions, or depend entirely on antipsychotics to banish them away. While engaging the client as a listening, healing presence, the therapist is at the same time providing the message, "I'll stay here, I'm the therapist, and you're the client." This is an important new experience for Ted in light of his previous two experiences with therapists, one who engaged too closely, the other not enough. It appears that Ted has sexualized intimacy, and has struggled with his self-image, his sexual identity, and his intense emotional longing for males in his life.

The therapist opened a window of help when he started, right from the beginning, by believing with the client that the fantasy life is a problem. It is very important for the therapist to set a groundwork that allows the client to come freely to the therapist with his truth, his experience, without fear of belittlement or shaming. The therapist is providing a holding environment that won't blow away or disappear while the client is gaining his strength, insight and tools for reframing his thoughts and acknowledging his feelings. This therapist is addressing Ted's whole person and, as a pastoral counselor, is called to be the Church for a while to his client, while bridging the client to the Church.

In part, the relationship between the therapist and Ted is itself a healing tool. The therapist is saying, "Lets talk about it," much like a spiritual father offering patient guidance toward spiritual growth. At the same time he is modeling for Ted a healthy self-discipline and appropriate boundaries and engagement around emotional intimacy, and distinctly unselfish, supportive motives, all within a same-sex relationship.

Pastoral counseling is a unique interdisciplinary ministry that is clinically sensitive yet spiritually informed. Pastoral counselors are typically trained in both psychology and theology and acknowledge the healing, listening presence of the Holy Spirit as the primary therapist in the room. Orthodox Christian pastoral counselors understand the Spirit's presence as a gift of grace and mystical response to human need which can lead a client who is willing to commit to synergistic participation in the process of salvation toward cure of both body and soul.

The case refers to the Orthodox understanding of *logismoi*. It might be useful to give a brief definition at this point. In Metropolitan Hierotheos Vlachos' book *Orthodox Spirituality*, he defines the psychological and carnal person as "the nonspiritual individual, who is deprived of the Holy Spirit" (1). He defines *logismoi* as "the thoughts which are connected with images as well as with the various stimulations originating from the senses and the imagination. They are called *logismoi* because they act in the reason (*logiki*, in Greek). The thoughts are created to naturally turn to God the Logos, but some may instead devolve to sin. The intellect, desire and will turn away from God to something else and become a passion, or what psychology might refer to as a fixation (2).

Fr. Vlachos characterizes the three stages of spiritual cure for humankind as, first, cleansing of the heart from its passions (*praxis*) to prepare it for illumination (*theoria*) – the second stage, which is nothing else but the vision of God (3). *Theoria* may come to one as a gift of the Holy Spirit when the will opens the heart and surrenders it to the grace of the Holy Spirit's healing presence and action within. The process of participating in this grace of God is the third stage, called *theosis*, a becoming by grace of what God is by nature (4).

Participating in God's grace and receiving Christ's healing is effected through the Sacraments and through ascetic practice. Through the Sacraments, the heart receives the uncreated grace and energy of God. The Sacraments offer us a transfusion of the life-sustaining Holy Spirit, to neutralize the illness of sin, and to heal and restore our hearts toward God (5). Ascetic practice strengthens us through the therapy of discipline and the medicine of faith. *Purification of the heart* involves the three faculties in the human soul: the *intelligent faculty*, consisting of intellect; the *appetitive faculty*, consisting of desire; and the *incentive faculty*, consisting of the will. All three faculties, when functioning according to their God-created natures, are directed toward God. The intellect seeks God, the desire longs for God, and the will must do everything to achieve this communion and union with God (6).

Purification is the cleansing of the heart from the passions. Passions consist of various thoughts *or logismoi* which dwell in the reason, but do not descend into the heart. Instead, when a *logismos* or thought comes and a person is not sufficiently attentive and spiritually alert, it does *not* enter the heart according to its created nature, but becomes distorted and turned away from the heart to give rise to desire for something other than God. Then the *logismos* or thought proceeds from the intellect to the appetitive desire and the incentive faculty or will *outside* the heart, where, if allowed to be realized, it develops into a passion. This malformed *logismos* then enters the heart as a passion.

As Orthodox Christians we believe that God's grace permeates all members of the soul with joy, peace and love. God's grace is rooted within us, even when we are sorely tempted, battered, and seemingly overcome by the Evil One. The Fathers clearly emphasize that the heart can be cleansed of *logismoi.* Deliverance begins with repentance from them. When all such *logismoi* are dismissed and the heart is cleansed, the person becomes more sociable and balanced, behaving properly within society, because selfish love no longer commingles in the heart with love for God and love for humankind. Only Christ, the true Physician of the interior person, can cure humankind, healing the soul and adorning it with the garment of His grace in this way. What is cured first and foremost is the human heart. This is what sets the Church apart from secular psychology. Pastoral counseling is clinically realistic and spiritually informed in understanding its contributions as well as the limitations in its ability, like John the Baptist, to make straight the way for the Lord's mystical healing.

In some ways, secular therapies offer intervention strategies which share in the idea of departing from negative thoughts, but which fail to address the spiritual depths affected by those thoughts. Cognitive therapy might say that Ted's thoughts are affecting/ infecting his emotions and behavior, and might offer some thought-stopping techniques, like twanging a rubber band around his wrist. Together with the therapist, Ted might develop an alternative script that could be carried in his pocket, or memorized, to interrupt those thoughts. Rational Emotive Therapy might propose that distracting Ted into another more balanced thought is a useful assumption. A family systems approach might reach out to the voices or and attempt to deal with them systemically, approaching them with clarity in love, much as Christ approaches us sinners, and promoting interior dialogue to gain new insights. Purely medical models might divorce themselves from the idea of *logismoi*, treating them as a hallucinatory symptom of sickness but never addressing their ability to distract a heart away from God. None of these, however, address the power of God at our center for cure of the soul. This brings us to the question, with what exactly is the therapist replacing the old fanstasies? If the *logismoi* are to be cut off, what will serve Ted in their place?

Pastoral counseling has emerged as a discipline within the context and culture of Western Christianity. In his recent book, *Hope in Pastoral Care and Counseling*, author and pastoral counselor Andrew Lester argues that pastoral theology (as well as social and behavioral sciences) has neglected to address effectively the predominant cause of human suffering, which he identifies as a lack of hope and sense of futurelessness that leads to despair. He proposes that "pastoral theology at its best allows mutual critique between knowledge generated by the human sciences on the one hand and the wisdom of the Christian tradition found in biblical, historical, ethical, philosophical and systematic theology on the other" (7). Clearly, for an Orthodox Christian, this model will not be adequate to cure Ted, since its cure is once again in the intellectual realm of human understanding.

Perhaps the technique of replacement can be used for spiritual cure of the soul if the process directs Ted back to some religious structure for containment – a rule of prayer, a Scriptural regimen, or reading some works of the Fathers. Again, while a good start, this falls short, for a structural approach to evicting the *logismoi* from their polluting presence in the heart is not adequate to Orthodoxy's mystical foundations. It is the experience and personal relationship with Christ that these structures might evoke which can bring healing.

For Orthodox Christians, what will replace the fixations and reform Ted's heart is the life of the Church. The role of regular Eucharistic participation and prayers of healing from the Church are central. Small steps of self discipline repetitively practiced as engagement with the sacramental and prayerful life of the Church could gradually develop the muscles of Ted's will. And the support of the prayers of oth-

ers as well as their goodwill could only be helpful. But Ted
has a panoply of voices bursting forth from him through his
voices. A whole variety of disciplines might be needed, with
different practices at different times for each of the voices
within.

In coming up with a treatment plan, it is important for therapists to know where they are going. In helping Ted to refo-
cus his attention away from his fixations, the goal of pastoral
counseling is not the cure itself, but the cure in God. If the end
point is God, then the use of secular tools can be most helpful. But for Orthodox, the cure is not just in God, although
that is a fine start. The cure is becoming one with God. In this
task, the secular tools finally become superfluous.

The Role of Grief

Not only is Ted's life out of control, his grief and anxiety
may be heightened by his cancer diagnosis. Grief is about
a broken heart, not a broken brain. Efforts to heal the heart
with the head can start the process but eventually may fail
because the head is the wrong tool for the job. We are dealing
here with the issue of broken trust and how it affects people.
When trust is shattered, people may decide rationally to just
carry on, but find they do not want to get close to anyone because of the fear that they will be abandoned. Such isolation
invites deepening mistrust and heightened anxiety.

With any life-threatening situation comes loss of trust in
the status quo and fear of the unknown, and the crisis may
yield an urgent sense of need to understand and even contain
the coming loss. Psychology and behavioral sciences can
work with anticipatory grief as a rake or hoe to assist the client in clearing away the tangled debris of his life. The Holy
Spirit may go further, frequently using anticipatory grief as a
plow for rendering a hardened heart suitable to receive seeds
for new growth in Christ, which must then be watered by the
tears of authentic repentance.

The goal of therapy is recovery and completion, not avoidance or isolation. Incomplete grief creates hyper-vigilant self protection from emotional pain, and reluctance to establish new friendships because of conflict experienced in past relationships. Does Ted trust anyone? Any of his voices? Whom do his voices trust? Will he be able to trust the therapist to guide him toward realizing the transformative potential of this life crisis?

Often people deal with unresolved feelings by transferring emotions to other areas. In this case it's possible that each voice is carrying one of Ted's split-off emotions. Recovery is defined as the point in the grieving process when one is able to participate in new relationships fully. Is part of the therapy getting these voices in touch with the God in Ted? Must they be purged, or can their appetites be weaned, and their hearts converted? For Ted to enter into new relationships with his voices, and with his God, he will have to develop new, useful habits, unlearn old unhelpful habits, and gradually replace them. But more important, he will have to learn to trust God, and to place his hope in Him.

Moving through grief can mean dying to the importance of self. This is a spiritual issue. Self-esteem must be established as a foundation for a healthy life, yet later becomes an obstacle for life in Christ. In the world, we are taught to acquire, but not to lose. We are taught to build up our low self-esteem, but not to diminish the importance of self for the sake of others. The human person becomes the actualizing center. We see losing and diminishment as cause for grief. So the question becomes, is Ted's problem only psychological, or is it connected to something deeper? Can Ted be healed by psychological restructuring alone, or might he actually hope for a cure of the soul? Outcome and progress in grief work is measured in behaviors, attitudes. But when one can transcend illusion and gain understanding of the true nature of progress, one finds it is measured in the human heart's capacity for love.

On Demons and Sexuality

The casting out of demons is tied scripturally to knowing the name of the deity. When you know someone's name, you have control. God gave Adam the task of naming the animals, and in that way gave him dominion for stewardship over them (Gen 2:19-20). God revealed to Moses no such name as we have, but answered his question "I Am" (Ex 3:14). The demons cast out by our Lord in Mark told him their name, "Legion," and they knew Christ as master over them (Mk 5:9-12). One may know something intuitively, but to name it and define it gives one power over it. The ability to objectify and not be identified with, consumed, or even obsessed by the demons must begin for humans with naming them. The sources and voices of Ted's sadomasochistic fantasies provide a challenge to cognitively and perhaps intuitively discover their names, their motivations, their goals, their fears, their tasks, their obsessions. How far have these spontaneous voices turned toward intentional avoidance of God? How strong are they in controlling and directing Ted's natural inclination to use his free will for following God? When and how have his healthy sexual desires been perverted to *logismoi*? The answers to these questions must take into account the complex history of the interaction in the Church between the two ways of dealing with human sexuality, celibacy or marriage, as well as Ted's reports of his own sexual experiences, and conclusions about the meaning of those experiences.

Who has asked Ted what his feelings were when his mother dressed him in girls' clothing, or about his troubling memories of his father's physical contact? We learn to live from our parents, but that doesn't mean we learn correctly. Has Ted ever named feelings of betrayal by his parents? How does he feel about his homosexual tendencies? Is he active in sexual relationships? Does he have a repentant heart, or is he just seeking relief? Pastoral counseling might ask who has asked him to describe his reactions as a physical image, or taught him how to ask the Holy Spirit to help him mentally blow that image away until it disperses. Orthodox Christian pastoral counseling might ask who has helped Ted to name the power and reality of the demons he battles, and the spiritual way of life and prayers that can disempower and expel them.

How could Ted's sexual fantasies toward the therapist be reframed and used productively for the therapy? How could one find *anything* in the sexual fantasies that is for the good, for God? Traditionally, there is no one process emphasized in Orthodoxy. The answer provided as part of a holistic spiritual process recommended by the Fathers, particularly the monastic ascetics, has been to cut off fantasies by the use of ascetic practices. I am unaware of any articulated patristic practice for reframing the issue to look at the underlying emotional causes and needs they are serving. It appears that in the patristic explanation of the *logismoi*, the negative or destructive thought is distinct from the God-centered thought, in that it has fallen prey to the power of the Evil One's distortion of the truth. For both psychology and spirituality, the disengagement from destructive energies is the goal. The two disciplines are not mutually exclusive, but each has its own special tools.

A pastoral counselor could explore another approach than "cutting off," which would tend to keep the subject or "presenting issue" of the sexual fantasies central, while helping the client with techniques for interrupting their power over him. This would be to assist Ted in discovering the links between his voices and the particular needs of the voice which is possibly attempting to contain and control this therapist by using techniques that worked before in deflecting Ted's previous therapists.

Depending on the severity and the possibility of a multiple personality disorder diagnosis, the therapist might try to explore really listening to and re-engaging with the voices, each of whom is desperately acting out in its ambivalence between the expression of longing for intimacy with other humans and ultimately with God, the illusion of control gained from the sadomasochism, and the shame underlying it.

If the fantasies were initially creations of Ted's mind, but later took on a "life of their own" as he stated, this could be reframed as a positive projective technique that the client has clearly mastered already. The problem lies in his failure to *use* the technique toward the good, his inability to control the technique being co-opted by the Evil One, and his lack of knowledge and experience in directing the use of the technique.

Extracting oneself from the bombardment of everyday thoughts by interior return to the Jesus Prayer is the "technique" outlined in *The Way of the Pilgrim* (8). Orthodox Christians believe there is power in the name of Jesus Christ. A pastoral counselor can encourage Ted to learn to depend on that power by practicing the Jesus Prayer or memorizing and reciting Scripture. Also chanting, fasting, or any number of small, repetitive, positive practices could help Ted to develop his will's ability to direct his intellect, emotions and behavior toward constant remembrance of God. Accountability would likely be an issue at the outset, and the therapist's firm but supportive guidance and presentation of new information to correct distorted thoughts would be important.

Ritual and Symbol

The ritual and symbols of Scripture, Liturgy, and Sacrament are powerful doorways to healing that provides structure and direction to the soul, while inviting the Holy Spirit to engage and direct the process. When a therapeutic technique is grounded in the awareness of the presence and action of the Holy Spirit, and is consecrated to that purpose by a person's heart and will, it is possible for it to be transformed into more than a 'technique,' and it can become a ritual gesture in the fullest existential sense of Orthodoxy. If ritual, symbol and liturgy, like icons, are windows to the Kingdom, it is intricately bound up with the fact that they bear the prayerful energy, meaning and intent of the Christian community.

Devoid of these, they can become empty, meaningless gateways to hell. It is up to each of us to constantly keep vigil and nip any buds of *logismoi* which could sprout and comingle with the goodness God has placed in the garden of our hearts. Here, the therapist acts as a spiritual father, guiding the client by his own experience and example, to also prune away all obstacles to God.

Praying with icons could be called a mode of doing theology, yet it could also be identified as a projective technique: the icon has a content of its own, and it speaks to me according to what I bring to it. But placing the 'technique' as such under the safety of the wing of the Holy Spirit allows praying with icons to bring one into contact with deeper levels of holy reality. The client's demons, whether fantasy or actual, are leading him instead across widening breaches away from the reality of God. If an icon begins to speak to him, he must test the spirit using the tried and true methods of stating the name of Christ, and adjuring the spirit to depart, using the name of Christ, most usually accomplished by fervently reciting the Jesus Prayer and focusing on the prayer entirely. St. Anthony reported actual physical battles with the powers of evil. Although his encounters occurred toward the end of a long life of spiritual struggle, it is possible for a client not yet strong in prayer to experience a physical response to engagement with fantasies or evil spirits.

One problem I have experienced with similar patients is that their understanding of prayer is frequently bound up as tightly as is their ability to respond freely to God. For a long time in the beginning, prayer seems mechanical, with little consolation in terms of affective or interior response, and an obsessive concern for "doing it right." But if prayer is "pre-scribed" by the therapist with the same level of regularity and strictness as one would expect for the ingesting of chem-ical prescriptions, the structure gained eventually provides a calming effect and a growing sense of self-control over the fantasies and negative passions' ability to drag him back down at will. Deeper personal engagement with Christ may come, according to the client's need and the Holy Spirit's movement. Ritual is also a mode of doing theology, a formal behavior which invites the reality of the Kingdom of God to reveal itself through the Holy Spirit as present and active within the worshiping community.

The Divine Liturgy, the Eucharist, the Prayers of the Hours, all involve ritual gestures and posture, whose function is not simply some symbolic transmission of meaning-making, but more importantly to engage the deepest parts of ourselves more closely with the Divine Presence. Similarly, the meta-phors and parables of Scripture are verbal gestures, bridging and carrying the person from one reality to the next, e.g., "The Kingdom of God is like..." etc. And Scriptural inter-pretation, according to Origen, offers yet another bridge be-tween a literal mode of awareness and an ever-deepening spiritual awareness of Holy Wisdom's presence as revealed in and through Scripture as the bread of life.

Ritual as a doorway to the Spirit carries within it the ability to transform. Repetitive and stylized patterned action, when repeated in a community context, especially a community of prayer, not only leads toward but also instructs us toward a larger meaning than what we can find on our own. So too can the spiritual life and prayers of a community provide that sense of acceptance and belonging which humans must experience in order to open to God's love. Orthodox ritual does not just symbolize another reality, it actually opens the door and invites our engagement with it.

Perhaps one aspect of the pastoral care plan for Ted might

suggest he try taking up chanting, reading, or singing, a repetitive ritual action of sound, or better yet, some fasting, the first rung of the ascetic spiritual ladder. Certainly, struggling against allowing the fantasies free reign, and eventually against even allowing them to enter into his consciousness spontaneously without any restraining exercise of will on his part, is foundational to the long-term goal of Ted being in charge of himself enough to preempt being controlled by the fantasies.

This therapist has given Ted room to be in process and growing, even though Ted hasn't yet moved out of his fantasies. The therapist has not cut Ted off. Ted's desire has not been cut off. But as a spiritual father, the therapist is training Ted about the appropriate use of his desires and longings for that which is healthy for him. He is being shown the goal and true prize of sober and moral mental life, while at the same time is being mercifully encouraged to lessen his attachment to the fantasies each day. He is being guided and given practice in allowing the mind to descend to the heart, and remaining vigilant to its distortion by the appetitive passions.

In some cases the use of guided imagery or dreams can be valuable, particularly with clients who have artistic or symbolic tendencies. Engaging the different voices within in a conversation might help Ted come to terms with them. Uncovering within Ted the aspects of self which embody the strength and goodness of God and can welcome the attention of the Holy Spirit, can be very encouraging and empowering to him. Discovering the real power of guardian angels, and the power of turning to God in times of extreme fear, stress, or danger, are well documented in the faith, and can be another source of strength against temptation.

The Logos indwells in Ted, and he is still related to God, even if he is fantasizing and fearful. Evidence of this is already apparent, since Ted has brought himself into the office to continue seeking therapy in order to rid himself of the fantasies and his perceived need for them. Ted may be dimly and vaguely aware of the proper meanings of agape love as voluntary self-denial for the sake of the other, and eros as passion for the good, and this awareness has caused him to persist in therapy, despite the risks to his status quo and the past experiences of exploitation.

It might be useful to explore a systems approach, to reveal the distorted relationships in Ted's family of origin, and understand the old messages he has been carrying around. A genogram of the relationships between his voices, and consideration of the symbolic meaning of each of the celebrities' faces which speak to him might also reveal some of Ted's interior mental landscape.

An overall approach of inviting the Holy Spirit's presence and action into the room, and into the interrelationship between therapist and client, is key to pastoral counseling. For Orthodox, however, the focus may shift to the Holy Spirit's presence and action within the heart and soul of the client. The interior relationship of the Holy Trinity is the basis for all relationships, a humane model for the ordering of society, and a bulwark against incursions into the heart by unhealthy passions. The strong bond of total self-giving to "the other" in agape love, when that "other" is Christ, is the healing power which has destroyed, continues to destroy, and will destroy the power of evil in our souls. One thing is clear: Ted must work on changing his behavior. The psychological and behavioral models of the social sciences linked to theological understandings for meaning-making will whiten the outside of the cup. But like the Pharisees, the change will not be complete unless the heart that motivates the behavior is cleansed as well. The right combination of social, behavioral and psychological techniques, while frequently powerful, sometimes still doesn't heal, even when couched in theological underpinnings. For Orthodox Christians, what is needed is the full transformation of the soul, which requires the fullness of Orthodox sacraments, worship and spiritual life for purification of the heart from all *logismoi*.

In his book *The Heart: An Orthodox Christian Spiritual Guide*, Archimandrite Spyridon Logothetis, Holy Transfiguration Monastery in Nafpaktos, Lepanto, Greece, devotes a beautiful chapter to "Purifying the Heart." With numerous patristic and scriptural references, he summarizes what is needed for your heart to be cleansed: First, acknowledgment that the act of purification is not yours, but is the "purifying breeze of the Holy Spirit." Next, earnest repentance – focus inward toward scrutinizing your heart, with honesty and humility. Then, the help of a spiritual father (or mother) who knows the depths of your heart quite well. Then prayer, repentance, tears of mourning and grief for your sins, to cleanse your heart and mind with tears, and thus make you able to see God's heavenly gifts. Next, grace, the sacraments (especially confession), and knowledge of the word of God help you to purify the heart by applying God's commandments. Finally, sincere effort to dismiss unhealthy passions, and constant remembrance of God. For beginners, certain conditions of silence, calm, and escape from temptations are also helpful, and for some, there is the possibility of a call to monasticism (9).

Final Questions

Some final questions from a pastoral counseling perspective which the case study leaves unclear:

• What denomination of church congregation has he joined? Does he agree with the image of God and the definition of what constitutes Godly life that he learns there? What draws him to that church?

• Does Ted believe the Holy Spirit is in him, or does he see himself completely devoid of good? What is his image of God? Is it an idol in the image of the uncaring God who did not protect him or answer his prayers as a child?

The answers to these and related questions may reveal criti-

cal factors – how is Ted seeing himself in relationship to God
what is the nature of his best personal experience of God as
well as his experience of church, what spiritual tools might
he best use to recover some balance and self-control in his
life, and, ultimately, does he trust God is there for him?

• What other kind of fantasies is Ted having besides those
mentioned? Are they strictly psychotic or could they be an
outgrowth of his homosexual tendencies? It might be useful
to mirror some of his comments and reflect together on the
possibility that, "Gosh, maybe you're homosexual?" and explore those implications. Or would this encourage him in the
wrong direction? Knowing the client and using discernment
would answer these questions. What is the creative tension
for Ted between leaving something behind and moving on to
something entirely different? For each client, such answers
are as unique as their individual life experiences.

• What family of origin information is pertinent beyond
what is mentioned? What various forms of sexual abuse
have been taken into consideration or missed? How would
you assess Ted's ability to recognize and acknowledge abu-
sive behaviors in his past?

• Could there be additional diagnoses of ego-dystonic homosexuality? What is the nature of Ted's fantasies about
this therapist? How are they dissimilar from other fantasies?
What counter-transference issues are not specified? Who is
prescribing the antipsychotic? What is the nature of the support or services Ted is receiving from that person? Are those
modalities complementary with the work the therapist is doing with him, or do they conflict?

Summary

Pastoral counseling and spiritual life in the Church share
the same goal – the healing of the person through the restoration of hope. But early psychology and many modern
humanistic psychologies are not useful for healing the whole

person, including the soul, because in them, it is the human person who becomes the actualizing center for growth and choice, and sometimes even the human therapist who carries the hope. Secular psychologies of the past addressed remission of illness or alleviation of symptoms. Both psychology and the Church address symptoms, and both may use cognitive and behavioral tools as helps to intervene with obsessive, negative, or self-destructive thoughts and behaviors.

Yet there is a difference between humanistic psychologies, western pastoral counseling, and the psychology of the Church. That difference is in understanding the purpose and goal of life as actualizing the authentic self by realizing God within, and re-engaging with the true joy which only hope in God's grace provides. Nevertheless, the recent growth in transpersonal psychologies is beginning to bridge what used to be a chasm. Particularly the Psychosynthesis model of Roberto Assagioli comes to mind, which posits a source of wisdom and healing energy outside the psychological, social self, but which is connected intuitively to the deepest realms of the human soul.

On their own, techniques tend to steer clients toward the secular, humanistic, medical model. But pastoral counselors believe a simple "how-to" won't cure. It may loosen the bondage, but is not enough for healing unto salvation, because it depends entirely on the energy of the client alone. Rather, for Christians there is a double struggle, one that is interior, and the other exterior. The exterior struggle consists of humankind withdrawing from worldly distractions. The interior struggle takes place in turning away from evil attractions within.

For Christians, the power to entertain both struggles comes from the grace of God. But for Orthodox Christians, the inner struggle of askesis is meaningful not for any cognitive or therapeutic reasons, but because it is a part of the inner journey of prayer, where mind descends perpetually into the heart. In purifying the heart, the Christians relearns to trust, placing that trust entirely in God, uniting oneself completely with God's hope and love, and ultimately transforming life into constant remembrance and witness to that Uncreated Light Who knows each of us by name and cures us by the grace of salvation. This is the hope and prayer of an Orthodox Christian pastoral counselor, for Ted, for self, and for all the world: "Behold I stand at the door and knock: if any man hear my voice, and open the door, I will come in to him, and will sup with him, and he with me" (Rev. 3:20).

Notes

1. Archim. Hierotheos Vlachos, *Orthodox Spirituality: A Brief Introduction*, trans. by Effie Mavromichali, (Levadia, Greece: Birth of the Theotokos Monastery, 1994).
2. Ibid. p. 56
3. Ibid. pp. 59-60
4. Ibid. pp. 56-57
5. Ibid. p. 66
6. Ibid. p. 63
7. Andrew D. Lester, *Hope in Pastoral Care and Counseling*, (Louisville, KY: Westminster John Knox Press, 1995), p. 6
8. Anonymous, *The Way of the Pilgrim*, trans. Helen Bacovin, (New York: Image Books, 1978), p. 78.
9. Archimandrite Spyridon Logothetis, *The Heart: An Orthodox Christian Spiritual Guide,* (Nafpaktos, Greece: Brotherhood of the Transfiguration of our Saviour Jesus Christ, 2001), pp. 61-80.

THE JOURNEY CONTINUES: POSTSCRIPT ON "TED"

Stephen Muse

As of the printing of this volume, Ted continues his journey. His cancer is in stable condition and his main concern now is that he "not die alone without anyone really knowing me." The loneliness he has lived with all his life is the primary axle to which are attached the other issues like spokes of a wheel: sexuality, trauma, betrayal, and life's meaning.

Ted has read each of the responses to the bare facts of his life presented in this volume and discussed them as part of his therapeutic journey. He said his choice among the three respondents, if he were to see one of them for therapy, was Fr. Stephen Plumlee, because he thought the theological dimension seemed to be foremost in Fr. Stephen's response. Significantly, Christian faith remains at the core of Ted's orienting with regards to relationship, identity, meaning and value in this life.

Because Ted's affective congruence has always been 100% on target, there has never been evidence of psychotic overtones to his presentation. Rather, his "voices" appear to have been more along the dissociative dimension, underscoring the impact of trauma compounded by isolation and accentuated by the appetite suppresant he frequently took to "pep him up." Schizoidal traits at the personality level appear prominent and the effects of a lifetime of isolation have had a significant impact on shaping Ted's behaviors and thought processes. The comments of Jeff Rediger alluding to realities of altered states of consciousness that cannot be fully subsumed under either psychopathological labels of "psy-

113

chotic" or "dissociative" disorders remain relevant in this regard.

Ted no longer experiences nor conjures up for himself sadomasochistic sexual fantasies, nor does he masturbate or express his sexuality in any genitalized form. Ironically, it was when he finally announced decisively, "I am gay," that he reported no longer experiencing sexual desires and fantasies. Some months later he challenged his assertion in this regard, but his sexual orientation has not subsequently been the major focus of his therapy in the last year, rather his loneliness in the context of what he thought was his impending death. This too has changed as Ted now suggests, "I thought I was going to die and now I appear to have much longer to live and I can't make up my mind which way to go."

Given the anemia that is prominent in his physical condition, his physical stamina is certainly decreased and it is unclear to what extent this is playing a role in the lessening of the intensity of his libido. Where did the eros dimension of his life go? Was it grief at losing his friend? Did it happen because of a chemical straightjacket? Is it an effect of the anemia? Or is it more that he "cut it off" as a response to his affirmation of his core spiritual perspective that such fantasies are destructive and go against his understanding of Christian teaching?

Perhaps there is more "dialogical reality" taking the place of frustration in that regard, as Ted is now regularly attending church, meeting with a group of friends in the evenings and taking trips with a woman friend he has known for many years. Taking a view of mental illness as proportionate to a person being unable to break free of the self-enclosed autoerotic world of the psyche into authentic "I-Thou" dialogue with others, Ted has made progress. He is no longer interpersonally isolated and confined to a world of pure projection of the contents of his own mind dialoguing only with a fictitious or projected 'other' which effectively kept him stuck within himself like a cow chewing its cud and swallowing the same unresolved issues over and over again until they build to a climax of unresolved tension which threatens to disrupt his psychic equilibrium. Ted has to some extent broken through into true dialogical prayer with the Eternal Thou in the context of a relationship with other human beings with whom Ted has chosen to become emotionally available and transparent.

Fr. Stephen underscored the importance of the fact that Ted was developing a relationship (non-sexual) with another man. I believe it is significant that this occurred as he was also developing a relationship of more transparency and emotional availability with the therapist which while healing, was at the transferential level, also threatening and frightening (thus anger in the voices at the time were to some extent related to feared exposure and vulnerability) for him. Furthermore, the man with whom he was developing the relationship was someone known to and knew Ted's therapist and Ted knew this, possibly adding a certain vicarious link with the therapist that may have been a significant factor. He once reflected, "You two are tied together in some way."

Fr. Stephen's suggestion to encourage Ted to connect with other males is a good one as is Dee Jaquet's observation that it is not enough to simply "cut off" destructive thoughts, but it is appropriate to understand their dynamic purpose and to replace the hidden functions they may serve with healthy alternatives such as koinania and Sacramental life of the Church. Dee points out she is unaware of a Patristic practice that encourages "reframing the issue to look at the underlying emotional causes and needs they are serving." which is one of the key aims of psychodynamic psychotherapy which values the integration of split off aspects of psychic life. The Palamite perspective which aims more at transfiguration of the passions, rather than their elimination may be supportive of this. Certainly this is a critical area for further dialogue between patristic teaching and modern psychology in terms of healing and the full development and growth of persons.

The Greek story of Odysseus' journey is something of an analogy of the forces with which we are contending. At one point in his journey, aware that they were approaching the place inhabited by Sirens whose irresistible voices lured all who heard them to their deaths on the rocks, Odysseus ordered his men to fill their ears with wax while leaving his own open and tying him to the mast of the ship, so that he could hear their enchanted voices, while not succumbing to destructive acting out. This and other stories which act as psychological roadmaps suggest that this perspective was not unknown to the ancients. Keeping in mind the variety of lenses through which to observe the same thing, it is also important, as Jeff Rediger points out, that the pastoral clinician avoid giving way to reductionistic thinking.

Nor are the two dimensions "psychological and spiritual" to be seen as separate or antagonistic, thus Dee emphasizes the value and rightness of inviting God into the consulting room and pointing to the presence of Holy Spirit through prayers and incense as visible, intentional reminders of the larger context in which psychotherapy unfolds. If the quality and origins of the logismi and our vulnerability to identifying with them and/or eventually compulsively acting them out, are to be studied to determine the extent to which they are potentially carriers of a psychological virus of sorts as distinct from being indicators of fragmented memories and unacknowledged feelings associated with childhood trauma needing to be heard and acknowledged, care must be taken to establish appropriate conditions for study of both. This is the realm not only of a therapeutic alliance of quality with a good psychotherapist, but for the activities of worship, asceticism, prayer, repentance, confession, experienced spiritual guidance and life within the full community of the Church – all of which are the subjects of the last two sections of this book.

In the final analysis, whatever psychiatric and/or spiritual labels are used and theories drawn upon to help persons, I am convinced that the most fruitful context is for the therapist to hear the whole of another person's behavior, feelings, understanding and intentions – their total life held in sum – as being the most poignant prayer he or she is able to manage, with all its mixture of despair, anger, longing, frustration, sense of betrayal, and all the rest of human passions and potentials, deception by spiritual evil as well as yearning for Christ which are aimed all at once like an arrow into life straight to God's heart.

The pastoral psychotherapist must approach a person's whole indivisible life-in-relationship as a living prayer of great depth and multiple overtones. Life's meaning and prayer itself, when separated from each other, divorced from the concrete lived existential context of life and relationships with others, amount to nothing but an empty shell of appearances calling out "Lord, Lord" and hiding confusion and uncleanness within or on the other hand, turning away from God outwardly, precisely because of the ache to be embraced by God that is at the core of all the person has suffered in life. So we can say that in Orthodox Christian pastoral counseling, the therapist is attempting to truly "meet" the person in dialogue in the presence of God and to "hear" this prayer of a person's life which is being offered up to God (consciously and unconsciously) for all who have "ears to hear." To the extent that this occurs, and the "prayer" begins to be understood clearly for what it is – the heart's longing to respond to the love of God which has brought it into being, powerful relational healing forces are brought to bear inviting communion with God, self and others. Healing occurs. Meaningful life emerges. Captives are freed.

In this sense, good psychotherapy, like all the Sacramental mysteries of the Church and its Divine Liturgy, are meant to uncover how persons are oriented to the living communal context which reveals the divine *image* in which we are each made and woven together as one people, healing and transforming us into the *likeness* of God. It is by remaining faithful to this primary existential context of dialogue with God over a lifetime, as we are able, in solidarity with others who face the same human challenges, that we are formed aright and healed in our depths. We share one Way, one Life, one Truth, even though by as many separate paths as there are unique persons. One helps another for as Harry Stack Sullivan once remarked, "We human beings are much more alike than we are different." The great message and medicine of the Gospel is that in Christ we discover that God, though eternally far beyond us and as different from us as Spirit from dust, is yet not unlike us in any way whatsoever. In this "meeting" of the holy Eucharist with its many overtones, both liturgical and practical in the "liturgy of life," we are healed and turned toward life and others with the same love that God in Christ loves us.

Chapter 5

CHRISTIAN ASCETICISM
AND COGNITIVE PSYCHOLOGY

FR. GEORGE MORELLI

A monk of Mt. Athos has been quoted as saying, "The holy monk is the one who is with the world in his desert, and in the desert when he is in the world." As Christians we are called to follow and serve God where He can be found. This is in the "heart of the world." Our Lord does not ask us to withdraw from the world, but to keep ourselves from evil. We know the Father sent Jesus into the world; so too, we are sent into the world. As Our Lord has told us, we have to flee from the spirit of the world, but be immersed in the reality of it.

As pointed out by Delfieux (1), our Church Fathers have given us some directives on how this could be accomplished. St. Basil in his Longer Rule admonishes us to be close and bound up with others yet keeping distance and remaining solitary. Following our Lord's command, the spirit of St. Benedict's rule is his monks focus on the needs of others, while at the same time longing for God alone. The Western spiritual tradition could describe this as acting at the same time as Martha and Mary. To accomplish this goal we need purified intelligence of direct seeing (*nous*) and reason. St. Paul tells the Corinthians: "I will pray with the spirit and I will pray with the mind also; I will sing with the spirit and I will sing with the mind also." In the *Philokalia,* St. Maximus the Confessor informs us: "A pure mind sees thing correctly.

A trained intelligence puts them in order."

One of the foundations of how this can be accomplished is to be "open of heart." In *Spiritual Direction in the Early Christian East,* Hausherr (2) tells us that this is not only openness of conscience but more importantly openness of thoughts. The ancient spiritual father would have his spiritual children reveal their actual dispositions, which would be inferred from the movements of the heart. This is surely not unlike psychotherapy, in which the patient has to disclose his or her inner feelings and thoughts to the clinician. Early ascetical psychology noted a difference between "suggestion of thought which is free from blame, (cf. St. Mark the Ascetic, *Against the Messalians)*, coupling "an inner dialogue with the suggestion (temptation) which may end in victory or actual sin." Repeated acts produce passion and captivity of soul.

Cognitive psychologists, using their own technical vocabulary, have demonstrated empirical evidence for such processes. The automaticity of irrational thoughts leading to dysfunctional emotions is well-documented (3). The difficulty of challenging or disputing these thoughts, thereby modifying both feelings and behavior, is delineated by modern scientific cognitive-behavior therapy. The initial step in the challenging-disputation process is pinpointing distorted cognitions. Typically, with the help of the clinician, the patient writes out a list of his or her irrational thoughts. Without this important step, cognitive-behavioral change cannot take place. In a similar manner, the spiritual church fathers emphasized the importance of this disclosure in a complete and systematic way. For the Spiritual Fathers this is done with *nepsis* (vigilance), watchfulness and the guarding of the heart. Haucherr quotes an anonymous old man.: "When evil thoughts harass you, do not hide them, but tell them at once to your Spiritual Father. The more one hides one's thoughts, the more they multiply and the stronger they become." The reason for this revelation is to provide the Spiritual Father with the basis for *diakrisis* (discernment). It appears the Spiritual Fathers knew the importance of disclosure, and extended this to actual techniques not unlike the disputation processes whose efficacy has been demonstrated by modern cognitive psychological researchers.

The spiritual writers considered that in *diakrisis* a spiritual father was required. The danger of illusion and exaggeration would lead to theoretical and practical errors on the part of struggling Christians, both young and old. This discernment process is so important that St. Anthony said, "There are many who broke their bodies by asceticism, but ended far from God because they lacked discernment … in their delusion they ignored the command that says, 'Ask your father, let him teach you" (4). While there have been a proliferation of self-help books even in scientific cognitive psychotherapy (e.g. Burns, 1980; Beck, 1988; Ellis & Harper, 1961; Gottman, 1994), frequently the authors who write such guides suggest readers consult trained clinicians in dealing with their problems. Burns, for example, points out it would be "unreasonable" to expect to improve or recover after reading his book. What is needed is "the additional help of a mental health professional."

The ascetical spiritual writers from a modern psychological viewpoint seemed to have grasped the connection between thoughts, emotions and behavior. Metropolitan Hierotheos Vlachos states, "It is in the intelligent part of the soul that evil thoughts operate which excite desire and attempt to capture man's *nous* so that sin is committed. The development of sin starts with thoughts."(5) He goes on to further pinpoint what thoughts are by appealing to the division made by St. Maximus the Confessor who distinguishes between simple and composite thoughts. Thoughts not producing passions (emotions) are simple. Composite thoughts consist of a conceptual images accompanied by passion (6) A question arises: How do the church fathers teach us to deal with these "thoughts"? St. Maximus the Confessor states: "[the separation of thought and passion] can be made through spiritual love and self control."(7) The author of *Unseen Warfare,* edited by Nicodemus of the Holy Mountain and revised by St. Theophan the Recluse, summarizing the Church Fathers on this subject, suggests methods such as effort of will, appealing to our Lord Jesus Christ, and doing something opposite of the thought. Appealing to our Lord of course is essential for any Christian, because he is the source of our life and strength and all that we do in his name is blessed. The other techniques from a psychological viewpoint could be labeled as cognitive techniques of thought-disruption. These interventions works with some patients. However, the plethora of other cognitive techniques, used in the name of Christ, could be added to aid in the spiritual and psychological healing of the patient/prodigal. This would be in the spirit of the Spiritual Fathers as well as using psychological techniques shown by research to be efficacious.

Christians perceive themselves as created in God's image called to be like Him, created with body, mind and spirit. Based on current understanding of how the mind works, they can apply this knowledge to their psychological and spiritual growth. Knowledge of the cognitive distortions and how they apply to our own lives is among the important uses of cognitive psychology in the spirit of the spiritual fathers. This list includes eight cognitive distortions.

• *Selective Abstraction,* is focusing on one event while excluding others. In one of my recent cases, "Jack" an engineer, selectively focused on a reprimand he just received from his supervisor, while ignoring the praise he received the previous week from the senior project manager. This irrational perception led to his depression.

• *Arbitrary Inference* is drawing a conclusion unwarranted by the facts in an ambiguous situation. The same patient men-

tioned above, the engineer, concluded that his next evalua-
tion (given by his supervisor) would be unsatisfactory. This
led to further depression.

• *Personalization* is blaming yourself for an event you are
not responsible for. Another patient "Linda" became depressed when during a business meeting (attended by her
section, comprising about twenty five people), her supervisor made a statement that "some in the section are not "team
players." She immediately "personalized" the statement,
of course with no evidence that the boss was directing it at
her.

• *Polarization* is perceiving or interpreting events in-all-or
nothing terms. "Cynthia," another patient of mine, became
depressed after receiving a 'B' in a college course. She "polarized" events into two categories, good student/bad stu-
dent. A grade of 'B' caused her to fall into the bad-student
pole. She failed to see that all events can be graded on a
continuum between two poles. On such a scale a 'B' is closer
to an 'A' that to an 'F', for example.

• *Generalization* is the tendency to see things in always-or-
never categories. Another patient, "Mary," became depressed
during marital therapy, when she irrationally concluded that
her husband will "never" change and will "always" be the
same. Her dysphoria led to a self-defeating pattern of behavior which further distanced her and her husband and set
herself up for the very thing she did not want: a poorer marriage.

• *Demanding Expectations* are beliefs that there are arbitrary laws or rules that have to be obeyed. "Kim" came into
treatment because she was depressed over her son talking
back to her. She irrationally believed that there is a "law in
the universe" that says that children should do what mothers ask and if not she has the right to get upset. She did not
see God "asks" us to obey Him. He gave us free will. Christ
Himself respected the free will of the creatures he created

as shown by the gentleness of His admonitions. Like Christ, parents should prefer and constructively work toward reasonable obedience from their children. A program of rewards for appropriate behavior and punishment for inappropriate behavior, administered without anger, anxiety or depression, would be constructive in bringing about good behavior instead of *demanding* it. Preferences would be substituted for demands.

• *Catastrophizing* is the perception that something is more than 100% bad, terrible or awful. "Kim" erroneously reacts to her son's talking back as the "end of the world." With cognitive intervention she would discover that on a scale of problems she might have with her son, talking back would be evaluated as decidedly low, surely not a catastrophe.

• *Emotional Reasoning* is the judgment that one's feelings are facts. Sandy has a "feeling" that her new boss does not like her. When asked how she knows this, she responds that her "feelings are always right." She fails to distinguish a feeling as real, which it is, versus a feeling proving something, which is impossible. For example, I tell patients: "No matter how strongly some people 'felt' during the time of Christopher Columbus that the world was flat, it did not make it so."

After identifying these cognitive distortions, clinical research has shown they have to be disputed. This is not dissimilar to the Spiritual Fathers who said evil thoughts have to be acted on. What modern psychology has done, however, is to give us more tools to do this. The church fathers would surely have welcomed such procedures. Teaching the patient/prodigal the "Challenging Questions" and engaging them around these, is quite effective in the disputation process and has its parallels with the spiritual guide:

1) Where is the evidence for or against the idea or thought?

2) Is there an alternative or any other way of looking at it?

3) Is it as bad as it seems. What is the worst and best that could happen? Could I live with it? What is the realistic outcome?

4) What is the effect of holding onto my distorted thoughts? What would happen if I changed my thinking? For example, an eighteen year old young woman comes to counseling very despondent. Her Beck Depression Inventory indicates severe depression. She is feels hopeless. During the initial session she reveals that she had a previous abortion and is currently two months pregnant by her father. She is overweight and did not immediately discover the pregnancy. Furthermore she has been sexually abused by her father since she was a young teenager. She sees herself as ugly and blames herself for the sexual abuse. She is convinced that she can never be forgiven. She has been abandoned by Jesus and anyone decent. At some after trust between her and the counselor has been established, the "Challenging" can begin.

The girl can be helped to identify her cognitive distortions. She is *labeling* and *polarizing* herself as "bad," she is *arbitrarily inferring* that she is "damned and cannot be forgiven." Combining both cognitive and spiritual approaches would involve integrating her faith in the "Challenging" process. The passage from the Gospel of St. John on the woman caught in adultery could be given to her to read and explore how it can be applied to her life. Jesus' words: "Neither do I condemn you; go, and do not sin again." (John 8, 11). The teaching of the church on forgiveness and the sin against the Holy Spirit can be examined as it pertains to her. Each of her cognitive distortions can be examined by finding alternative explanations and their consequences. There are a host of other scriptural and pastoral teachings of Our Lord and the saints that can be used. As the "Challenging" continues, the process has to be enlivened by the love and spirit of Christ.

The world is something that should be loved. God made the world and it is good. (Gen 1:10) As the psalmist states:

"The heavens declare the glory of God and the firmament proclaims his handiwork" (Ps 19:1). What is to be rejected in the world is that which separates us from God and our love of one another. Our task as Christians, using the admonition of St. Paul, is to be "wise as serpents and harmless as doves." We use our intelligence, by which we are like God, to be "watchful" and "discern" that which is good and leads us to God and one another, versus that which is evil and separates us from God and one another. Our calling as God's children demands this. This is the wisdom of the Spiritual Fathers whose ascetical practices have much in common with the scientific findings of modern psychology.

Notes

1. Pierre-Marie Delfieux, *The Jerusalem Community Rule of Life,* (Mahwah, NJ: Paulist Press, 1985).

2. Irenee Hausherr, *Spiritual Direction in the Early Christian East* (Spencer, MA: Cistercian Publications, 1990) and Aaron Beck, *Love Is Never Enough,* (New York: Harper and Rowe, 1988).

3. Aaron Beck, "Cognitive Therapy: A 30-year perspective." *American Psychologist,* 46, 368-365., 1991; Judith S. Beck, *Cognitive Therapy: Basics and beyond* (New York: The Guilford Press, 1995); and David Burns, *Feeling Good: The New Mood Therapy* (New York: Avon Books, 1990).

4. Op. cit., p. 158.

5. Metropolitan Hierotheos Vlachos, *Orthodox Psycho–therapy: the Science of the Fathers* (Levadia, Greece: Birth of the Theotokos Monastery, 1994), p. 214.

6. G.E.H. Palmer and Philip Sherrard and Kallistos Ware, *The Philokalia,* Vol. 2, (London: Faber & Faber, 1980), p. 79.

7. Ibid, p.89.

References

Albert Ellis and RobertA. Harper, *A Guide to Rational Living,* (New York: Lyle Stuart, 1961).

John Gottman, *Why Marriages Succeed or Fail,* (New York: Simon & Schuster, 1994).

E. Kadloubovsky and G.E.H. Palmer, trans. *Unseen Warfare,* (London: Faber & Faber, 1952).

HEALING THE HEALERS

The great illusion of leadership is to think that humans can be led out of the spiritual desert by someone who has never been there.
– Henri Nouwen

The Creed does not belong to you unless you have lived it.
– Metropolitan Philaret of Moscow

We have experienced that no psycho-analyst goes further than his own complexed and internal resistances permit; and we shall consequently require that he shall begin his activity with a self-analysis and continually carry it deeper while he is making his observations on his patients. Anyone who fails to produce results in a self-analysis of this kind may at once give up any idea of being able to treat patients by analysis.
– Sigmund Freud

The Fathers say that Christ dwells in our hearts through faith. He becomes incarnate in us when his commandments are observed. He is crucified when the pain of asceticism bends and cuts the passions. And he is resurrected when the Christian, freed from sinful passions, experiences spiritual visions, ascents and delights.
– Monk Moses

Chapter 6

POLLUTION OF THE SOUL: THE DANGERS OF LITERALISM AND PSYCHOLOGISM

JOHN PERKINS

In Princeton, New Jersey, last spring, Bishop Kallistos Ware speculated on Christianity's focus in the twenty-first century. In the twentieth century, he reminded us, the chief preoccupation was ecclesial: the theology and the shape of the Church itself. In contrast, the chief center of attention of Christianity both East and West during the twenty-first century, would be, in Bishop Ware's estimate, the theology of the human person.

If I might be permitted to narrow this even more, I would say that as far as human personhood is concerned, the most vital area of consideration ought to be the acknowledgment and the understanding of the human soul. For it is in the human soul that God and man come to meet each other in greatest intimacy and in greatest creativity. Our whole program of social action and communal relationship requires first that we come to terms with the human soul as the psychological region of actual spiritual events and spiritual transformations. It is here in the human soul that we first discover the perishing image of God, according to which we were created. And it is here, in this same soul, that mankind fights the battles and forges the difficult relationships that may lead first to inner peace and then to outer, worldly peace, so that all of creation may be restored in the image of the Creator.

Both outer physical reality and inner spiritual reality make an equal claim on us. Both are real and both are essential aspects of the nature of human beings and of our lives in this world. Jesus was a supreme psychological expert regarding the human soul. He often spoke of the Kingdom of God or the Kingdom of Heaven. Asked by the Pharisees when the Kingdom of God was to come, Jesus answered them by saying, "The coming of the Kingdom of God does not admit of observation and there will be no one to say, 'Look here! Look there! For you must know, the kingdom of God is among you" (1). This quote is from the Jerusalem Bible. But the King James version, which English-speaking Orthodox read as the Orthodox Study Bible, translates the phrase as "the Kingdom of God is *within* you." This was the preferred translation from ancient times until the comparatively modern era.

Inner and outer. The difference between *among* you, or *in your midst*, compared to *within you* may be an indication of how far our disposition has shifted in more modern times. *Among you* lends itself to an interpretation that the Kingdom of God is a corporate, communal and social phenomenon between persons, an interpersonal reality. The Kingdom of God, though not of this worldly political realm, is still a hoped for phenomenon of those persons who constitute the Body of Christ which is the Church. This is a great and valid truth. The translation *within you* calls forth the mystery of the human soul and of the deep and mystical interiority of the individual human personality, a realm of profound spiritual events that is hidden from normal, ordinary, everyday awareness. This level is not interpersonal, but precisely intrapersonal. This is also a great and a valid truth.

My belief is that both of these spheres, the outer and communal: the Church, and the inner and the individual: the soul, are legitimate scenes for the coming of the Kingdom, but with this requirement: they are each in their own way sides of a single reality in which each becomes a distortion without the other. The Kingdom of God without the individual experience of a dynamic human soul is nothing less than a type of tribal conformity, a collective institutionalism that absorbs and stifles any kind of unique initiative or creativity in response to God. On the other hand, the human soul without the holistic community of the Church prescribes a Kingdom of God that is really a kingdom of isolated and detached eccentricity, where everyone goes his own private way.

The soul is the psyche. Psychology means the study of the soul. Psychiatry means the healing of the soul. Unless you are a psychologist that has succumbed to a rationalistic, mechanistic and ego-centered paradigm, it is obvious that all religious experience including that of prayer and the discernment of spirits is quite psychological indeed. But in saying that religious experience is psychological, we need not assume that it is *only* psychological or *merely* psychological, or that psychology in some manner "explains away" religious experience.

The soul or psyche is not a closed system invented by human intelligence and made by human hands. The soul is a vast realm, an open-ended domain that is the medium for the profoundest experience. Think of our consciousness as a house with a front door and a back door. Out the front door is the world reaching from the sidewalk of the local community as far away as the deepest reaches of outer space millions of light years away. Out the back door is the realm of transcendent spiritual reality, somewhat personal and individual in its nearest elements, but limitless and transpersonal in its vast extension. Here, in this house of our ego consciousness, we live, at the intersection of these terrifying realms. Origen put it so well when he said, "Know that within you is another world in little, in which are the sun, the moon, and all the stars." That is the soul and the spiritual reality that lies beyond it. Origen meant to give his hearers a sense of the incredible and unlimited cosmic reaches of the human soul. With such a magnificent sense of soul, it is impossible to psychologize or reduce religion to some closed and mechanistic psychology. Neither is it possible, in such an open system as Origen suggests, to interpret human nature as a merely inconsequential atom in a vast and impersonal universe. For like the Theotokos, we contain the heavens even as we are contained by the heavens. We should never forget that we are just like the Theotokos, the Mother of God: Our soul and her womb are the same, for she is the archetype of the human soul and the model of its response to God.

Inner spiritual reality is not *just* psychology or *just* mythology, though it is psychological, and the soul experiences itself in universal terms of myth and symbol that point beyond itself, linking the earthly and the heavenly, the human and the divine. Outer, hard-fact physical and social experience is not all there is.

Jesus appears to have been equally balanced between an extroverted approach to life and an introverted approach. He comprehended both the solitary soul alone with God and the community together with God. These are mirror images of each other. I believe that when he spoke, particularly in his parables about the Kingdom of Heaven, Jesus was often alluding to the outer and the inner worlds at the same time. He was speaking paradoxically, of the ethic of the human community on the one hand and of the dynamic events of the human soul on the other. For example: "Happy are those who are persecuted in the cause of right: theirs is the Kingdom of Heaven" (2).

On the surface this points to the inner certainty and faith that is a great comfort to those who suffer actual, worldly persecution. No problem about that. But there is another realm of persecution, and that is within the human personality where one's own egocentricity is the tyrant, and where valid parts of our human nature as intended by God are abused and misused, depreciated or just plain ignored by our one-sided prejudices and our stubborn pride.

"I found myself in a dark and damp corner of an abandoned subway corridor in Harlem," dreamed a middle-class white man. "It was made known to me that I was scheduled to attend a rich and festive luncheon on the East Side of New York City. But in order to prepare properly for access to it, I was required to walk the breadth and depth of Harlem and observe first-hand the terrible plight of the poor black folk, particularly the homeless people. As I felt my way along the dark corridor, the nauseating stench of urine and human waste reached my nose. Then, abruptly, I stumbled upon an old sick black man lying in a pool of his own urine. He was feebly trying to eat a dirty torn-off slip of paper with the word 'sandwich' written on it. At that moment I was filled with an overpowering feeling of disgust and despair at the way this man had been treated. 'How dreadful it is for these folk,' I mumbled under my breath, 'No one is helping them. This poor man is being left to die!'"

Before we can sit down with God in the festival of the Kingdom, we must first locate that Kingdom in ourselves. But many of us will be in for a rude surprise, for just as the image of God in which we were created is darkened and tarnished by our fallen nature, so does the Kingdom itself appear in the depths of our own souls in its present *actual* condition, as the persecuted, ignored or abandoned part of ourselves that is dying of illness and starvation in a slum. This is a wonderful dream example because it demonstrates the validity and the truth of both the outer and the inner situation. It is an interpersonal social comment, but it is also an intrapersonal sort of x-ray picture of the condition of one man's soul, a man whose collective conformity and egoism are guilty of starving the Kingdom of Heaven to death in his own self! If the dreamer, like the good Samaritan, had embraced the sick old man, tended to his wounds, fed him real food instead of lip service, helped him up, and given him a home and cared for him, then he, the dreamer, would be instantly in the Kingdom at the heavenly banquet, and his whole life would be changed and reinvigorated. He would have a moment of heaven on earth, as the promised luncheon signified. So the kingdom is both inner and outer, but always simultaneously and paradoxically! "I have come to save that which was lost," says Jesus. These are the lost and abandoned people in the world, but also the lost parts of our inner selves. Outer social justice can never be achieved in a community of people who have ignored the demands of the inner justice of the soul. As James Baldwin once said, "The racial problem will never be solved until the white man comes to terms with the black man inside of himself." Entrance into the kingdom requires the destruction of the old, ego-centered personality, and the revelation that, from God's holistic point of view, what appears to be the lowest and the most despised in all of ourselves or in the surrounding community, is in fact the highest and the most valuable. Or as C. G. Jung was heard to say, "God loves the shadow within us far more than he loves us... and he continually stands us on our heads!"

"You therefore must be perfect as your heavenly Father is perfect." The word perfect means complete, brought to the end state, finished. Perfect does not allude to perfectionistic, idealistic, fastidious; to a fussy, one-sided pureness that is above it all. It is precisely our whole and healthy and earthy spiritual life that God is after, rather than imprisoning us in rigid ideals of flawlessness. God leaves that to the Pharisees and to the intolerable show-offs among us.

When it comes to the soul, we must remember that the Christian life of faith is a journey toward wholeness, because that is what holiness really is, to be like God, one and complete. This journey is profoundly paradoxical. It is at once a quest, an adventure, an arduous task, that requires spiritual sweat and endurance on man's part in order to reach the goal. But the journey toward the Kingdom is also a discovery, where God finds us and validates us, and we are then known and acknowledged by Him. The Kingdom is both the highest and the deepest value in ourselves: the pearl of great price in the soul, the holistic image of God according to which we were made and which can really be found within us. But the Kingdom is also the one who finds us and values us, our Father, the creator, because he is the King of All.

Consider these two somewhat different parables from Jesus' own lips: "The Kingdom of Heaven is like a treasure hidden in a field which someone has found; he hides it again, goes off happy, sells everything he owns and buys that field"(3). And again, "...the Kingdom of Heaven is like a merchant looking for pearls; when he finds one of great value he goes and sells everything he owns and buys it" (4).

In the first instance the Kingdom is a thing that we discover after a long search. We ourselves find it. We are the seekers. That is the quest dimension of the Christian journey toward holiness and wholeness. We find the Kingdom of Heaven or its equivalent, which is the image of God in our souls, and we submit everything to it as the most valuable and the most important. But in the second of these two parables, it is the Kingdom of Heaven itself, in the form of a merchant, that discovers the treasure; and that treasure is our essential and aboriginal selves in the depths of the soul, the true and greatest value of humanity. It is as if two searches and two quite different discoveries by different agencies are occurring at one and the same time, and are united paradoxically. We find the divine image of our humanity, and it both seeks and finds us. This is the synergy of our joint effort with God. When God created man in his own image, God made a self-portrait, in which two phenomena occur. God comes to see himself reflected as in a mirror, and thus comes to know himself more fully in some hidden manner that is connected with the most dark and mysterious purposes of the creation and the incarnation from God's side of the picture. One may not speak much about this. And at the same time, we discover who we truly are as formed by and from the divine. In this mandorla or partial overlap, we are God and God is us. Such a treasure is not the human ego, nor its vanity or pride, but the divine treasure hidden in the unconscious personality, and this treasure longs for the light and to be discovered and cherished, like the sick black man in the subway passage above.

"I was hungry and you gave me food; I was thirsty and you gave me drink; I was a stranger and you made me welcome; naked and you clothed me; sick and you visited me; in prison and you came to see me... I tell you solemnly, insofar as you did this to the least of these brothers of mine, you did it to me" (5).

Today we live in a supposedly egalitarian society where our welfare system attempts to care for the poor and the unfortunate. But this will come to naught; even become a strange kind of self-idolatry that expresses the superiority of the rich and the competent, unless the same thing occurs within the soul of every human being. Every one of us has a stranger hidden inside himself, the one whom we do not yet know, and for whom we have not yet learned to care. That shadow person is the part of our God-given humanity that must be discovered, valued and integrated if the image of God, the Kingdom of Heaven, is to be realized within us as well as among us. These two spheres must be indissolubly joined and recognized as one, both the outer and the inner.

It would be a great mistake to assume that, if one speaks of the psychological reality of the spiritual realm, that one thus reduces spirit to the "nothing but" level of materialistic science. Since the word *psyche* is in fact the Greek word for soul, the equivalent of the Latin word *anima*, which is literally "breath of life," the assumption should go quite the other way!

When Christ reiterates that his Kingdom is *not of this world*, he does not mean that his Kingdom has nothing to do with psychological experience, or that his Kingdom exists in some split-off ethereal region that is entirely inaccessible to human mentality. Christ means that his Kingdom is to be identified neither with the profane political realm *per se*, nor with intellectualized concepts, nor – witness Nicodemus – with prosaic, matter-of-fact, literal occurrences. This Kingdom points rather toward an interior and dynamic sphere of events, to that mysterious well of the spirit inside the human personality, that can only be approached through the agencies of living symbols and parables, through bodily participation in sacred ceremonies and rituals. Here Christ promised that a rapturous fountain of living water would spring up, leading to eternal life. Such a transformation occurs as one's conscious awareness is immersed in the divine mystery that exists beyond ordinary egoistic awareness. Human consciousness is dissolved. One's attitudes, values, concepts – one's entire state of mind, even one's personal and cultural identity – is taken into the symbolic underworld, which we today associate with the realm of the deep unconscious psyche. As St. John Chrysostom explained Baptism by water and the Spirit, "It represents death and interment, life and resurrection... When we plunge our head beneath water, as in a sepulcher, the old man becomes completely immersed and buried. When we leave the water, the new man suddenly appears." Our baptisms are extended and reenacted repeatedly through every stage of our psychological and spiritual development, as we encounter the unconscious psyche.

One of the major problems we have today in the Christian Church is that many people are limited to a second- or third-hand spiritual experience. Too often there is talk about religious matters – especially rational talk with vague sentiments. We have also witnessed altruistic impulses, or the external imitation of pious gestures, or the need to maintain gnawing guilt or a sense of groveling inferiority, or a finicky obsession with the fine points of church order or a sense of power and importance. In short, the subject matter of religion and the institutional structures used for ulterior demonic purposes replaces dynamic inner spiritual encounter. Such a borrowed pseudo-religion is completely unlike that of the desert fathers, who really struggled tooth and nail experimentally toward the immediate and vital realization of God in their lives. The desert fathers were wild and adventurous, not piously conventional or obsessed with detail!

The most important messages that come to us from Christ and the vital holy people who followed him are addressed to the inner man, to the soul, to the intuitive spiritual faculties of interior perception. Yet most modern folk live on a completely different plane, the level of egoistic conformity to the standard life of society, "just like everybody else," where we all consider ourselves relatively decent and sincere people. Thus, few really experience those radical psychological levels that can register the numinous and powerfully transforming energy of God – the Breath of Life of the Spirit as its mighty wind blows through the deepest reaches of the soul.

We live a kind of mass-transit psychology – in common with others – and it rarely occurs to us to get off the bus or the train and visit the wilderness, especially the wilderness within, where we might encounter vital spiritual reality first-hand. In other words, the soul, the faculty of actual religious experience, has been repressed and devalued in the psyches of most modern Christians. A Russian bishop, Philaret of Moscow, reminds us that the Creed does not really belong to us until we have lived it. There are no armchair travelers in the realm of the spirit. Kallistos Ware says that God has children but no grandchildren. We can't live through another person's religious life. We can't travel toward God by reading a book, even if that book is a theological work written by a world-renowned scholar. We must travel firsthand in actual psychological experience. God wants originals, not clones! God wants us to be ourselves for the very first time. Information about our faith and the workings of church machinery gives us an illusion of relationship to God. But it is not the true thing. It is merely a pale, thirdhand reflection, like eating the menu instead of the meal. We cheat ourselves if we believe that union with God is an occurrence that can happen only *after death*. To the extent that we don't meet God face to face *now* in the very depths of our lives, we never shall afterward!

In some very important respects, Jesus, in the tradition of the prophets, was the first individual person who possessed an appreciation of the scope of human interiority, which we call soul or psyche. His prophetic requirement is that following rules and regulations and putting on the outward airs of holiness, obedience and rectitude will get us nowhere. We must come to terms with God directly and immediately in our souls and in our hearts, often in our own unique and painful ways; in this manner we will gain the freedom to love and to serve our fellow men. The new individual divine human being that Christ is and we must become is equipped with the discernment of spirits by the power of the Holy Spirit of God. This discernment of spirits is the task of Christian psychotherapy, where, rather than conforming to a rigid code of laws, together with wearing a mask of sophistication in the community, the human being is given the possibility of a creative existence in imitation of his divine Creator. In this way, his life is renewed each and every day, and his unique selfhood, as intended by God, is first revealed and then given a chance to live abundantly. Here he is able to recapture what has been lost, even as he is simultaneously saved from above. He may find the stone that was rejected by his phony big ego and his prideful self-esteem. Or he may stumble upon it quite by accident, as if God laid a trap for him. At some points it may be a terrifying journey, where things go out of control, and events ensue that he had neither planned nor least expected. Often the Kingdom of Heaven takes us by force.

A very successful big-city clergyman, in charge of a rich parish with many impressive programs, had the following dream: "I am driving my late-model sedan down the avenue, hurrying to an appointment, and suddenly I seem to lose control of the car. The vehicle swerves, begins to roll over and crashes into a light post. The impact is so violent that I am thrown clear of my car and land in the gutter. But before I can catch hold of myself, I am washed down through an open sewer grate and am carried by the current of waste water a long way underground. It is a terrible place and stinks to high heavens. Finally I am washed up at the edge of the stream, and as I look around in the darkness, I think I see a small door in the wall of the sewer. Believing this to be an exit to the street used by maintenance workers, I try the door. It opens easily, but to my utter surprise, I discover that it is a door leading into a small chapel, where I see candles lit as if for Mass. I venture cautiously inside, and as I turn the corner into the chapel itself I am confronted by a man with penetrating and luminous eyes, who gazes steadfastly at me. Panic seizes me as I realize that I am standing in the presence of my Lord and Savior Jesus Christ Himself! With a look that seems a mixture of irritation and compassion he says, "Do you realize how very long I have been waiting here for you!?"

Such a dream is, of course, specifically pertinent to the life of the man who dreamed it. Outwardly, he was a successful and a competent, worldly man, respected by the community. But his prophetic and warning dream showed that in his pride, this venerable minister of God had flushed true religion down the toilet, and that is precisely where he had to go once again, quite against his willfulness or his conscious intentions, down again into the sewer to find God. We are mostly all of us in the same predicament. We must work up the courage, summon the will, and then fathom the depths of the human soul. It is a long, long way down into the sewer from the high place of our inflation and our pride. Spiritual development, like all good psychotherapy, is invariably unpleasant, even frightening, and extremely hard work, though its rewards are great.

Now is the time for us to give this neglected realm the attention and the value it deserves. By acknowledging it in all humility, by stooping way, way down and by embracing it, by taking it seriously and giving our inner, non-ego world of the psyche and the real psychological events that occur within it top, high-level priority, we repair and cleanse and renew the sacred vessels of our hearts and minds, nourishing and renewing and healing the soul, so that it may become a fitting home for the King of All.

Notes

1. Luke 17:20-21
2. Matt 5:10
3. Matt 13:44
4. Matt 13:45-46
5. Matt 25:35-36, 40

Chapter 7

SPIRITUAL WAR:
THE RELEVANCE TO MODERN THERAPY OF THE ANCIENT EASTERN ORTHODOX CHRISTIAN PATH OF ASCETICAL PRACTICE

Jamie Moran

Take your mind down into the heart, and stand with
your mind in your heart before God.
– Monastic Injunction from
the Egyptian Desert Tradition

Keep your mind in hell and despair not.
– Christ to St. Silouan of Mt. Athos

He who knows himself is greater than he who raises
the dead.
– St. Isaac of Syria

Something is only true if it can be lived.
– F. Nietzsche

PART ONE
THE ASCETICAL YOKE – ENTER THE FURNACE

Why ascetecism is so vital, and necessary
Asceticism is not some exotic extra, but is central to
Christianity, and other 'spiritual' religions. This is because

of its power to reach the place other 'religious things' cannot reach, and effect change there – in the *deep heart* of the human being. Being a nice guy, even the conventional well-meaning religious person, simply does not get to the place that needs to be changed. We have a tv ad here in England, "Heineken lager gets to the parts other beers cannot." This is the claim for asceticism, thus why it is central, and thus also why religions without asceticism (which operate mostly through beliefs and morals, and good intentions) differ fundamentally from religions with asceticism. For example, Eastern Orthodox Christianity is in many important respects closer to Shamanism, Northern Buddhism, and Hasidic Judaism than it is to Western Christianity, because all of these four Traditions follow a Yoke, a Practice, a Way, that is *mainly* ascetical. Not only St. Paul refers to askesis as necessary, but Christ does repeatedly in the Gospels, especially in the Sermon on the Mount. The claim that asceticism is an Oriental import into Christianity is rubbish. Equally rubbish is the claim that it is only for monks and nuns in monasteries. It is for all Christians who want to be melded into the Cross of Christ.

What asceticism is

It is important to distinguish between a more broad and a more narrow definition of asceticism. Broadly defined, everything in Orthodox life is ascetical in some manner. Thus, in most of our ceremonies we stand rather than sit, take a long rather than a short time to complete them, and are meant to use body, mind, heart and soul in a certain way so as to be fully present in that ceremony, alert to it, offered to it, and able to share it with others (both those who are there with us, and those who are absent). Or, at certain moments in the year we fast, and at other moments we feast; when meant to fast, feasting would be breaking the ascetical yoke, but equally when meant to feast, fasting would be breaking the ascetical yoke. There is a distinct discipline to this, but also an ethos that informs it. There is a practice, but also a way of doing it that is inspired and informed by a certain spirit: it would not be any benefit to throw away the practice, yet equally useless would be to do it in the wrong way, e.g. with the wrong spirit, or no spirit. Neither anarchic self-expression, nor formulaic rule-following, are any help.

Narrowly defined, asceticism refers to a varied set of 'spiritual disciplines' crucial to the walking of the religious path, when that path is seen less as about obedience to an authority whom one pleases in a way of living, and more about the following of a way of living that leads to a radical transformation in those who bind themselves to it and faithfully keep it as a practice. It is because of asceticism that you get the *wicasa wakan* or 'wounded healer' in Shamanism, the Buddha or 'enlightened one' in Buddhism, the Zadik or 'proven one' in Hasidism, the Staretz or 'spiritual elder' in Orthodoxy. Indeed, it is even more radical than this: we follow the path Christ has left us in order to grow more like Him, in order to allow God to change us, already in this life, from the fallen Image to the actual Likeness to Christ. A disciple is not one who 'conforms' to authority to escape punishment and gain reward; nor is a disciple one who 'exercises' spiritual muscle to grow into a superman – there is nothing punitive in asceticism, nor is there anything athletic in terms of spiritual accomplishment. *A disciple walks a path that can change him into who and what he is following.* This is why Christ says to us: "If you love me, keep my commandments." We may have the intention to get closer to God, but unless we practice as a way of life those things that **weaken** what **separates** us from God and that **strengthen** what **unites** us to God, this intention remains merely theoretical, never finding realization. We remain ambivalent, conflicted in our depths, however much we put a good face on that at the surface.

The aim of asceticism can be put in a host of ways, such as to become purified, or to become humble, but basically it aims at holiness: as Syrian Orthodoxy puts it, not just God's occasional "visitation" *to* us, but God's permanent "dwelling" *in*, and *with*, us. We are called to love as God does, by virtue of that love living and acting in us. For as an Athonite elder has said: "He who does not love has no peace, even if they were to put him in Paradise."

But this switch from visitation to dwelling has to be prepared for, and freely. Ascetical practice is what we offer to God's gift: it is our gift because it makes our whole being and existence in the world capable of incarnating God, after the pattern of the divine-humanity of Christ. In Lakota medicine man Frank Fools Crow's image, we must become a 'hollow bone'; in Buddhist terms, we must die 'the great death'; in Hasidic terms, we must be 'reduced to nothing'; for Christians, we embrace the Cross of Christ, that we may be raised into His Resurrection. I am not claiming that there are no differences in these four ascetically-produced experiences of radical spiritual transformation in the human being, only that a similar pattern undergirds all of them. One thing (very precious to us) must **decrease**, that another thing (more basic but hedged round by doubts, weakness, secret agendas, and escape clauses that tempt us to not pursue it) can **increase.** To be anything but sober about this, trusting of the potentiality but respectful of the gravity, is foolish; there is no room here for romanticism, idealism, or triumphalism. This process is too terrible for any of that. Fear is the beginning of wisdom; and it is a fearful thing to fall into the hands of the living God. In asceticism, we let God's fire burn us to ashes: we encounter the daemonic God, the God who destroys and brings suffering and loss. In the throes of this process, "deep cries to deep," as David says in the Psalms; Bodidharma said that over the course of it, "you will bear the unbearable and endure the unendurable."

Asceticism is, then, a method for crossing the disabling and dispiriting gap between promise and fulfillment. This gap is the deep place, the beautiful and terrible place, the place of ultimate glory and grief, where most people never venture. Asceticism situates us in this place, rather than the more comfortable and distracted places at a distance from it, where we usually (half-) live. In this place is the real hell, the hell in the deep heart, but in this place is also the seed of the kingdom. The deep heart is also the heart ground where all human beings stand, in possibility and tragedy; for Christ, this was the killing ground to which he staked his life and his death. Only here can everything be gained, but it is also here that all is lost.

Ascetical practice is already a 'taking up of our cross' for us. Yet just as ascetical humility is less profound than the humility of Christ, so too the ascetical cross is less profound than the Cross of Christ, but it is the former discipline that opens up a road toward the latter spiritual reality.

How asceticism works

Ascetical practices are often hard and pained, go against common sense and our supposedly 'natural' inclinations and feelings. Anyone who has tried to meditate in the nous, contemplate in the soul, and pray in the heart ('stay in your cell'), as well as fast and work physically, and the host of other things we can do, including practices that pertain to how we are with other people ('bear your brother'), knows from experience how arduous this kind of life can be. But arguably most challenging is simply to be constant, and thus stable, in one's practice, however simple or complex it may be (the desert fathers recommend we try a few rather than many of these things). Ascetical practices cannot be taken up and put down, on a whim or if one feels up for it or down about it: they need to be done on a regular, day in, day out, basis. Moreover, they are life-long. They are in one sense pointed at a stupendous and dignified goal, yet in another sense they are also simply an end in themselves, since in this life we are never given any assurance the goal has been reached, and it is wiser to operate on the more modest assumption it has not been, even if that entails accepting it may be unattainable for me (this does not mean it is unattainable for others). The fact that we are aimed at that outcome, truly vowed to it, is far more vital than how far we get; what really matters is (a) the striving, and (b) the persistence. A peculiar effort is needed. If we make this effort, we get help from God and the spirits who do God's service, but if we shirk all such effort, no 'magical rescue' saves us. The effort needed to hold firm through real ups and downs that stretch us to the limit, and break us to remake us, comes from our spirit (e.g. our strength), and does not resemble the usual, fallen ambition. Tradition calls it a synergy with God and the creation; it is neither relying entirely on our own power, nor that passivity or defeatism in which we rely on a power beyond us and refuse to act from our own will and guts. St. Theophan the Recluse: "Do not grow faint. God will not forget your labor, as He did not forget that of others who labored…"

The sought-for outcome of asceticism cannot be guaranteed, but when it works, perhaps three things account for its unique power of transformation. For one thing, it is **practical.** Life is action; our life is what we 'do' with our existence, on the ground, in the wonderful and harrowing situation in which we are placed. *Whatever we practice (and any form of living is in this sense a practice) is who and what we become.* Western rationalism has always mistakenly valued theory over practice, seeing practice as merely the 'application' of theory. But practice is a domain on its own, and so the practitioner discovers things, and undergoes things, that the theoretician either could never have imagined or dreamt of, or even if they were partially foreseen, they prove importantly different when they emerge and are encountered on the ground. Practice takes the lid off all hidden realities, sacred and profane; yet it only does this by testing us. We must go blind, with faith, courage, generosity and self-control, through this 'walk.' There is a trust in not knowing and not being in control, a passion and a pathos.

Practice as a concrete way of action puts difficulties upon us, but the measure of this is less their severity and more how we are changed as a consequence; those who speculate, and merely talk a walk, are not changed in the least, but reinforced in their opposition to such change. But if you walk, then you soon learn to curb talk altogether ('Guarding the tongue' is a major ascetic practice), and you cease being impressed by that failing of the sophisticated that their talk often exceeds their walk: to hear some of us talk, you would think we were gods already. But in the throes of the practice, we cease this sort of untried arrogance; we learn to stick to a humbler stance, yet one more open, and indeed more bold. Practice produces experience, a direct knowing of human and spiritual depths, and this experience shows us both how we get lost and how we find ways through. The traditional name for such 'learning of life lessons' is Wisdom. Asceticism presupposes a need for a degree of Vision; but its main thrust is with what produces Wisdom. Light does not just come down from the sky; it also comes up from the ground, as we walk.

For another thing, asceticism is **disciplined.** The Lakota say "a person of great heart has generosity, bravery, and self-control." Self-control does not mean, as it is so often misunderstood, self-inhibition. To control oneself means to take responsibility for one's existence, to see honestly its potential yet distortion. But in the ascetical context it also means to see that more is at stake in existence in this world than just me and my woes. We are all in the same boat together, and something profound is endangered, something that needs to be saved, and transfigured, to liberate its potentiality. Taking responsibility is an awakening to the suffering world in which all beings, creatures and things dwell: the opposite of the young Galahad who, confronting the sick king and the sick land, neglected to question this. Responsibility is to do with being moved by the fate that befalls oneself and others; it is a kind of compunction, and if potent enough, can engender the desire to repent. This repentance is not about right and wrong, or juridical guilt; it is the sudden perception of a more ultimate concern in all things, and a biting sense of failing this, yet wanting to serve it. To fear being in the wrong and wanting to be in the right is nothing to do with this deep moment of opening to the actual state of things. When we do this truly, an awakening comes that we are failing the human dilemma, and thus it is first of all we ourselves who must change to become a healing, creative, redemptive presence to it.

In short, we accept our own need for fundamental alteration because of wanting to serve something greater than ourselves. Curbing our current life and way of being in the world is an act of love, an act motivated by our response to a divine call. A discipline serves something, it does x, y,and z, rather than a, b and c, because it has a noble task to take on, and it comes to the understanding that x, y and z will serve this task while a, b and c betray it. For example, as a psychologist, I discipline my actions because I serve the promotion of my subject, my discipline; I want to do what contributes to its thriving, and not do what adds to its burdens and in fact drives it into a worse condition. Ascetic discipline has this rationale: *we curb ourselves, so that a different self can live and act in the world, for the sake of the world.* Self-control is about restricting the lesser in us for the purpose of freeing the greater. It isn't even only our love for God that drives this, but our love for the existential situation in which everything is put at fundamental risk. "He who loves acquires another self," says St. John Chrysostom.

These two features of asceticism explain why this path is called, in the Orthodox desert tradition, 'the practical life,' and also, 'the life of virtue.' Virtue does not arise except through practice; and a practice that does not glimpse the supreme value in things fails to grapple with the virtues that address and actively pursue this value, and the vices that either ignore or damage it. In short, the practice of virtue, and resistance of vice, must be undertaken as a 'discipline', like a vow that is not to be broken, but faithfully kept through thick and thin. We are not born virtuous; it is an accomplishment, born of practical struggle and travail.

This brings out the third, and most vital, reason why asceticism works. It has a **strategy**, a concrete way in which it plays down the one thing in order to play up the other. The implication is, mostly we skate over this whole deeper fulcrum in us, occasionally and haphazardly tapping into our potential greatness and call, but often letting our fallen and broken condition blot out the former, to promote its own mischief and mayhem. Mostly, the true conflict raging in our depths is evaded. Instead, a fragile crust of decency sits over a hell of potent derangement, a sickness of life and evil of passions, and we have no method of access to, nor do we even trust, the deeper heaven within that hell. This type of self-division in which the 'nice' precariously sits on the 'nasty' – so well unpacked by Freudian psychoanalysis (and by Sartre, who called its self-deception "bad faith") – is not at all how the self-control of asceticism functions.

The self-control of asceticism functions through a strategy perfectly summed up by the following, real incident. A Lakota holy man was asked about his inner life by a visitor to the reservation, who no doubt was expecting some reply that would conjure up mystical vistas. The reply he got was more prosaic, and truthful. The old man said, "My inner life is two dogs constantly at war, a good one and a mean one." Probably thrown, the questioner flippantly reacted with the immediate question, "Which dog wins?" The old man thought for a moment. His answer was, "The one I feed the most."

Normally, we hardly feed the greater (we don't know how to feed it, and a lot of our attempts to feed the greater actually feed the lesser: we know we are hungry, but we hardly know where the food is), and though we may not feed the lesser too blatantly, we feed it in secret. Polite eating masks devouring; what we really need, and want, is feasting. Asceticism dispenses with polite eating altogether, and proceeds to put a brake on devouring, and an accelerator on feasting. This has a revolutionary impact on us. Take a lion you've been tossing choice bits of meat to in secret out in the back streets, hoping thereby to keep him happy and quiet, no threat to the cozy living room where you stroke the tame cat; now put him in a cage and cut off the supply. What happens? He roars and shakes the cage with such ferocity, you start to sweat in your previously impervious and impregnable little chamber. The old game of compromise and containment is up. You have to take the lion on. But with what resources do you face this challenge? You fear to be eaten, but actually when you relocate to the cage with the lion, a mysterious process begins.

Another story, probably based on a true incident. To get relief from the withering heat of the desert, a monk went into a cave. A lion already there began to roar. The monk turned to him, and said in a fierce voice, "If you cannot share this place of shade, you'd better leave." The lion did.

When we enter the cage with the lion, we should know there is no exit. We are now in what the Eastern Christian Desert Tradition names 'the spiritual warfare.' Not only our greater heart is there with our lesser heart, but God is there, as is the evil one. A battle in the deeps has begun. We will fight it, henceforth, until the day we die. The obscure and twisted side, in us and beyond us, will protest mightily at its curbing, but the light and fire already in us will, encouraged by nourishment from outside itself, start to really engage the enemy. This enemy will be watched, and understood; and by resistance his power of temptation and persuasion weakened. This takes time; it is slow, it has steps; it makes progress and has setbacks; it is, at times, just in hell, though at other times it can discern the heaven being planted in hell.

Asceticism contains a strategy for feeding the greater and starving the lesser which has the effect of (a) eliciting the hidden conflict in us between greater and lesser, (b) containing and holding it (so it doesn't spill over, or just explode outward) while intensifying and clarifying it, and finally (c) undercutting the lesser at the same time as enhancing the greater.

PART TWO
NEPTIC WORK – STAY IN THE FURNACE

Inner work

Asceticism implements this strategy of nourishing/starving by dint of many practices, but especially through the *inner work* referred to in such injunctions as, "Still the mind," "Take the mind down into the heart," "Guard the heart," "Stand with the mind in the heart before God," and "Pray in silence."

In the Desert Tradition, those persons especially experienced and skilled in ascetical inner work were called the Neptic Fathers. *Nepsis*, in Greek, indicates a state of wakefulness which is the converse of drunken stupor. Palmer et al. in the glossary of the *Philokalia* (Vol. 2) summarize it as "spiritual sobriety, alertness, vigilance. It signifies an attitude of attentiveness whereby one keeps watch over one's inward thoughts and fantasies, maintaining guard" over the mind and heart. The Neptic Tradition developed techniques for 'watching and guarding' first the mind and then the heart. These techniques constitute tools, virtually weapons, for conducting the spiritual warfare that a person is thrown into, if they seriously keep the strategy of asceticism of getting in the cage with the lion. To try to pursue this strategy without these tools would probably be fruitless, and maybe even dangerous.

Nous

Watchfulness begins with the mind. A technique was developed, similar to that in Buddhism, for stilling the mind, so that whatever is present there can simply be watched in bare attention. This is what Buddhism calls 'meditation', and should not be confused with the contemporary Western Christian and Roman Catholic activity of the same name, which employs a host of words, thoughts and imagery. None of this is wanted in the present context. But this watchfulness of attention (known as mindfulness in Buddhism) awakens a latent faculty of mind called the nous, which is remarkably different from mere analytic intellect, or even synthetic reason. The nous, ordinarily asleep or blinded, has a penetrative power of direct seeing. It sees through the veils and glamour by which evil disguises itself, never showing itself to us openly. Thus, the coming into being of the acute awareness of this nous allows us to begin to see through, and distance ourselves from, the way in which evil gets a hold over our whole existence. This is mainly through mental fantasy. The practise of just watching in meditative awareness, without defence from or indulgence of the gripping scenarios of fantasy, starts to weaken the usual link between fantasy and action. The fantasy ceases being a compulsion to action. We know, for example, that serial killers all entertain violent, sadistic fantasies, long before they begin acting on these in their killing sprees. Normally, fallen action is instigated by seductive fantasy, and therefore fantasy is the reason why certain actions gradually become irresistible. Fantasy takes us over, and so acting on it becomes inevitable. By weakening fantasy's power in the mind, the ability of fantasy to compel action is also weakened.

The full-depth psychological analysis that the Neptic Tradition gives speaks of three stages by which evil becomes ingrained, from the point of initial suggestion or provocation, to the point of captivity or, in modern parlance, addiction.

First, there is demonic provocation deep in the heart, or the rising of a fallen impulse. This cannot be prevented. Next, there is a second stage in which the provocation or impulse enters the mind in the form of a fantasy image or 'thought' (*logismi* in Greek); at this point we begin to entertain the image, turn it over in our mind pleasurably, parley with it, yet still hesitate to act on it. But, the more we 'couple' or 'commune' with the image through indulging its fantasy in our mind, the more inevitable becomes the action it suggests. Such fantasy is like the projection of a delicious menu, seemingly offering the most exciting, wonderful, satisfying food. Drooling over the menu finally persuades us: Yes, we say, I'll have that. The third stage, then, is when we assent to the action that is required to go out and grab the food. Even though it turns out to be a poisoned chalice, and despite the fact we usually 'know' that in the abstract, such is the power of fantasy over action that we cannot desist. The more we act on fantasy, the more of a habit the action becomes. This force of habit makes it difficult for us to resist temptation.

We cannot stop the arising of fantasies; but we can cease to entertain them and enjoy them. In the Desert language, we 'de-couple' from them. When we do this, such fantasies start to lose their seductiveness. And when we are no longer caught up in attraction to the fantasies, then we can withdraw our assent from them; their existence in the mind no longer exerts a pressure to pursue them in action. Indeed, they become a way of clarifying the heart, for if we will look with the nous at fantasy, neither indulging it nor just intellectually analyzing it, then secrets of the hidden heart start to be disclosed. Gradually, penetrative direct seeing into the depths becomes possible; through this activity, the Neptic Tradition uncovered the eight fallen passions, and their underground hiding places and obscure maneuvers: greed, lust, gluttony, hate, discontent, accidie, vainglory, pride. The lesser heart was discerned. Such discernment produced amazing depth-psychological knowledge of 'sin,' and its 'workings' deep within. This discernment is more than speculation about the heart, based on drawing inductive conclusions from the data provided by fantasy (the method of all modern depth psychology, starting with Freud). Moreover, not only does the nous see into the dark depths in a manner intellectual analysis cannot, it can also renounce the fallen impulses, or the evil that provokes them, in a way no mere 'ego strength' can muster. Indeed, there is a first kind of ascetical 'dispassion' achieved here: the nous allows us to withdraw from the lesser heart, to stand back, to no longer be captivated, interested, driven. This stilling of mind and birth of discernment causes us to stand back from many pursuits people normally follow. A certain detachment from 'delusive cravings', (as Buddhism aptly names the fallen impulses of our being) begins. A wisdom about the fallen heart, which goes with ceasing to employ it so much, comes to the fore.

Equally, the deeper impulses of the greater heart begin to break through; restraining evil passions 'makes space' for good passion. Wisdom and compassion, as Buddhism contends, arise together. Thus nous cannot awake without this engendering a degree of new freedom of the greater heart. This is why some Desert Ascetics do not really much distinguish nous from heart, or refer to nous as the 'eye of the heart'; once there is Light, Fire follows. Nonetheless, many of the Neptic Fathers, and especially the so-called 'heart' tradition of St Macarius of Egypt, state that stilling the mind is easier than stilling the heart: watching and guarding the mind is the first step, but the second step of watching and guarding the heart is far more problematic. Stillness is close to purity; thus purifying the nous is not the same as purifying the heart. The nous is not fully in the deep heart yet. There is a descent down into the heart, and a further battle in that place.

Purifying the attention is necessary before we can purify the intention: but the latter is more arduous than the former. In the nous we contend with the flowering of evil, but in the heart we contend with the root of evil.

Heart

A host of subtle, and hard, sayings refer to this tussle with the root of evil deep in us, starting with Christ's answer to St. Paul, who wanted his own evil of heart surgically removed. Telling him this thorn in the flesh could not be removed, Christ said: "My strength is revealed in weakness." St. Silouan, after living in hell for fifteen years following a huge mystical experience, was told by Christ: "Keep your mind in hell, and despair not." The mind referred to is the nous, and the hell is that which is lodged in the heart's depths. A strength that is forged only by bearing and enduring weakness, a heaven born only from hell, is a very different kettle of fish from the puritan strategy of good triumphing over evil: good excising evil. Even the Neptic strategy of detaching from the evil heart to break our assent to it, and thus break its usual unconscious capture of our life, is not as radical, or strange, as this. Here we have one of the Desert's oddest and most elusive, yet important, injunctions: "Take your mind (nous) down in to the heart." And: "Stand with the mind in your heart before God." This last is the real meaning of the 'prayer of the heart', which in its deepest form becomes 'the prayer of silence'. We go into the very root of hell in us, and offer all of this pain and joy, this terror and beauty, to God.

We collect the heart, to stand with all of its depths, before God.

I am not convinced that Buddhism 'takes the mind down into the heart' in this sense, nor goes all the way through the process of final battle there in which the heart becomes singular, through a reversal of all our normal instincts about good and evil. The Cross of Christ enacts this reversal in the world; but we are called upon to undergo such a reversal in our depths. If we don't, it is not just that we cannot follow Christ in His final challenge of Love to the world; it is also that we will never, in ourselves, taste or understand that Love. It must be victorious in our depths for us to grasp even a real inkling of why it is victorious in the world.

Even in the Desert Tradition, not all Neptic Fathers could take this second step, where meditation and prayer conjoin, and where prayer reaches the ultimate of what it can be: the deep crying to God, and the deep acceptance. Evagrius was rejected as a 'spiritual guide' by the Eastern Church because he taught the stopping at nous, rather than taking the final plunge, and risk, with the heart. Of this St. Macarius said, "The human heart is an unfathomable abyss." For the Christian who wants to follow Christ all the way to the Cross, then into hell, and finally to the Resurrected existence that emerges only from a very peculiar embrace of hell, there is no alternative but to jump into the heart's abyss. This is a trusting of our human passion; the lamp of nous can illumine, but it cannot leap. Only passion makes the final leap of faith, into the depths where heaven and hell contend for us. Bodidharma said, "You will sweat white beads." Christ sweated blood.

Nous acutely watches how the evil implanted in us moves from impulse into fantasy, and from fantasy into action. This helps us discern, and resist: but it does not, in itself, fully clarify the root of sin in us, nor does it cut that root. In the depths of the human heart is everything that seeks to separate us finally from God, including what has damaged us; to be united with God in that place is to be unbreakably united, and this in turn enables us to be unbreakably united with the world. We can accept it, in passion and passion's suffering and loss, as God does, in Christ's Cross.

In the first nous step, the evil dog stops biting, yet can still bark; in the second heart step, the evil itself has to be transformed, not simply deprived of energy, or we will never reach the wholeheartedness whereby our passion understands, accepts, and acts from the passion of God.

Thus the sign that the heart is stilled, and pure, is that the heart becomes entirely trustworthy: instead of standing back from the heart's fallen activities, we commit to and engage with the world out of a 'singular' heart impulse, a singular will and passion. This signifies a heart which has been fundamentally changed, not simply from evil to good, but something more paradoxical and profound. Out of the conflict of good and evil in the human heart, a radical and total love is born, a love that has to go deeper than good to undercut evil, yet in this process must also bear and endure evil, not triumphing over it, but being tested and taught by it, and forced to go into the mysterious place where evil attaches itself to us and takes root: the place called 'the deep heart.' Only here can the final victory of love be won – or lost.

In other words, the 'good' that must go deeper to undermine evil at root is a greater good than the good which tries to rise above it into some abstracted realm (spiritually effete transcendence), get rid of it (puritanism), or compromise with it by the usual human strategies of defense (in effect we bargain with the lion, 'I'll maintain you if you agree not to invade my comfortable house and embarrass me in front of my friends"). Something deep is happening here. The heart is undergoing a strange alchemy. What is this deep process in which the greater does not rise above, smash, or skate over, the lesser? This is the final meaning of the fight – the

Spiritual Warfare – we make in our depths. This fight insti-
tutes a mysterious healing. In one way, this is a Redemption;
in another way, this is a Transfiguration. Healing encompasses both.

It is the process of healing that is incomplete at the nous,
and can only be fully accomplished in the heart.

A last story:

An old man went to a spiritual elder, and said to him, "All
these many years I have kept what little practice I could; I
have prayed, fasted, kept watch, and given away all my possessions to the poor, and tried to offend no one. What more
must I do?" The holy man raised his arms to the sun, becoming translucent, and said, "If you will, you can become all
flame."

PART THREE
THE PLUNGE INTO THE CHASM

*The strange process asceticism kicks into motion in our
depths*

The alchemy the heart undergoes in the final struggle in the
depths by which we go toward the origin of our dividedness
occurs as a result of a certain kind of mingling of the wheat
and the tares. There is a mingling of greater and lesser in the
deep heart of the human being, even as Christ mingled His
divinity with our humanity. Hippolytus, referring to the latter, uses words that perfectly express the former: "...having
mingled the corruptible into the incorruptible, and the weak
with the strong..." In one sense this process starts by achieving a separation: the greater gets out from under the lesser
and learns to resist the lesser's inducements and pressure; it
withdraws, and refuses to play. This is where dispassion begins. But in another, more paradoxical sense, as the process

continues *the greater suffers the lesser, like a wound. And out of this wounding, the greater is broken and remade in the depths by its confrontation with the lesser.* The signs that this is happening are a growth in strength, compassion, understanding, patience, humility and wisdom. But oddly, all these virtues imply that, in an entirely unexpected manner, *the greater in us only becomes greater because it wrestles with the lesser.* Finally, there is but one heart, one passion, one action of love, and thus a total involvement, a total commitment and engagement with God and His suffering world. This is where dispassion ends. It begins when we can refuse to partake of evil, but it ends when, by virtue of suffering evil in ourselves in a certain way, we can suffer evil in others, indeed in the entire world, in that same way: and this means that dispassion ends as the ability to love everything and everyone, without favorites, without hindrance, even if that entails suffering everything and everyone. Suffering *for* evil says we no longer suffer *from* evil. Love has conquered, in the depths.

In this process of healing, we enter upon very fearful and wonderful terrain. We confront that in ourselves which is the real sticking point. Greater and lesser hearts wrestle in some new, more total way. The very basis for our rejection of God, our opposition to God, our moral and metaphysical disapproval of God, is exposed, and given its head. Will any heart, in us or in God, be able to prove itself deeper in the face of this powerful root of evil? The heart has its reasons, Pascal said; and the heart has reasons why evil is meaningful, even precious, to it. Something must be given up, let go, surrendered; yet to allow this 'precious jewel' in us to break, we cannot just throw it away. Something in us, and God, must embrace it, and prove through the test it subjects us to, that the greater heart really is better than the lesser.

In the deep place, only God can help us. Yet it is here we experience God's absence, and feel abandoned. Here, we cry to God in the extremity of our being, yet also stand before God in absolute silence. It is only in such extremity that we find out what deep prayer really is. Meditation allows us to be attentive – watchful and vigilant – but prayer is a reaching out from an edge where ultimate dereliction and ultimate coming through are very close.

On the heart ground of danger and opportunity we retain the practices and techniques we have used to get this far; we still require the tools and weapons of spiritual warfare. But in another sense we are alone with God, and the evil spirit. We are alone with our heart.

How do we proceed?

Places on the desert road

The Desert Tradition always refused to provide a formulaic road map of the deep heart ground. But the way through the barren sands – there is no way above, or around – has to be won, again, each time it is ventured. But there are way stations that I want to try to flag up, since hopefully they give a flavor of the alchemy of radical change that alone can win the heart's depths: win them wholly, for God and hence for the world. The conclusion to be derived from Eastern Christian asceticism is that *if these depths are not won in this mysterious, suffering manner, they remain unredeemed, and holiness as a result remains outside us, and evil inside. If they are won – not transcended, not suppressed – then holiness is inside us, and evil outside.* It may arise, still, like an old root that throws up a few shoots; but the evil dog can neither bite nor bark, because the old clash of good dog versus evil dog has been replaced by a different heart born of that clash, but no longer subject to it. This is the 'new heart' prophetically foretold in the Old Testament. It is the 'singular heart', which is also known as 'the heart of fire'.

Way Station 1 – Finding the place of the heart

But how is this strange fight, and alchemy, in the depths accomplished? It is accomplished through a mysterious synergy between God's unknown presence, and energy, at work in our depths, and certain steps we take. There are many ways to describe these steps, but none does justice to the experience. Every human being must undergo this search, and experience both its battle and journey *personally*; this is the only truth and meaning of having a 'personal relationship with God', since only in the deeps do we really face our rejection of God and really overcome this in final acceptance. But to come to this point requires that we first must pass through much affliction and tribulation of heart: we have fierce battles to fight and long journeys to make in the heart's depths. This is a struggle, on an edge, in a gap, and no one can make this struggle for anyone else, or really tell them what it is like. Each of us must go into the chasm and embrace its stark radicalness. The experience of being stretched, broken and remade in the deeps cannot be removed from us, and no words can really capture what it is to experience this. It is the struggle to be real in relation to God, to stop faking it on the surface and remaining paralyzed, or at best ambivalent, deeper down. And in this struggle to be real toward God, out of being real to our own heart, we cry out to God, and this cry is our personal relationship with God, and it is our prayer, because true prayer can only be uttered from the extremity of our depth. Words fabricated from the surface of our being are not prayer; even emotions, if added to these words, are not prayer, because emotions signify nothing but a shallow over-reactivity, a surface perturbation. We only begin to pray when we have reached the hidden, deep place of the heart. Prayer keeps us in the struggle in that place, asking for no shortcuts, no escapes, no leaping free in a single bound, but only the strength to undergo the suffering that embraces the deep things of God and of the human heart. The evil spirit is the perverter of this suffering. He either convinces us it is God's punishment of our unworthiness, or he insinuates we should flee it and console ourselves with worldly pleasures. But if God's will is done, then remaining in this suffering is crucial to the final victory in the depth.

In short, prayer is needed to help us find our footing in these unfathomable depths. But it is needed even to locate the place deeper down where the heart dwells. The Desert Tradition warns it is sentimental to claim we 'have' a heart, as routinely happens in common sense and everyday parlance. Instead, Desert Tradition tells us we must locate the place deeper down where the real heart resides in us. In prayer, however halting its attempt to descend from the surface, we search for the place of the heart. This searching is a work; praying is the work of heart even as meditating is the work of nous. We need to make daily, and repeated, attempts to go from conscious, mental prayer – which only receives the name because it is a first step – to the passionate yet "inarticulate speech of the heart" that is not so much spoken as uttered from the edge on which we stand in the depths, which constitutes true prayer. We must find the 'deep heart', as did the Eastern Orthodox Christian ascetics who hunted it and wrestled in it and suffered its torments of hell out of faith in its heaven.

God gave us this heart; only God knows why, only God knows what we are to make of it and what we can make from it. Prayer is our deepest stance toward the depths that torment us, undo us, enthuse us, raise us. The awareness of the nous, awakened by meditational practice, lights and stills our way to the real heart place where we need to stand, helping us not to trip over either the more superficial heart level of emotional reactivity (which blows us off course), or even the deeper heart level of evil illusions (which crash us on to the rocks). But only in the burning of prayer do we really stand in that place, and fully assume its responsibility and burden. In meditation, we come to *see* deeper into the heart. In prayer, we *experience* the deep heart. Thus in the 'Jesus Prayer' of Eastern Orthodox Christianity, the nous settles its watchful and vigilant concentration on the heart, and is aware of both the heart's breathing and its utterance of words. Gradually, the 'mindful awakeness' of the nous actually descends from its initial situation in the head, and relocates further down the body, at the heart; but the physical heart is only the gateway for the entry of awareness into the dark and deep real heart. This is like being aware of crossing a threshold into a new terrain, unlike any ever seen, felt, or met with, before. The breathing and the uttering of the heart reflects the fact that prayer occurs both in the Spirit and in the Logos of God.

In effect, no prayer equals no deep heart. Meditation, on its own, is not sufficient to reach, and remain in, that new 'mystical land', as the Desert Tradition calls it. Yet meditation of the nous, once descended into the chasm beneath the furnace of the desert heat, can help the standing in the heart remain watchfully and vigilantly concentrated on the heart. It can help to 'hold' that place. What occurs is actually a blending of meditation and prayer which the Desert Tradition calls 'contemplative prayer' (confusingly, because contemplation is used of a very different activity of the soul as well). My chosen terminology is 'meditational prayer'; this blending of nous and heart creates a pervasive quieting that reveals the core and ground of the heart's passion, and therefore releases the heart to make its cry to God. This cry of deep to deep is prayer. It is our heart's 'cante jondo', as flamenco calls it; our deep song. When we call to God, out of the core and ground of the mystery and agony of our deep heart passion, God comes to us. We breathe in and out a new air; we speak and hear a new language.

If nous is necessary but not sufficient for the way of heart, what then of the soul? Is the soul also necessary but not sufficient?

In the Desert Tradition, it might be argued there are three neptic practices in all: meditation of nous, prayer of heart, and contemplation of soul. This last, as St. John of Kronstadt sums it up, is "the contemplation within oneself, in people and in nature, of the works of God's wisdom, goodness, and strength." This differs from meditational 'emptying' because the content, even form, of what is seen by the soul in contemplation is sacred: it is the real essence of everything, the real shape and the real movement. Moreover, such vision should not be confused with everyday perception of the world: it is no mere detached observation, but an involved participation, that heals our alienation from all that we encounter. Heidegger speaks of the soul that is 'contemplative' toward reality, as contrasted with the egoic mind which is 'calculative', as in a state of 'abandonment' or 'releasement' (gelassenheit); in this condition we are 'permeated by existence'. What 'really is' enters the soul, and the soul joyously welcomes it, ravished by the sheer fact it is. Such immersion in the divine providence, and beauty, at work in the creation nourishes the human being as nothing else can, bringing to the soul which thirsts for the 'life more abundant' a foretaste of future (eschatological) beatitudes. The Greek Fathers of Eastern Christianity assert that such vision of and unity with Life, Goodness, Beauty, Wisdom, is the real desire of human 'eros'; thus the cure for seeking unity with illusory 'goods' (lust, avarice, vanity, envy, despondency) is to shed them for the genuine article. Such a state constitutes the 'cleansing' of the soul. And this cleansed soul is thus a channel to the Sacred which acts like an oasis in the parched desert. The heart needs water as well as light. A heart never touched by soul runs the risk of becoming too heavy in its journey and battle; a necessary 'light heartedness', even in the midst of what is difficult, is lost. Moreover, a heart without soul runs a worse risk: of missing entirely the larger context within which its struggling is placed. There is a disclosure to the contemplative soul of the potentiality of goodness at the Beginning which will come to flowering, in a new way, at the End. The soul knows the wine of the spirit, and that the whole creation is on its way to a wedding. It was the soul, in the person of Mary, who sparked Christ's mission, when she brought to his attention at the wedding of Cana, "They have no more wine." The soul tells us where we have come from and where we are going.

But only the heart can get us there.

Neither the nous, nor the soul, even in their respective illumination and cleansing, have yet plumbed the depths of the heart. The quickening light of nous and the enlivening water of soul gives the human being a sense that everything is 'already meaningful'; yet the burning of the heart is something more than this, something stranger and more awful, yet also more amazing. For the heart aches and burns with the deep knowledge that the entire world has been placed in some radical and ultimate risk by God, such that even the meaningfulness already present in it can be lost, if what is at stake is not 'saved'. There is a terrible, haunting yet moving, precariousness in the very ground of existence which only the heart can face up to and take on, as a challenge it is fated to engage. The fate that befalls the world befalls the heart, and the heart's choice is either to let this jeopardy, in which everything stands and by which everything could fall, affect it, open it, pierce and penetrate it, so that it is committed to the redeeming of the endangered possibility; or to be deaf to the world's cry: "We need your stand, help, sacrifice." The heart is called to accept this commitment to saving the world, not letting it be lost, through its courageous, generous and suffering passion of love. In the depths this passion is both what the heart most wants and what the heart most dreads. For, to follow the former rather than the latter strips us of all we think we can possess, think we can control: it costs us everything.

William Blake's picture of "God creating Adam" captures the mystery at the root of the human heart. In the very act of creation, God is seizing Adam in an embrace that is at once terrifying, powerful, passionate, binding the creature to the intent, and energy, of the Creator. In this furnace is the heart forged. God's face is sorrowing yet at peace, assured both the risk and all that must be undergone to render it finally fruitful is worthwhile; while Adam's face is utterly agonized, signifying that he is in a state where he is wholly gripped and cannot evade what has taken hold of him, yet cannot have any assurance about it. He has to receive it, like a blow, and carry it, like a weight, at depth. He has to proceed with faith and passion, or seek some illusory escape that diminishes the heart. Thus are we "fearfully and wonderfully made," as the Psalmist proclaims.

Jacob had to let go his slippery and trickster heart to enter the deep heart arena where he had to fight the angel for a blessing and receive a wound. The wound to the thigh signifies the heart's acceptance that its deep struggle with the paradoxical and suffering depths at its own root must be shouldered before eros can be fulfilled; Jacob's eros is wounded so that his heart's feet and hands may be restored. Jacob prefigures the Passion of Christ, in which the divine passion and the human passion interlock, contend with one another, and finally are reconciled.

In what sense, then, is it also the destiny of the soul to descend into the heart, as was the case for the nous? The true destiny of the nous is to serve the heart, to become ever more mindful of the heart, finally becoming a 'heart-mind'. Hence, a nous which evades going down into the heart is a mind state, however potent and alert, which is literally 'heartless'; and this makes it easy for the nous to become spiritually puffed up, even given to having its head turned by 'prelest'. Such is the 'proud mind'. What is the heartlessness of soul? This is a state in which the soul abuses the many and varied gifts entrusted, using them to build an ontological 'security in meaning' that defends itself from any more underlying existential insecurity of meaning. Such a soul, even if ripe with the talents granted by divine providence, becomes selfish and enclosed. Such is the 'vain soul'. This soul wants the cry of the heart extinguished, and will use every kind of good, life, wisdom, joy, falsely to pretend that what the heart struggles with can be sidestepped. By contrast, the true destiny of the soul is to comfort and enable the heart's battle and journey: the soul must come with the heart, away from the rich mansion out onto the dusty, barren road. This soul becomes a refreshing balm in the midst of severity. This helps the heart bear the unbearable and endure the unendurable. It is a cool hand on the fevered brow.

But for the heart struggling with itself, and thus with its stand, or fallenness, towards the wound of existence, this can only be a renewing oasis in the fierce heat of its trials and tribulations; a place to pitch camp, to get sustenance for the battles and traveling still to come, not a place to remain in so as to evade all battle and traveling. It is in this spirit of sustenance – not a false paradise – that many spiritual masters in the Desert Tradition seamlessly meld nous meditation and soul contemplation into heart prayer.

Thus it is clear that neither nous nor soul can resolve the heart's burning dilemma: to pronounce a final no, or a final yes, to the fate God has laid upon it – the fate which is the source of all its dignity yet at the same time all its dereliction. Prayer alone expresses the heart's recognition of the dilemma in which it is positioned; for it both acknowledges the great honor God has bestowed upon it as the pillar and flame sent to uphold and change the world, and the nothingness out of which it came, which renders it a nonentity, a being with nothing to call its own. Thus does the heart stand before God humbly and in gratitude, as a supplicant.

By contrast, pride prevents prayer, because in it we are in an illusion of self-sufficiency and self-reliance that credits all our strengths to ourselves alone; vainglory prevents prayer, because in it we are in an illusion of self-empowerment and self-giftedness that not only neglects the divine power upholding and raising us up, but seeks glory only for itself. The more ardent the prayer, the humbler and more modest the heart's stand before its own mystery and the Great Mystery in whose passion it was made. The more insensible and indifferent the prayer, the further from any authentic stand, or even struggle to stand, the heart is. Prayer is the heart's "audacious conversation" with God about the heart that links God, the world, and the human being, in a connection made of fire, blood, and earth. The nepsis of nous and the nepsis of soul might save those in whom these states happen; but only nepsis of the heart can save the world, in its past, present and future. Only the heart is decisive for everything.

Prayer can include meditation and contemplation, but the person who refuses to pray will never enter the deep heart, fight the battle there, travel the journey there, and be a witness of and participant to the paradoxical victory won when heaven only emerges from hell.

Risking to go into the place where hell takes root in us, which alone can become the root of heaven; offering all our depths of pain and joy, grief and hope, tragedy and possibility, to God; collecting the heart, and just standing with all our depths before God; all this – and in a sense only this – is what the Desert Tradition of Christianity calls 'prayer'. This is 'prayer of the heart.'

Such praying is no childish demand for rescue, or some false hope in magical escape. It is no self-satisfied self-congratulation that I, or some few I identify with, am all right, even if everyone else is not. Such praying is dragged out of us, squeezed out by being between a rock and a hard place, and is the only authentic response of the heart, in depth, to its own depth. We do not offer our depths to God to be rid of them, but because on our own we cannot solve the mystery of the unfathomable depth out of which our heart arises; we give these depths, in all their power and vulnerability, their openness to being indwelled both by the spirit of evil and the Holy Spirit, or just left 'empty', back to God, who is their source. They are the ultimate defeat of us, and the ultimate remaking. Alone with them, we cannot but fall; we will let them become the reason for our preference for evil, or just be paralyzed before them, unable to act from the heart when this entails walking over abyss upon abyss. Often the evil must be closing in, or the paralysis total, before our heart will break free of its chain to stretch forth to God. We beg God's help in our extremity. When things are too easy, or going too well, it is easy to hide from the extreme position we are actually in at depth. Then prayer ceases, or does not begin.

Prayer is a deed of our depth, arising from our heart-ground where we are potentially at our strongest and greatest yet actually at our weakest and worst; prayer is a cry from our depth to God's depth, and it is an anguished cry whose whole 'statement' anguishes over depth: anguishes over the human depth that is being contested by the Spirit of God and the evil spirit. Such a cry is often despairing, and always savagely angry, but most of all bereft. It comes from that in us really hurting, and this hurt between God and us cannot be explained away, consoled, or fixed. It must just be. No one and nothing can take it away. It is only between God and us, and will make or break our relationship. Prayer performs many 'deep' heart 'actions' which are left undone if we meditate with nous, or contemplate with soul, but refuse to pray. These deep heart actions – of praise, and thanksgiving; of asking help for oneself; of asking help for others; of acknowledging our heart's betrayal not only of God's depth but of its own human depth, and repenting of and turning from this betrayal – are not needed by God, but they are needed by our heart, and properly understood, they are all just one deep action.

This is the absolutely necessary action of gathering together all facets of our being in the heart, then opening the ontological and existential dilemma of the heart's depths to the God who is the Author of what is deep in existence. This, and this alone, is why it is useless to beseech, or pray to, any other god. These other gods may grant light to the nous, or water to the soul, but they have nothing to 'say' to the heart in its mysterious agony, because they can do nothing about this. The abyss is closed to them. This is why, also, such gods are usually amoral, dealing in powers and gifts, but never truthfully connecting with the central heart issue of standing and falling. That our depths can be filled by both the Spirit of God and the evil spirit, and that we ourselves can experience them as an unfathomableness before which we stand intimidated, and frozen, is a torment to us, yet also a strange profundity. We cannot embrace or reject such a fate. Yet in prayer we bear and endure these depths, and we open them and give them back to the only One who is deeper than they are, the One whose enigma alone can bear and endure, uphold from 'below', their enigma.

Thus, (1) praying is the deep heart's standing before God, collected and concentrated, from this place of our most terrible dereliction where our life has become a shabby wreck, and come to naught, yet paradoxically which still contains our life's great hope and latent pregnancy; (2) praying is the deep heart's giving of the whole paradox to God, returning the gift to the Giver; (3) praying is the heart's opening of that paradox to God and acceptance of 'the Way it is' – of the way existence is and the way the heart is, and the way God works in this existence and in our heart, and does not work.

This deed of our heart is free and loving, but more precisely, it is passionate.

This final acceptance is what truly calms and quiets the heart from its agitation and anguish in its dividedness; it 'rests the heart.' It also brings tears, which signify a deeper step even than crying out to God: a step of letting God act, because of letting go all resistance to the unknown, all resistance to suffering, and all resistance to not having power over or being in control of one's existence. These tears take us further into the mystical land of the heart's abyss where there is a new heaven and a new earth. Only this final acceptance 'quietens' the heart's basic restlessness over its own 'situation' in this existence. Silence ceases being a state we are in; it becomes, instead, a Presence with us.

For, God answers prayer.

God comes to the heart, even before it prays, to help it begin the ferocious battle and the long journey in the human heart's depths that will end only when they are filled by God. Thus our heart's passion cannot be quieted from Above, but must plumb the furthest reaches of hell, passing through a terrible struggle, before heaven can loom up from the abyss Below. A prisoner in Auschwitz wrote on one of the walls, "I can say without hesitation I saw everything that I can see and experience in heaven and hell." Whether this proved redemptive, even transfiguring, we might assume, but do not know for sure: there is no further record of this person. Frankl, also in the concentration camps, and speaking from that heaven and hell, disputed that it is we who question life; he asserted it is we who are questioned by life. The deep heart's passion is our reply to the questioning.

Is it for hell?

Is it for heaven?

There is no heaven, if it does not emerge from the embrace, struggle with and suffering of hell.

This is the way of heart.

It is a great thing to "become all eye," as a neptic holy man instructed his disciples on his death bed; this could apply equally to the single eye of the nous, or the many eyes of the soul. But it is a greater thing to "become all flame."

To have acquired the mind, and soul, of Christ is an accomplishment not to disrespect. Yet only to acquire the heart of Christ is really to be a follower and lover of Him who lived the deep pain and the deep joy of the human situation, as both God and human.

Praise be to the Passion of Christ.

Way Station 2 – It is my problem, not yours

The Desert Tradition says, the closer we get to God, the more aware of our own sinfulness we become. We are moved to repent. Repentance has to be lifelong, and so too its practice, confession. But people often miss the motive for repentance alluded to earlier, as well as the spiritual state it creates, if its truth is plumbed. St. Isaac of Syria refers to this when he says, "He who knows himself is greater than he who raises the dead." We know, in a personal and direct manner, our own fallenness, and how serious this is. In the throes of honestly facing it, and wrestling with it, we lose all concern with the failures of other people. It is not that we are ignorant of these, or are pretending they do not exist; it is, rather, that accepting our own failures, errors, destructiveness, follies and the rest, so *humbles* us, that we realize it does us no good – in fact, it does us harm – to judge, even bother over, the evil of others. We stop 'projecting', in modern parlance. It is this humbling involved in the true recognition that we are fallen beings, or have major evil in our inward parts, that causes the Desert Fathers to pronounce such sayings as "Only I am a sinner", or "Only I am lost" or "Only I will end in hell." This is not reverse narcissistic grandiosity, etc. It is truthful self-knowledge, the kind of self-knowledge needed if salvational power is to reach us from God, and our own greater heart be roused from its slumber, lethargy, despair. Metropolitan Anthony of Sourozh once said, God can save and divinize the fallen being we acknowledge we are, but not the saint we pretend to be. Thus we should understand, and put into practice, the words the priest speaks when he brings out the chalice for communion, and refers to himself as the 'chief' of all sinners. This is what each one of us is, if we take our salvation and divinization seriously. The state of you, or the world, makes no odds to my fallen condition, if I truly want to change. My own failure is existentially paramount, once I become determined 'to seek salvation.' I can only decide that I want to change; I cannot decide this for others.

The marks of progress here are the diminishing, or fading away, of those three prime evils that often possess the heart and disturb the mind (if their voices and fantasies constantly and repeatedly fill our conscious sphere, we are unconsciously in their power): (a) the Satanic **accusation** whereby we judge and *condemn* people all the time, executing them in our minds if not in reality (if we 'assent' to the fantasy thoughts in the mind, it is as if we have done the evil, even if we don't act on it, say the Desert Fathers); (b) the Luciferian **superiority** whereby we admire our self – and people we identify as like us or worthy of us – and disrespect others, making *comparisons* among people all the time; this elevation and dismissing of the beautiful vs. the ugly, or charismatic vs. the ordinary, or the rich vs. the poor, elects a select few while jettisoning everyone else; (c) the Mephistophelean (from the Faust legend) **abstraction** of ourselves by virtue of seeking knowledge (whether scientific or metaphysical) that puts us, so we think, beyond the pain and pathos in the human heart; all this does is to make us *indifferent* to both our own, and our neighbor's suffering and struggle (condemning is the evil of the heart; comparing is the evil of the soul; being indifferent is the evil of the mind).

A traditional Lakota prayer perfectly encapsulates the true meaning of repentance.

Truth is coming
It will hurt me,
I rejoice,
You can heal me.

God will not reject a broken and contrite heart. Such a heart is never turned away. St. Silouan was told by God, "The proud always suffer from devils."

Way Station 3 – The wounded healer

One of the major dynamics of our fallenness is the way we pass on to others the damage, the problems, the hell, inside our own heart. Whatever pseudo-morality we operate out of – whether that of rising above, triumphing over, or compromising with – the evil supposedly 'defeated' in these various ways always leaks out of us and pollutes others. In fact, this cannot be otherwise. The above-it-all gorges on food, the puritan sneaks off to prostitutes, the liberal has intolerant rages, etc. The wounded person wounds others. We cannot but affect and be affected by one another, such is the inter-relational passion by which each of our hearts lives and acts. But once we are dedicated to the Spiritual Warfare raging in our interior recesses, then it becomes possible to effect a remarkable change in this dynamic. The leakage can genuinely be plugged: we cease to 'pass on' damage and evil, hurting and tempting others, but start to carry it 'inside' us.

In part, this is based on simply admitting the truth about our inwardness, but it is also a holding of it, in therapeutic parlance; a bearing and enduring of it in the heart. If ascetic humility is our first crucifixion, then this ascetic long-suffering is a second crucifixion. But it has wonderful results. When we "bear it in the kidneys," as a flamenco dancer told his students who wanted to stop a pulverizing training session, we start a healing, not only for ourselves, but also for others. Spreading sickness and evil to others keeps us all imprisoned. If the buck stops with me, however, then I can begin to open my inner conflict, confusion, brokenness, to God's power. A new inner knowledge of what has affected and tempted me becomes possible. A new strength to patiently bear and endure through this also arises, as does greater compassion towards others, caught in the same drama of glory and grief, potentiality and ruination. We extend to others the same kindness and clarity that has been of help to us in our struggle. This kindness and clarity is rooted in deeper understanding of the realities of the heart: it is nothing like harsh judgment or lax condoning, which arise when we are still dark and disturbed in heart. Moreover, we bear and carry the pains of others, in the same way we carry and bear our own.

The ultimate of this process in which we cease to pass on what has diminished and damaged us, and pass on only what has been of help in redeeming us, is seen in the figure of the Wounded Healer of Shamanism. In Siberia, shamans are of two types, and even wear white and black respectively to signify their different callings: the white-robed 'priestly' shaman conveys the vision of what will be, and draws everyone together on its basis, acting in a pastoral way to his people; the black-robed 'holy person' shaman risks losing this vision, because to heal others he must go back down into the heart, and again go through the mysterious battle in the deeps which transmutes woundedness into healing, evil into love. Should this descent into the matrix of the human problem go wrong, he might emerge as a 'wounded wounder', and thus such a person constantly returns to the edge where humanity really dwells, but most people refuse to go. The wounded healer must be wounded by what afflicts all humanity at depth, yet in coming through it to the other side in his own life, he also is living testimony to hell becoming heaven, to death becoming life, when our everyday experience is usually that there is no reversing the universal journey from heaven to hell, from life to death. Whatever else Christ was, he was certainly a Wounded Healer in this Shamanic sense. In many primal cultures, the power to reverse the one-way traffic of the human tragedy, the power to heal the ancient sorrow corroding our existence, is rightly seen as the primary activity of holiness. The wounded healer is remarkable because he does not become whole and well for himself alone, but returns, again and again, for others who are lost. If even ninety-nine were found and one remained lost, the Wounded Healer would return, at any cost to his own completion and happiness, for that one. In this figure, and in this process, we begin to get the first inklings of the sacrificial Love that is greater than good and evil, because it will suffer evil to find and redeem good in one and all.

Put at its simplest, the nature of our suffering changes: it becomes a spur to relieve the suffering in every being, creature and person. But this is never automatic. An Inuit medicine person was asked what was required to reach holiness. He replied, solitude and suffering. Then he added, but solitude can drive us into madness, and suffering can reinforce us in evil.

Way Station 4 – Your fate is my fate

What is sin? No term is more abused, and distorted, in Christian history. Today the religious fundamentalists hold a harsh and condemning *sinful* view of sin, while the secular humanists hold a weak and sloppy, and thus equally *sinful*, view of sin as unimportant (Sin is explained away as psychological troubles or social iniquities). The Greek word for sin implies a 'failure to hit the mark,' pointing at an existential failure in our being in the world: we fail our sacred calling. The ascetical perception does not differ from this, but looks

into the subtle point of origin more. Sin is a spiritual condition deeply implanted in us, yet still foreign or 'not natural'
to us. It is deeply ingrained, and therefore potent in human
existence, but it is not in the primal ground of our being.
Yet, it becomes a plausible hypothesis, a dynamic tendency,
a glittering jewel we cling to, in our depths. Put simply, sin is
our attachment to self; in extremis, we will sacrifice God and
neighbor to preserve and enhance it. Sin deprives us of our
real nature and real personalness as 'ex-static'; sin makes us
'in-static': self-enclosed and unable to stand 'in relation' to
God, the creation, everything.

Thus, the most dramatic progress in the Spiritual Warfare
becomes evident not simply when this 'law of fallenness' at
work in me starts to loosen its grip, and I become capable
of attitudes and deeds of charity, but when in fact there is a
total revolution, a total shift, that indicates this fallen Law is
being shattered, and the Law of Love is taking its place. This
does not mean I am free of the former, but it does mean the
latter has been born in me.

But we need more existential language here: as Christ puts
it, "He who preserves his life shall lose it, but he who loses
it for my sake (the sake of Love) shall preserve it." Preserve
the self, and it deadens and goes evil; give, and lose the self,
for Love, and it lives and is good. But there is more.

In our fallen condition, we are 'bound to the self': selfishness is not a choice, but an inescapable state. But when
this revolution I am seeking to describe takes hold, then we
realize that we and other people are all one human race: all
'the Body of Christ', in Christian language, or in existential
language, all in the same boat together. Or as Shamanism
puts this fundamental truth of the human heart, we all 'share
a common fate.' What befalls you also befalls me, and vice
versa. There can be no winners and losers, no saved and
damned; all arrive, or none do. 'I' cannot survive, and pros-

per, if 'you' perish. John Donne said of this, "Do not ask for whom the bell tolls, it tolls for thee."

It is not at all that we 'choose' to be together. "Come together" is a false injunction. Rather, the real truth is that, ontologically and existentially, we already *are* together. In a sense, we all dwell in only one heart: God's heart holds us all, and we none of us reach God except that, in our own heart, we break through the wall of separation between us and find that human heart which is also only one. This is the heart of radical solidarity. This is the heart not only of bearing the brother, but suffering with him, and for him. This is the heart that still hopes in even the most twisted and deluded brother, the heart that forgives seventy times seventy. This is the heart that, if asked for a shirt, gives away the hat, trousers and shoes as well. This heart is spoken of in the old Gaelic saying, "It is in the shelter of each other that the people live." In the Lakota Way, it is spoken of in the ending to every prayer, "all my relatives." Every human being is my relative, because every human being stands on the heart ground where God loves all, upholds all, bears and endures, suffers and makes sacrifice for all. This togetherness is 'the community of all living', and we do not build up this community; we join it as already what is. Our choice is to extend it, or take ourselves away from it, and by doing that, fail it. *Sin is primarily the injuring of this community.* This is why in ascetical depth psychology greed is the start of our Fall, while pride comes last and seals us in. Sin is by no means simply a turning away from God: it is at the very same time a turning away from this all-inclusive community in which each of us lives with, by and through each other.

St. Silouan said of this, "My brother is my life." The underlying mystical truth is the most profound of all truths. God opened a wound in His own completeness, to share His riches with our poverty. Thus when we accept the wound entailed in losing our individual completion and riches to include the other in our very self, then and only then do we become more like God. Individualistic morality, individualistic spirituality, individualistic salvation, obscures the very nature and deed of God as Love: and it prevents us from receiving and living this Love, which can only be lived together. The Lord's Prayer is corporate, not individual: it prays for *us*. Many of Christ's most mystical and puzzling statements refer to the Give Away, and Reversal, entailed by letting ourselves be injured, or burdened, in order to allow the other *in* to our existence. The well, if it pours out ecstatically, is without bottom; if we try to preserve it, and measure it out meanly, then it runs dry.

Put simply, the day we die to sin is the day we rejoin the human race. Then, I no longer care if I die for the people; on the contrary, I am vowed to their fate, and so their life and death is my life and death. It might be added that this is the meaning of becoming an adult: thus it is also pointing to the child who must die if that adult is ever to live. The preoccupation with our childhood difficulties causes us to think adult life should be the fixing of these, to permit our individual flowering. This causes us to forget our vow to the people. An adult, especially spiritually, is someone upon whom others can rely.

Way Station 5 – Cutting the root next to the abyss

Keeping our awakeness and watchfulness in the hell of the heart, without despairing of hell, tells us that hell is not final. It also tells us that it is possible to enter hell, as Christ did after the crucifixion, to cut the root of evil in the deep heart. This is the significance of that dynamic Greek Orthodox icon in which Christ, with daemonic force, lays hands on Adam and Eve in the underworld, and drags them out. On the basis of my encounter with Christ, who took me into the depths of the human heart, I would contend that only Christ has wholly and irrevocably cut the root of evil in us, though any holy person from any tradition has begun this uprooting, and progressed as far with it as is humanly possible to go. There is no question of anything being lacking in any manifestation of holiness prior to Christ, or indeed subsequent to Him. For few Christians, if any, have gone all the way with Christ into the abyss at the base of the human heart. I could not. It is enough to speak of the struggle here; Christ's deed is universal because it clears a path. Maybe only in the future will people really walk down this road.

In Shamanism, humanity suffers and makes sacrifice for God; in Christ, God suffers and makes sacrifice for humanity. It is the movement from the former to the latter that completes the cutting of the root: the former begins this, the latter finishes it.

The abyss in the human heart is that 'unfathomableness' so deep only God can fill it. Leaping into the abyss signifies, therefore, the final letting go, the final trust and opening to God's Way, which allows God to dwell in the human heart. For God's heart has no other final and full entry into the world, except through the human heart. The human heart was created to be the face, voice and action of God in the world. But we fear this abyss at the bottom of us. "My Way is not your way," God says to humanity in the Old Testament, and this declares a truth. Something in our heart wants to leap, wants to go all the way, wants the abyss; the passion of our heart is 'the bird who flies into the abyss without knowing the principle of its flight.' Yet something holds us back, putting a painful restriction on this passion. It is not just that God's heart is too deep for us: it is, but the abyss is the place where the Divine deep supports and indwells the human deep. To be 'out of our depth' in God is fearful, yet not incapacitating. Jumping off the edge is our passion's great adventure, what it was created for, and what its burning to ashes releases. Yet still we don't jump. Why?

Near the abyss is the root of evil, because its premise and message, and dynamic, declares to us that God's Way cannot be lived in our way: God's Heart cannot be trusted, followed, lived, in our heart. The evil spirit does not resist God's greatness as such; *he resists it dwelling in and acting through our smallness*. Evil, at root, separates great and small, thus evil cannot grasp strength in weakness, or heaven born out of hell.

Why do we cling to this root? It is not only that we cannot let go of something in our self, to jump. It is that we cannot let go of something about God. We only half-believe our own passion, which tells us to jump. We also believe the evil spirit: God should remain great, and not become small. At this root, it is not the power of God we rebel against, wanting that power; it is far more subtle than that. What we cannot bear and endure, trust and accept, plunge into, is not the power of God, but the refusal by God to approach the human heart with power. It is God's vulnerability we reject. We do not want the God who leaves the heart free and allows innocence to be harmed, the God who loves and suffers for those who oppose Him, and continues loving even when they disparage His greatest gift. We want a god who suppresses freedom, to make everything good for all of us; we want a god who snuffs out those who oppose him, and brings to their knees those who disrespect him. That God's Heart will only come to full and final presence and action in the human heart entails the most unbearable and unendurable paradox and mystery of all: "a stumbling block to the Jews, and folly to the Greeks." The true God 'contaminates' incorruptibility by mingling it in corruption, and we do not trust that the small can be won, and can embody, the great.

What we have to give up, at the root on the edge of the abyss, is our disappointment in the Way of Love by which God's Heart operates in the human heart. We don't want this. Under the influence of the evil spirit, we believe this won't work. It is weakness, it is folly; the weakness is a scandal, the folly is contemptible. Yet God's Way says to us, "My weakness is stronger than your strength, my folly is wiser than your wisdom." In effect, following God's Way is less about submission to an Authority, and more about faith, hope and love for a vulnerability that reverses all our expectations about who and what God is.

At the root near the abyss, we demand to know if God has a heart, but God replies, "You can only learn my Heart if you dive into the abyss of your own heart." When we love, we encounter the Love that supports and upholds our love in its vulnerability, in its strength through weakness and wisdom through folly. God is Blake's 'tyger', burning bright in the forests of the night; but God is also the 'lamb' slain before the world began, as its foundation.

When I can trust this paradox and mystery as lived out to the end by Christ, then I can follow Him into the abyss. The Fall also means no human being, however spiritually evolved, can really jump all the way in. But in Christ, God's heart suffers the human heart's restriction, that the human heart can embrace the divine heart's limitlessness. In the Old Testament, it says the Holy Spirit tests the deep things of God and of humanity. In Christ's mingling of divine and human passions, the "deep things of God and man" are tested and proved.

God's Love is pure, it cares nothing for the regard of men or worldly consequences: it goes all the way. It makes any sacrifice and undergoes any humiliation to do what it has to do: to bind the divine passion to the human passion. When this Love is in us, we too can act with such purity of intent.

This is why St. Silouan says there are only two reliable marks of the person who has come through this terrible struggle at the edge and is leaping into the abyss: one is humility, the other is love for enemies. Such is Christian holiness. This is because it follows Christ's Love. This Love accepts its own denigration, being slandered and mocked by those it benefits, such is its Humility, and it embraces all and will suffer and make any sacrifice for all, such is its Passion.

When we can pray for all, not as some all too easy or sentimental piety, but as the result of passing through a furnace and entering an abyss, then we have come close to God. St. Silouan said we can use such prayer to measure how far from God we really are: he prayed for hours through the night, seated on a rough wooden stool, weeping that none should be lost.

If we are far from this kind of prayer, we are far from God. We have not yet entered the heart, nor learned to pray with the heart.

Let us be moved by Love to make the journey into the heart, and take the risk with the heart's depth. How else can we honor all the holy people who have struggled for our sakes?

How else can we honor Christ?

Frank Fools Crow performed miraculous healings for his people, but all he said about this was, "Anyone can do the things I did if they live the life I lived." This reveals the correct understanding of the ascetical yoke, the yoke Christ said is light, because when we bind ourselves to it, we find He is bound to it.

Way Station 6 – Tears

Though St. Silouan spoke of the two criteria of holiness, his own life demonstrated a third: the tears of the deep heart. These are not psychological tears of frustration, self-pity, or pent-up emotion. Spiritual tears signify not only our repenting, but also the breaking of the stone in the heart that is our last resistance to the Way of God that we judge as not good enough, too insecure, too unworkable: too ineffectual, immoral, foolish. Out of that rigid "No" to God comes a river of tears, when our mourning becomes an acceptance, a final

"Yes." Tears come when we cease all *judgment* of what is 'right and wrong,' cease all *comparison* of what is 'better and worse,' and embrace and dive into it All, finally accepting the contradiction of good and evil, life and death, strength and vulnerability, meaning and absurdity, joy and sorrow, by carrying its weight and paying its cost. Tears pour out of the breaking of the heart of stone, signifying that we have ceased our war with God. We have leaped – leaped into the fathomless abyss under our feet, leaped ahead onto the hard road that carries our feet toward the final destiny to which we are called. In the heart, the Abyss and the Road are two sides of one thing: our human passion's reconciliation to, and unreserved acceptance of, the Divine passion. Thus the leap into the abyss puts us on the road to Jerusalem, where the ultimate testing and proving of the Divine Passion in the human passion occurs. Our union with God is our union with the Passion of Christ.

The ascetic tears of our breaking and remaking, deep within, become the tears of God for humanity when "Jesus wept." Tears shatter the heart of stone only to place in our depths the rock of God's original promise; the promise not to abandon the world, no matter what sacrifice and suffering is needed by God, and by humanity, to save it. Now a new grief afflicts us. We comprehend, and answer the call of, "the man of sorrows acquainted with grief" because of what he loves. The sorrow of detaching from the world to embrace God becomes a sorrow for the world that embraces it in a new manner: the desert brings us to abandon ourselves unreservedly to the fate of the world.

Now we begin our struggle with the Cross and Passion of Christ.

This is the struggle Christians have funked, down the centuries, generating in this process the degraded and disgraced history of Christianity, West and East. This is the final struggle.

From the desert we return to the city, to live out and enact the Cross, and Passion, of Christ. Christians have not put God's Way to the test. Thus they have not proved it. The deep things in the heart of God must be tested and proved in the deep things of the human heart, but this can be done, finally, only in the world. It is done in the world for the world.

The Love that is deeper than good because of the Way it suffers evil and gives good for evil must be lived out and enacted in the world, because only this Love can save the world.

This is God's Way.

This is the way of heart.

PART FOUR
RETURNING TO THE CITY

Eastern Christian Tradition affirms St. Athanasius, not Augustine or Calvin: "God became man, so that man might become God." But the deification Christ offers is no private or otherworldly mysticism.

Ascetic discernment of the difference between what is true and what is false ends in a Holy Love that goes beyond discernment, because of the way it suffers for what is loved. It takes the hit for those who cannot stand the blow, it assumes the burden for those who cannot carry the weight. It pays the cost for those who cannot overcome and struggle through. This love is the richness that pours itself out for poverty. It judges no one as found or lost; it compares no one as better or worse. It puts its shoulder to the common wheel, and walks the difficult, uphill road to Jerusalem that Christ walked, to be crucified with him, in order that this wheel may turn for the benefit of all. For only the unreserved suffering of love breaks humanity's fallen attachment to a kind of benefit that is always for the self at the cost of others, and for some at the cost of the rest. Only suffering love includes all, by paying the cost of all.

But to live this in the world means having to face and take on worldly evil.

The way of the world

The 'world' as evil is not just the multiplication of individual sin: the sum total of the sin of each adding up to the composite sin of all. The world is more than this sin of every individual. It is more powerful than that. Certainly the world plays on the sin in every individual, but it plays on it by drawing it into something bigger and more harmful. Thus the world amplifies the single sin of each and the additive sin of all in a much worse evil that is totally pervasive, capturing each person, but only so as to govern the community in which all persons live together. Decrying 'the evil of the world' has nothing to do with dismissing either nature as created by God, or God's desire that human beings interact with nature to co-create a world. In another sense, the 'world' is where all divinely created and divinely inspired natural and human potentialities come to actualization. But, this cannot happen, and indeed becomes ever more remote, while evil 'rules the world.' Evil is the system that runs and drives the world, and by virtue of this, enslaves and dominates humanity as a collective. It is reminiscent of the Borg in Star Trek who travel all over the universe and assimilate entire races and cultures to their uniform way of being, pronouncing to those they swallow up that "Resistance is futile." Paranoiacs and political radicals have accurately perceived this collective system that acts like a huge machine devouring, restricting, distorting, damaging, corrupting, destroying, everything that human beings are, and human beings do, in their life in the world, but diagnosed it incorrectly.

Who, or what, built it? How can it be torn down? We return to the world to answer these questions. If they are not answered, spirituality might be able to save us from the world, but it could not then save the world.

Christ's answer to the first question echoes the Jewish prophets, who saw that human error alone is not potent enough to produce the evil machine that runs the world. This collective system is compounded of two things: human error and spiritual evil. The 'extra' horror at the heart of the world is the spiritual being called the 'devil'; the devil is 'prince of this world.'

Christ's answer to the second question departs from, and indeed reverses, the Jewish prophets. The Way in which God fights the actual evilness of the world to save the potential goodness of the world clashes with all our expectations. It disappoints us, and we conclude that it cannot work. But in concluding this, we are affirming we believe the way evil 'conducts its business' in the world to be more true, more strong, than God's Way. Thus the majority of people unconsciously and docilely go over to the devil's way of ruling and running the world, since the root of evil in the heart is the love of invulnerable power: they see the devil as 'on top of the game' and able to grant them a successful life. They enter the devil's machine, learn how it runs, and then run it for him. Some get to the top, becoming more devilish as they 'rise', but many are content to get on with the job at the bottom of the heap, simply working the levers, going along for the ride. A smaller band of holdouts regret the way things are, but see no alternative, and thus capitulate, even if they don't like doing so. Only a handful really fight the good fight, trying to keep the jaws of hell back a little, but these people often underestimate the error gnawing away at the base of each of them: thus they make mistakes, lose resolve or trip up over their own unacknowledged and unchanged investment in worldliness. In the end, the saying that "the road to hell is paved with good intentions" becomes true of them. These people often have big hearts, not small hearts like those who appease and those who condone, but their own small heart, still in the error created by unacknowledged and unchanged sin, fatally undermines their efforts. Greek and Shakespearean tragedy portrays these bigger people who fall in the end, either because they sell out at the last moment, or because their bigness is inherently flawed, simply not sufficient, on its own – without the radical alteration brought about by the spiritual process of the desert – to withstand the world. Idealism, romanticism, even prophetic battling, all fail. For, any good-hearted person will be, whether through damage or temptation, pressured by 'being in the world' to give in and give up. No human hero, as individual or group, can fight the devil, and the vast mass of sad humanity fooled and in thrall to his way of 'making things work', entirely on their own. They need God's help.

But this help comes only through a Reversal.

This Reversal is a stumbling block to Jews and foolishness to Greeks.

The devil's rule over and running of the world is a way of doing things which presents itself as the best path ahead, indeed as the only path that will get us ahead. It is promoted and widely seen as the only way forward. Though it uses sin to build its kingdom, it is compounded not only of human error, but also of spiritual evil. By contrast with the desert strategy which first cages, then gets in to the cage with, and finally gets down to the real root of, sin, the devil's strategy is to 'play' with our error, in such a way as to lead it much farther down his own bad road. This is why the fallen passions are far worse in adults than in children (not to recognize this, or ask why it is so, is the major untruth in psychoanalysis). The devil is a spiritual master who knows how to make sin look good in childhood and youth, then subtly entrench and further develop it in adulthood by drawing us towards an ever more sophisticated and 'pure' evil that is spiritual in origin, not human. Such pure evil is a Lie about how things are and how things function which 'appears' as Truth.

The implication is that sin is still human, and hence redeemable, but this increasingly pure evil is spiritual, and thus more difficult to redeem. The devil has both a face of inducement and a face of intimidation in drawing adults into his way. Many people resist while still in innocence of the world, but the loss of innocence upon entry to the world convinces them to be 'realistic.' They give way. They join up to the devil's kingdom. This is why Christ speaks of the need to be like children in order to enter the heavenly kingdom planted in this world that operates differently: in children, sin is mixed with every other heart factor, and so is open still to change of heart. But in the worldly, sin has 'advanced' and 'grown' toward pure spiritual evil. The most worldly are the most akin to the devil. These are the big wheels, the movers and shakers, of money and its power. This is the Mammon that Christ said we cannot serve as our master if we want to serve God. For centuries, Europe tried to have both God and Mammon, but was uneasy about it. England then found the way to rationalize and justify their coexistence. In America, this compromise ceased because God was confused with Mammon. At last, Mammon was the master. America is the leading edge of worldly evil not because Americans are the first people to live for Mammon, but because they are the first to make this into a religion.

The two aspects of worldliness, human and spiritual, need to be disentangled, to be able correctly to read the total package.

Sin has been looked at in three levels, going from mistrust of God at the base, to self-love in the trunk, and thence to all the varied and different evil passions of the branches. But this means something for our being in the world that remains to be clarified.

In essence, the Way of God in the world is not a way of preserving; it is a way of not preserving. It is a Way of giving and losing. Mistrust of God at our inner base entails mistrust of this Way of Vulnerability in the world. We want life, not death, good, not evil, joy, not sorrow, gain, not loss. We resist the existential contradiction fundamental to existence. Already, something in us wants "to get ahead." We want to be preserved, and enhanced. We want the positive, not the negative. Existence seems to us flawed because it includes the down in the up; we would like to 'reinvent' it, so we can evade all loss, and obtain nothing but gain. The Old Testament says that if a person wants his or her name written in the Book of Life, he or she must accept, experience and live "the sufferings and raptures of the Spirit." But we do not want this paradox. We fear it as a death to all hopes; we resent it as a restriction on our happiness. We want what the American Constitution grants, a "right to happiness." We want freedom from loss, and freedom for gain. Safety, success, fulfillment, should not be subject to jeopardy and uncertainty; safety, success, fulfillment, should be guaranteed. We do not want to have to be involved in, and undergo, existence's 'fate.' We want, instead, to have what E.G. Howe termed "power over" existence: power over any 'other' that might invade and diminish the self. The self wants not to be injured; the self wants to be whole.

This is already a failure of passion, a cowardice and meanness; this already fails the call to a task that marks our passion from its inception. Already we start counting cost, and reckoning consequence. Cost and consequence diminishes our passion by placing conditions on it: I will follow passion but only on condition that at the point where it costs too much, or the consequence becomes too much, I can stop. Then I will back off and back out. I prefer to be closed down and shut in, than put up with the fate that is out of my control, and over which I cannot get power. We refuse to wrestle with the wound of existence authentically, as Jacob did with the angel, but prefer a false notion of heroism. We must win, we must triumph. The wound of existence is to be conquered, not suffered.

In America, they invented Superman instead of Christ.

This resistance to the paradox and anguish of existence – its affecting existential dilemma – is what the devil plays on, and enhances, to take over the whole world process, engendering James Joyce's "nightmare of history." For the devil whispers, "You must get your happiness, no matter what happens to anyone else as a result." The devil began by placing himself above God, and he counsels each one of us to put our own self above the self of any other. The human sinful desire for gain, not loss, which already rebels against the existential blow God daemonically inflicts on all of humanity, becomes something more purely evil. It becomes the sinful desire for my gain, even if this turns out to be at the expense of your loss.

The devil, with a cleverness so acute we can hardly discern its moves, links escaping from the existential dilemma with obtaining individual advantage. *Self-preservation becomes equated with individual advantage: every person seeks to escape the down side by breaking ranks with his fellows, and getting a better position for himself, or those few with whom he identifies.* This turns into a kind of self-indulgence, not just a self-love. Suffering any loss to the self is resisted, but suffering loss to the self so that the other can gain becomes religiously and politically, socially and psychologically, heresy. That the self's increase must be decreased to let the other in, cannot even be countenanced. In effect, all demand for 'liberty' is really the claim to an unimpeded self-indulgence. Anything I want to do, I will do, no matter whom or what I hurt. Doing that is my 'right.' If you don't like it, that is your problem. I have every right to absolutely whatever I deem is needed for my happiness, safety, success, fulfillment. I'm

looking out for me, you look out for you. But this self-indulgence becomes, then, a sense of 'entitlement' to whatever 'I'
want, and need to do, at any expense to 'you': at any expense
to other people, to nature, to God.

So if I come from poverty in my old situation but find you
already occupying my new abode, it is perfectly feasible that
I shove you out, and make you poor so I can get rich. Such
entitlement is a recipe for the destruction of the interdependence not only of the human community, but also of the balance of nature. Entitlement takes a knife of greed, ambition
and violence, to the "one body" of God constituted by nature
and by humanity, and slices the body up, grabbing the choic-
est cuts for itself and its cronies. But as this goes on it gets
worse. My individual gain, or that of the few with whom I
identify, becomes absolutely paramount. In the end, nothing
else matters. The result, that advantage to me and mine, giv-
en the interdependence of everything, inflicts more and more
disadvantage on you and yours, is not important. *Indeed, it
is not even noticed.* I have to look out for me, you have to
look out for you. Some will rise, some will fall; some will
get the lion's share, some will get slim pickings. That is the
way things are. It's the way things run. It is rational. There is
no other way things can be made to work.

Mammon is the only god in whom we trust.

Money and its power becomes the way to resolve humanity's existential dilemma, and as such, it is the golden calf
on whose altar the winners make a bloody sacrifice of the
losers. In this way, existence judges some as of worth but
many as worthless; in this way, existence compares some
as better but many as worse. In this way, some are included
but many are excluded; some escape paying any cost, many
pay a heavy cost. The result is that all common humanity
is destroyed. In the end, we lose any sense of common interest, and experience each other not as fellow sufferers of

existence's wound, so I feel your fate as my own, but rather as threats to each other's advance and advantage.

Ordinary human love can modify this law of competing interests, but not challenge its basis in human error and spiritual evil. This is what has happened to the churches: they have let the devil occupy the center ground of the world, while they stand at the periphery, trying to damp down its worst effects, by resorting to some shallow and utterly compromising niceness. Love's bite, and its punch, is avoided; its Sword that challenges the devil's way, and its Cross which pays the cost of the world's existentiality and communalness, are rendered nice stories we tell our children on Sunday, but no one tries out for the rest of the week. Christ expects people to be extreme, but we always seek a compromise.

Indeed, nothing could be more heretical to worldliness than suffering for love. It is not 'justice' that I pay for you if you cannot pay for yourself; and it drags my 'elevation' down into your mire.

The Way of God

God's Way operates through existential vulnerability and self-giving because it is communal, not individualistic. We all lose, no one breaking ranks, so that all may come to gain. We share with each other, we put up with each other, we make sacrifice to each other, for the sake of nature, and humanity becoming the one body of God. We are "a part of it," as Native Americans describe our connection with the Sacred. We are "in relation," as Martin Buber describes our communion with the Holy.

St. Basil the Great:

> What keeps you, now, from giving? Isn't the poor man there? Aren't your own warehouses full?... The command is clear. The hungry man is dying now, the naked man is freezing now, the man in debt is beaten now – and you want to wait till tomorrow? 'I'm not doing any harm', you say, 'I

just want to keep what I own, that's all.' Which things, tell
me, are yours? Whence have you brought them into being?
You are like someone who sits down in a theatre, and would
prohibit everyone else from entering, saying that what is
there for everyone to enjoy is for himself alone.

St. Clement of Alexandria:

He who holds possessions as the gifts of God... and knows
that what he possesses is for the sake of others, is blessed
by God.

There is a Cross at the heart of the world, where existence
is wounded. Beneath that Cross is the abyss which is hell,
but can become heaven. Black Elk said, "The Great Spirit
has made the good road and the bad road to cross, and the
place where they cross is holy." We were created by God to
go into that holy and terrible place. Hell ends in our hearts
when we accept this wound in existence as Christ did and
perform the same deed of suffering love to save the world
from becoming and ending in hell.

The Cross is the guardian of the whole earth;
The Cross is the beauty of the church.
The Cross is the strength of kings;
The Cross is the support of the faithful.
The Cross is the glory of angels and the wounder of demons.
(Matins of the Feast)

When in the Old Testament God says to humanity, "My
Way is not your way, my thoughts are not your thoughts,"
this refers not simply to our proclivity toward sin, but our
wavering before spiritual evil as the Solution, and Answer,
to all our existential worries and woes.

The evil passions have been discerned as our blind rebel-
lion against the spiritual, or our delusive attachment to the
material. Both descriptions have a point. But a more incisive
description would be that these sinful passions are all diverse
ways of eliminating the terrible and holy place in the center

of the world. We are trying to re-engineer the fate at the heart of existence which tests us to the maximum of what can be undergone. We try, in all the fallen passions, to 'improve on' or 'make better' the affecting dilemma that moves and drives existence in the world. This is 'progress' – psychological, social, political, economic, religious. We want out, and want it different. From the perspective of our way, God's Way is either indifferent to our pained existence, or impotent to do anything about it. Thus we 'go it alone': we say in our heart there is no Divine help, because this help comes through a Wound and heals that wound only through a Cross.

We will have our way, not God's Way. We will continue to improve and make better the existential Koan and existential Reversal that the Great Spirit placed at the heart of existence; a heart only embraced and lived through a different heroism: a passion not only courageous and generous, but also afflicted and struggling, yet which produces something awesome and marvelous. In our heart, we believe our way is superior to God's Way, despite the evidence that our road to happiness, safety, success, fulfillment, only produces more and more hell.

What those consumed by worldliness do not notice is that their 'brave new world' is becoming ever more a hell. The hell is outward, the hell is inward. The outer life of community is lost more and more to cancerous division. The inner heart is lost more and more to a shriveling: the stance of including and excluding kills passion. Outer and inner are in a dialectic. Each makes the other worse: the heart adds its hell to the world, the world adds its hell to the heart.

This hell consumes the city and spills out into nature, threatening to swallow the very earth.

Hell ends only when we accept the Way of God in our deep heart. But by pursuing the way of worldliness more and more, becoming stronger in its weakness, becoming wiser in its folly, we finally come to a collapse in which hell totally encompasses us. Hell is the deep heart when God is gone from its abyss, and we experience it as without profundity and inspiration, to raise us up and project us forward into dynamic motion. We experience it as just empty, and hence life as ungrounded and absurd. This creates that pervasive loneliness in existence whereby wherever we look, we see only a featureless landscape stretching out into infinity. We have nothing to do and nothing to say. We have nowhere to go. This is worse than any clinically described depression. It is a sense of total futility, all the way down, and all the way out. All we can sense is some intangible defeat at the base of us, for which we half blame ourselves and half blame God. All meaning and purpose is gone. All we can see wherever we look are the blots on the landscape. The flaw in everyone, and everything, alone grabs our attention out of the blur of featureless nothingness that emanates from an abyss of emptiness into which we fear to fall, endlessly. The only power that stirs in this deadness would be evil. Only evil seems able to conquer the abyss, but even this power may fail to move us. We are in a sense beyond good and evil, because everything has gone down a vortex of spiritual death where we are finally, and irredeemably, alone. This is the final abandonment.

When we are in hell, we have resisted God's Way to the point of outright refusal, and so God departs from the deep heart. We are left with what we insist upon, which is our way. We are alone with our way, and the evil whose way works on us to wholly follow it. Frozen in ice, the evil spirit offers us his flames as a way out. Many of the most truly evil people in the world are those who came out of hell too soon, taking the evil way as the only exit. Many of the most truly holy people in the world saw it through, remaining in deadness rather than follow the renewal of life offered by evil. They waited in the tomb.

The descent into hell, and remaining there for as long as it takes, is God's cure for our trust in worldliness as the Solution, and Answer, to our human fear of being in the world. We discover for ourselves where this ends, and we turn back.

Hell ends when we accept the Way of God and, by doing that, recover our own deepest passion for existence; this passion is not blocked, but sparked, set free, inflamed, by the Way that works through Sacrifice. Hell ends when we accept that the way things are, and the way things must be, is the way we want them also; hell ends when we trust our heart as well as trusting God's Heart.

Hell ends when, in loving the world as God does, we accept God's Way of saving it.

Hell only ends when we trust and believe it can only end for each of us when it ends for all humanity, and all creation. Hell ends when we go up to Jerusalem to be crucified with Christ.

The Way of God vs. the way of the world

God determines that God's Way will be fairly contested in the world by the world: it operates only through Love's Truth, Strength and Life. Its authority is only intrinsic, not extrinsic: it is authoritative but never authoritarian. It makes no resort to the coercion of dire threats, or the seduction of pleasing inducements. Nor does it have any truck with the liberality that masks indifference. The Way is. It is what is. In the beginning was the Way. The Way is the Tao of the Chinese, and the Logos of the Greeks, the Primal Harmony and the Suffering Road toward a dimly-appreciated but Greater End.

Even for Christ, the devil He overcame in the desert had to be faced again in the world, and defeated there.

In the world, Christ fought the devil.

In the world, Christ fought the devil for the world.

Even for Christ, the place ultimately holy and terrible was the place where existence is wounded and the two roads cross; there Christ made His real Giveaway, there He offered His fire and blood to the earth as a Sacrifice; there His Passion was tested and proved.

So must it be for us.

God's Way will not flatter, seduce or crush any human heart. This Way does not try to overpower reluctance, but must show us the 'cause and effect' between how we stand and fall in the heart and how this allows the devil to play his game and build his palace of false answers and false delights. Both Jewish reward and punishment, and Buddhist karma, are simply telling us that the heart's stand has a vast consequence not only for us, personally, but for the world, communally. If we fail to stand, and fall, this has consequences for everybody and everything. Only Love, at its final extreme of suffering for all that it loves, can overcome the law of cause and effect that obtains spiritually in the world. I harm you, you harm me, and it even goes down the generations. There must be an accounting, a reckoning, our heart demands, forgetting that if this ledger of right and wrong, of bad effects produced by bad causes, comes to us, we shall be judged by it, not saved. Indeed, if the ledger is to be the final law that rules everything, then "none shall stand." All will be judged wanting, guilty, as having failed. None will be saved. But St. Isaac of Syria asserted a different law, the Law of Love, when he said that love's suffering for what it loves is "a judgment on judgment." It is the end of good and evil: the end of right and wrong, the end of karma. It is the beginning of love. Love suffers for all, to include all. There is then no included and excluded, no innocent and guilty. All are innocent, all are guilty: all are suffered for and all loved. We suffer because of each other; we suffer for each other so that no one will be cast out, but all invited in.

But the Way of God, as well as a suffering for the world, is also a fight with the world. It does not hide its light under a bushel, but calls the world to awareness of what worldliness is in truth creating: nothing but hell, and increasing hell. The inward heart in people collapses in bored, restless, deadened apathy, while the outward heart running society becomes ever more the devil's playground. A dead heart faces an evil world: thus the former allows the latter to proceed unchallenged and unfought.

God's Way must fight the world for what will save the world's possibility.

We fight with God to be able to fight for God. The Jews began the former but only Christ completes the latter. For only suffering love can both expose the hell in the world yet not judge it; only such love can wield the sword of prophetic anger, pointing it at the humanly sinful and devil-corrupted heart running the world without giving up in the face of this hell at the base of things, and pronouncing some damnation on it that fixes its divisions forever. Christ was angry, but His anger was hopeful, not vengeful: it always held out to the other a way back, never pronouncing a final sundering. When we truly know from personal struggle the divine love that was angry for us to recognize the truth of our own condition, yet was always willing to carry and suffer us as we went through every reluctance and refusal, then we know from 'the inside' what changes hell into heaven, and then – and only then – do we believe love can change everything and everyone. What it has done for us we believe it can do for the world. Being a believer has little to do with mentally assenting to, or verbally declaring, doctrinal truths whose existential promises we have no experience of, and whose sacred power has not won us over, dwelling in our depths and upholding our action. The heart 'believes' when it trusts, in its action, a road on which mountains will have to be moved, and camels will have to pass through the eye of a needle. Belief is what we are prepared to do, to give, to risk, to lose, for love.

God's Way fights the world to save the world.

It fights the great and deep lie that the world has a heart, and is improving, and needs only to rely on human and devilish power to progress. A *warrior,* as the Iroquois word translates, "carries the burden and responsibility for protecting the sacred origins." But a time comes when fighting must defer to the sacrifice of love, which shows and risks a different Way to that which had been exposed and opposed. The warrior cannot kill those already in hell, adding another murder to their deadness and evil. They are already killed by evil and killing because of evil. The warrior has to show them how to bear evil like a wound, that love can defeat evil in the depths. The warrior has to fight enemies and the warrior has to die even for them.

The warrior begins by dying for the ones still struggling for the true heart, but in the end he also has to die for the ones who have given up on any heart. The sacrifice is his, not theirs.

This is the Way of God, lived out to the full by Christ.

A warrior is at peace when he trusts the Way that fights the world, not in order to judge it, but in order to save it. The fight begins by protecting innocence, but the fight ends by the sacrifice of innocence. Such was the Way of Christ in the world. He began as the Tyger but He ended as the Lamb: the innocence sacrificed to the world, initially defended by anger, becomes in the end an innocence sacrificed for the world, undefended and wholly given in gentleness. For our greatest and deepest 'no' to God's Way is the manner in which it allows the harming of innocence, our own and that of those we love. Our final 'yes' comes when we let the sacrifice of innocence in Christ become for us our own willingness to let our innocence and that in those we love become a sacrifice for the lost innocence in those whom we cannot love, and who cannot love themselves, but whom God loves. This is why God's Way will not give up on anything or anyone.

In this holy passion that Christ brings us to, we become the world's Tyger and its Lamb.

On the Cross, in his Passion, Christ suffers everything and everyone, and forgives everything and everyone, for all time, past, present, future. The suffering at the hands of the world, where our passion starts its entire struggle, becomes in the end, through the intervention of Christ's Passion, a suffering with and for the world. Only he who suffers has earned the right to forgive. This is the Atonement. "Lord, if Thou should mark iniquities, who could endure it?"

In Kierkegaard's tongue, passion literally means 'sufferingship'; a warrior is one whose passion is vowed, to go on suffering until the world is saved.

Such a warrior was Christ. In passion, I make a promise, a commitment, to the world: to take its hit, to carry its weight, to fight for it and to die for it, but never ever put the burden of it down – for comfort, or for supposedly higher things that are not bound to the earth. The sword Christ brought to the world is that promise, that commitment, of passion to save the world. St. Isaac of Syria said: "There is no passion more fervent than the love of God"; yet if we are won to the love of God, and believe in His Way, then we are fervently staked to the ground, committed not to judge and give up on the world, whether in the name of fallen passions or higher spiritual states, but to stay with it forever, whatever the cost and consequence to us not only in ascetic repentance and purification, but worldly patience and loss. We mix our blood, sweat and tears, in the ground of this world. The sword of Christ is the vow not to rest until the world is saved. This sword is not, therefore, just our ascetic struggle; it is a warning to the world that passion, both human and divine, will sufferingly fight for the world. The world is not going to be handed over to the devil. His rule is going to be broken in the world – not above or beyond the world, but in the world, for the sake of the world. In Christ's Passion, we encounter how the Above really descends into, and commingles itself with, the Below, knitting the two together, unbreakably, making them one. The 'issue' of passion that divided God and humanity creates a contention, but in the end this is reconciled, uniting God and humanity. This is the way of heart.

The Cross tells each and every one of us that our deepest irrational urge, its deepest impulse and energy, to leap into the unknown, into toil and tears, into death, for the sake of loving the world, is true. Christ has done what we funked, and hence his life, death and resurrection tells our passion, we can take love to the most holy and terrible extremity. By attaching to Christ, we can also do it. "He is the first born of many," the elder brother. Christ pays the cost we cannot, so that we can pay it. This is also the Atonement. Thus he has not done it for us, to absolve us; he has leapt into the abyss within and walked its road without that we may follow. We must be joined not only to Christ's ascetical yoke, but bound hand and foot to his burning Passion. The former exists only to free the latter.

God suffers eternally with and for us. God has postponed God's own fullness and peace until we are included. This is God's Sword and Cross. Only after we have passed through the Sword and the Cross will we find fullness and peace. Because only then do we know the divine heart has won the victory in the human heart.

Hence it must be understood that the desert takes us out of the world, not so that we may then ascend a ladder directly to heaven, but so that purified, cleansed and illumined, we can go back into the world, go back to Jerusalem to "ascend the Cross" and be crucified with Christ. Through the Passion of Christ, the heart leaps, the heart is raised up, the heart is handed over, the heart gives away and the heart goes all the way.

In Christ, both God's Heart and the human heart are glorified. The grief they share comes to a great joy.

The ascetical process of the desert is necessary to us, but not sufficient. It reaches its apotheosis, its reaches its destiny, in the city where we are crucified with Christ.

Let us go into the desert, to take on the task there. Let us then return to the city, to take on the task there.

The way of heart is too terrible and wonderful for any words. Its rewards are beyond all imagining.

To be one of those fiery ones suffering for the saving of the world, out of love of the world, is the heart's fullness, the answer to its anguished questions, the joy of victory, the peace that passes all understanding. The heart is a warrior, and this is the heart's only rest.

Praise be to the Passion of Christ.

Can This Ascetical Path
Be Integrated Into Modern Therapy?

Should the ascetical path be regarded as distinct from, or a potential basis for, modern therapeutic practices? How could it be integrated into these practices? Is a 'Desert Therapy' desirable and feasible? Would it be a wholly new and distinct kind of therapy, or might it be a resource that could underlie, inform and inspire, existing therapies?

The Ascetical Way, whether for monks and nuns or those 'living in the world', is not an abandoning of the world. It is an entry into the desert, so as to save the world: it is 'taking on' the clash between garden and hell that sits just a little below the city. Only in the desert of the heart can we recover the primal garden and move toward the eschatological, holy city. We go into the desert to undergo a process that has the power to reverse the whole balance of power in the heart. Without this fundamental alteration in the human heart, the world will continue to be an outward reflection of the inner hell in each and every one of us, just as the heart will be an inward reflection of the world's outer hell. Indeed, that hell is 'within' each and 'between' all. The struggle in a desert where only God and the evil spirit dwell is possible to, and in fact necessary for, all Christians, indeed, for all persons on a spiritual path. We must follow Christ into the desert, before we can go up to Jerusalem to challenge, and die for, the world.

Questions

• Ascetical healing traditionally occurs within a culture where everyone shares a common life-way. Therapy operates in a diverse culture, and must be open to all and sundry. How can ascetical practice and wisdom be open to that?

• Isn't therapy already ascetical in certain key respects? Disillusioning powerful illusions, undergoing loss, and showing patience, and many other such spiritually bracing factors, play a key role in most therapies. Might even the threefold journey of asceticism not be tacit in many therapies? At a certain point when our life has come to a dead end, and what is destroying it cannot be understood or stopped, we take on a way of life governed by a discipline. This is the first step of yoking. After a time, as St. Paul says, we discover that no outward change in our pattern of living is sufficient to change us thoroughly within, for we discover in our more "inward parts" that there is both good and evil, but the evil cripples the good: "..the good thing that I would, I do not, but the evil I would not, that I do" (Rom 7:14). Therefore, at this point, we have to begin the real work of the nous, which leads to the beginning of humility and knowledge of self – knowledge of our hidden motives. This is the second step of digging and dawning discernment. Then, at last, we get to the heart ground, which leads to deep repentance, and transformation, in the place where we are all together with God in the sorrow – and hope – of mankind. That place is where the heart is finally healed, or finally broken. Isn't something like this 'descent into hell' the course of therapy, when it manages to really approach a human being's sticking point, the point that is make-or-break for their whole existence in this world? For many therapies, heaven has only been recoverable in the midst of hell, and thus the ascent into healing comes up from below. Like the spirit of flamenco, the duende, it is a blackness that rises from the earth and into the soles of our feet, becoming fire in the belly and heart, and light in the mind.

• Isn't the Un-named often more effectual, spiritually, than the Named? As soon as spiritual things are given names, people either think they can know and control them, which entails putting them to some use that violates their whole nature, or people dismiss them because they stir up some ignorant prejudice. The Spirit often works best as a secret agent, unsung and unknown. All names and no names belong to this Spirit who moves in our depths, driving us from the heart back into the heart.

• We therapists are not, and should not aspire or pretend to be, spiritual directors in the traditional sense. Is this an advantage or disadvantage? Is this "the blind leading the blind," or in fact a door to practitioner humility? If we respect, but do not fear and try to conquer, mystery and danger, then won't these become the very precondition of our trust in the Spirit's guidance?

• Much of modern life is already ascetical in a very grey and inhibiting sense: we are imprisoned rats in a rat run. Given how little vitality, or real freedom, most people enjoy, how can we demystify their fear of the ascetical yoke as just another hairshirt they are supposed to like 'because it is good for them'? Can we show poverty, chastity, obedience, in their spiritual light, and as required by all of us? Poverty: to overcome individual greed, and a world polarized into rich and poor, so that brotherhood can be released; chastity: to overcome fantasy and its devouring selfishness, so that eros can be released; obedience: to overcome our own opinions and prejudices, so that the Way to deeper knowledge and truth can be uncovered and pursued, etc.

• Asceticism is radical, and fundamental. A survivor of the battle of El Alamein said, "War in the desert is total warfare; there is nothing to get in the way" (Black Watch, Highland Regiment). This captures perfectly the intensity of ascetical practice. The purpose of asceticism is to fight the spiritual warfare which alone enables us to reach the deep heart. Can we adapt ascetical practice and wisdom when many people today just want to be patched up, or fixed, so as to successfully return to the Fallen Way of the world? In particular, how do we as therapists prophetically and healingly stand against 'the American Dream' sweeping all the world, when we know it is not only evil, but virtually the Antichrist? Will Orthodox Christianity in America and in the West remain true to its life and death struggle through the desert, for the sake of the original garden of Nature's Sacredness and the final City of Holiness? Or will Orthodoxy basically succumb and become just a quaint enclave, but one in basic compromise with America and the West? Will we, in short, let ourselves become just another exotic version of the American Dream? Or will we stay true to our Yoke, adapting it, but not surrendering it?

Conclusion

Religion has, in the Western democracies, all but died out because it is too bland, anodyne and unchallenging. A working-class American guy who had lived many years with the Lakota once remarked to me, only half in jest, "If you want to avoid suffering, stay away from Indians when they start to pray." The pap regularly served up in everyday life, and in most current religion, disappoints us precisely because there is no 'blow' in it capable of getting us into the depths, and keeping us there. Asceticism has an answer to (a) what gets us there, and (b) what keeps us there. Does any other way of life, or healing?

The Desert Fathers were famously reluctant to make maps of the hard road they walked. Instead, they told 'wisdom stories' that hinted at the progress of the road through twists and turns; left (often deceptively) simple descriptions of their practices, and techniques and gave brief instructions in the form of injunctions (called 'giving a word', usually from an elder to someone less experienced). They wrote no theology and no philosophy. They had no interest in the theoretical, only in the practical and the experiential: they were not trying to build an abstract model of the transformation towards holiness, but to be dedicated in the concrete living of it. Maybe precisely this emphasis is what the present moment needs.

References

Anonymous Series of the Apophthegmata Patrum, *The Wisdom of the Desert Fathers*, trans. Benedicta Ward (Oxford: SLG Press, 1986).

Metropolitan Anthony of Sourozh, *Living Prayer*, (London: Darton, Longman, and Todd, 1966).

Archimandrite Capsanis, *The Eros of Repentance*, trans. Hieromonk Alexander, (Newbury, MA: Praxis Institute Press, 1987).

Archimandrite Chrysostomos, *The Ancient Fathers of the Desert*, (Brookline, MA: Hellenic College Press, 1980).

Archimandrite Sophrony, *A Monk of Mount Athos*, (Essex, England: Monastery of St. John the Baptist, 1952).

Nicholas Berdyaev, *Dostoevsky*, (NY:Meridian Books, 1957).

Nicholas Berdyaev, *Christian Existentialism*, ed. D. Lowrie, (New York: Harper and Row, 1965).

Roberta Bondi, *To Pray and to Love: Conversations on Prayer with the Desert Fathers*, (London: Burns and Oates, 1991).

Martin Buber, *The Legend of the Baal-Shem*, (New York: Schocken Books, 1955).

John Chryssavgis, *In the Heart of the Desert: the Spirituality of the Desert Fathers and Mothers*, (Bloomington, IN: World Wisdom Books, 2003).

John Chryssavgis, ed. and trans., *Letters from the Desert: Barsanuphius and John*, (Crestwood, NY: St Vladimir's Seminary Press, 2003).

Oliver Clement, *The Roots of Christian Mysticism*, (New York: New City Press, 1993).

Igumen Chariton of Valamo, *The Art of Prayer: An Orthodox Anthology*, trans. E Kadloubovsky and E. Palmer, (London: Faber and Faber, 1996).

J. K. Kadowaki, *Zen and the Bible*, (New York: Routledge and Keegan Paul, 1980).

Gregory Mayers, *Listen to the Desert*, (London: Burns and Oates, 1997).

J. Moran, and M. Moran, "The Battle for Person in the Heart", (*Parabola*, Oct, vol VII, No 4, 1982), p. 52-59.

Jamie Moran, "Beyond Intellect", (*Self and Society*, March, vol 23, No 1, 1995), p. 20-23.

John G. Neihardt, *Black Elk Speaks*, (London: Abacus, 1974).

Stelios Ramfos, *Like a Pelican in the Wilderness: Reflections on the Sayings of the Desert Fathers*, (Brookline, MA: Holy Cross Orthodox Press, 2000).

St. Isaac of Syria, *Heart of Compassion: Daily Readings with St Isaac of Syria*, ed. A. M. Allchin, trans. S. Brock, (London: Darton, Longman, and Todd, 1989).

St. Isaac of Nineveh, *On Ascetical Life*, trans. M. Hansbury, (Crestwood, NY: St Vladimir's Seminary Press, 1989).

St. Nikodimos, *The Philokalia*, vol 1, trans. G. Palmer, P. Sherrard and K. Ware, (London: Faber and Faber, 1979).

St. Nikodimos, *The Philokalia*, vol 2, trans. G. Palmer, P. Sherrard and K. Ware, (London: Faber and Faber, 1981).

St. Nikodimos, *The Philokalia*, vol 4, trans. G. Palmer, P. Sherrard and K. Ware, (London: Faber and Faber, 1995).

Paul Saliba and Joseph Allen, *Out of the Depths Have I Cried*, (Brookline, MA: Holy Cross Orthodox Press, 1979).

Columba Stewart, *The World of the Desert Fathers: Stories and Sayings From the Anonymous Series*, (Oxford, SLG Press, 1986).

Columba Stewart, "The Desert Fathers on Radical Honesty about the Self", (Sobornost, 12, 1990), p. 25-39.

Benedicta Ward, ed., *The Desert of the Heart: Daily Readings with the Desert Fathers*, (London: Darton, Longman, and Todd, 1988).

HEALING IN COMMUNITY

We are saved together but we fall alone.
– unknown

Chapter 8

THE SPIRITUAL LIFE AND
HOW TO BE MARRIED IN IT

PHILIP MAMALAKIS

As I prepared to write this article, I reviewed some notes I took at Holy Cross in a class on the sacrament of marriage. As I reread the notes, I became aware that notes on the theology of marriage mean something different to me now, five children and ten years of marriage later, than when I first wrote them. I know that the theology of marriage hasn't changed in those ten years, but I have. Within my own marriage I have come to know a little more about what love is and have experienced love in a way that was foreign to me ten years ago. I am certain that I love my wife more now than I did on our wedding day. It is not that I feel different. If anything, I feel less emotional now than I did in my first year of marriage. My heart does not speed up when I see her as often as it did ten years ago. I am certain that in ten years I have learned to love her more purely, more selflessly. One only needs to ask her. Within this transformation of my love towards my wife, I am a different person than who I was ten years ago. This is the mystery, the sacrament, of marriage.

We know that marriage, as a sacrament blessed by Christ Himself (John 2:1-11), is a revelation of the Kingdom of God(1). As such, it is sustained by the Holy Spirit and is a vehicle of the Holy Spirit. It is transfiguring. Marriage transfigures human love into a new reality of heavenly origin, it transfigures the unity of a man and woman into a reality

215

nothing short of the Kingdom of God (2). "Through the presence of Christ in marriage, the water of the natural passions is changed into the fruit of the vine, the noble wine that signifies the transmutation into the new love, a charismatic love springing forth to the Kingdom"(3). Within this mystery, we find our fulfillment as husband and wife as we become one in Christ and love with Christlike love. That perfection, naturally, is not simply an outward perfection of a couple that never fights and is happy, but an essential transformation of the persons of the man and the wife who participate through grace in the divine nature of God (2 Pet 1:3, 4). And that divine nature, we know, is love (1 John 4:16). "He who possesses Love possesses God Himself, for God is Love" (4). The result is, that through the mystery of marriage we come to love in a divine way.

If marriage transforms us towards the perfect love of the Kingdom of God, then marriage is a process of learning to love with perfect, Christlike love. We can infer, then, that this spiritual transformation of marriage towards perfection in Christ is far from struggle-free, for the Kingdom of Heaven suffers violence and the violent take it by force (Mat 11:12). However, the distinct nature of the struggle is not against our spouse, but against the flesh (cf. Gal 5:13-25). This marital struggle is a struggle for the salvation of our souls. The goal of marriage, then, is not self-gratification, endurance, or even happiness, but salvation, union with Christ, perfection in Love.

The fact that marriage is a process of becoming means that we are not there yet. In marriage we love imperfectly and, more noticeable at times, we are loved imperfectly. "Only the perfect person, with a perfect conscience, a perfect mind, and perfect power, can have perfect love. Such a person is our God"(5). The result of this fact is that marriage is the setting for each person's "struggle to be fulfilled, through relationship with God and with his fellow men, in his personal distinctiveness, which can only be realized through love" (6).

Marriage Counseling

This divine call, to love our spouse as Christ would, serves as the thrust or orientation of marriage (Eph 5:25 ff), and marital therapy. Couples therapy situates the daily struggles of marriage into the call to be Christlike, to become divine, to love with perfect love. Marriage counseling, like marriage, is a theanthropic endeavor.

The most common approaches to couples therapy focus on helping couples learn to communicate, to understand each other's feelings, to accept each other and negotiate personal needs. Counseling without an orientation towards the Kingdom of God risks missing the underlying issues that turn a husband and wife against each other. At its worst, such counseling can lead a couple off the path of salvation. Therapy can easily be a process focused on the faults of each person. Typically couples come to therapy reporting that they have a communication problem. Then each partner proceeds to demonstrate how disconnected they are, placing the blame on the faults of the other. Clients typically believe that if the therapist can change the other person, everything would be fine. By helping couples identify negative patterns and interactions and the emotions underlying these interactions, the therapist can subtly help couples identify the faults of the other. This heightened awareness of the ugliness of sin in one's spouse can feel disheartening and overwhelming, fostering a sense of hopelessness. A simplistic injunction by the therapist to accept the other's shortcomings fails to account for the depth of dislike that exists in many marriages. Problem-solving within therapy risks being reduced to a quid pro quo arrangement that has little to do with love, let alone divine love. Identifying feelings, alone, can contribute to a never-ending cycle of mutual hurt.

Therapy can become a setting for promoting the self-serv-ing desires of each person. In secular therapy, couples are able to identify the incompatible, competing desires of each person. This can lead a couple to the conclusion that they are "not meant for each other." A colleague consulted with me on a case where he had helped a couple identify their needs and desires only to have them realize that they were not in love and unable to meet each other's needs. He stated what seemed to be the obvious conclusion that they should divorce.

Therapy focused solely on teaching communication skills cannot address the deeper issues that couples struggle with and can intensify negative interactions as they become more skilled at communicating their dislike of each other. One highly-respected professional in the field of marriage and family therapy astutely identified that if the aim of therapy is simply to help couples to communicate, and it is successful, what is communicated can be destructive to a marriage. He himself acknowledged that, although he traveled nationally and internationally teaching communication, he divorced his wife in the process. The problem of secular therapy is not so much the failure of the resources or the research as much as it is the displacement of therapy from this call to become divine, to participate in the life of Christ within marriage.

Alan Jenkins (7), a therapist in Australia working with vio-lent men, found that most of the existing literature focused on violent men's deficiencies. That literature, he found, im-plied that some men had personal limitations that led them to violence, implying that these men were passive victims to their personal limitations. In his work he argues that if violent men were to change their behaviors they would have to take responsibility for them. He developed his theory that men were fully capable of relating to women in a respectful, sensitive and non-abusive way unless they were restrained in some way. Restraints, he continued, were habits, traditions, or beliefs that influenced their behaviors and kept them from taking responsibility for their harmful behaviors. The restraints do not cause abuse, but they prevent men from taking responsibility for their actions. His work focused on men taking responsibility for their behavior and overcoming all restraints. Consequently, rather than being focused on inherent limitations, men became preoccupied with their own competencies in challenging any restraints.

As members of the Body of Christ, husbands and wives, similarly, are fully capable of perfect love through union with Christ. It is our calling (Mat 5:48). Rather than focusing on individuals being passive victims of self-gratifying needs, or fleshly desires, therapy focuses on our call to grow in likeness of God, towards perfect love. Therapy is a process of becoming preoccupied with our call to love as Christ loves, to become perfect as He is perfect. Therapy is a process of identifying those beliefs, habits, or passions that keep us from taking responsibility for our inability to love in a perfect way. Marital therapy goes beyond, or beneath, simply learning how to communicate, negotiate, accept or share feelings, and into the depths of our own fallenness, our worldliness, our passions, and the restraints to love as we are called to love. Therapy is a process of helping persons become preoccupied with their own call to love as Christ loves, to become perfect as Christ is perfect. "Do not observe the sins of others, and do not behave inimically, inwardly or outwardly, towards those who sin, but represent to yourself your own sins, and heartily repent of having committed them, considering yourself in reality worse than all. Pray lovingly for those who sin, knowing that we are inclined to every sin" (8).

For most Trinitarian Christian faith traditions, couples exchange vows and commit to loving each other on their wedding day. Couples therapy is a process of identifying what each couple meant by that vow and in what ways each person struggles to fulfill that vow. When therapy is successful, clients become preoccupied with learning to love the other and fighting against any restraints to loving. Resources of contemporary psychology find their place and their fulfillment within the divine mandate to love.

The therapist, using patristic teachings of spiritual warfare and contemporary psychology and couple therapy resources, works with the couple to identify the restraints to loving. However, couples typically do not come to therapy and report that their problem is that they have not acquired perfect love for each other and would like to work towards that. They might know that they have to love, but they are not aware of what that means, or they don't know what is getting in their way. One of the unique challenges of marriage is that spouses learn everything about each other, including each other's sins and shortcomings. The initial commitment to love fades in the face of the newly-discovered habits, characteristics, shortcomings and sins of our spouse. The newly-discovered faults of one's spouse simply reveal one's own inability to love. The challenge for the therapist is to redefine the negative interactions as a failure to love.

Defining love for a couple

Couples therapy is about exploring how couples understand marital love. Within the marital bond love is lived and learned, and deepened. It is not uncommon for couples to enter therapy dissatisfied in their marriage, reporting that they no longer love each other. Some are more careful and share that, although they still love each other, they are not 'in love'. With a little exploration it becomes apparent that love is confused with infatuation or a feeling of warmth and closeness. What also becomes apparent is that each person entered the marriage looking to have personal needs met by the other and have come to the painful realization that it is not happening. The common conclusion is that it is the other person's fault. Within a conversation on what love means, a couple defines love in terms of its expression within the marital bond. Love is redefined and becomes the goal of marriage in addition to the starting point.

If both parties have a voice in this conversation, a couple can quickly come to identify how they would like love to be expressed within the marriage. Rather than defining love in abstract or theological terms, it is defined in terms of how a couple would like to be with each other. The end result is that the couple has identified their goal of marriage: perfect love. This definition of love serves to realign the marriage relationship. Conflicts, disagreements and daily challenges can be addressed from within this movement towards perfect love.

Within therapy, a reflection on St. Paul's words can serve as a starting point and would suffice to delineate the meaning of love or, more specifically, the expression of love within the marriage. In 1 Corinthians 13: 4-7, St. Paul writes that "Love suffers long and is kind; love does not envy; love does not parade itself; is not puffed up; does not behave rudely, does not seek its own, is not provoked, thinks no evil; does not rejoice in iniquity but rejoices in truth; bears all things, believes all things, hopes all things, endures all things." Based on the couple's experience, they can expand on this list to include whatever particular challenges they struggle with. For example, couples might identify that love does not mock or minimize the other. Love does not belittle, oppress, or subjugate the other. Love does not control, but seeks to serve. Love does not reject the other. Love condemns sin, but not the sinner. "Love every man in spite of his falling into sin. Never mind the sins, but remember that the foundation of the man is the same – the image of God" (9).

While St. Paul states primarily what love is not, within counseling the couple can expand and define what love is. Based on St. Paul's words, it quickly becomes apparent that the expression of love within marriage is synonymous with the pursuit of the classic Christian virtues of the Kingdom of God. To love my spouse is to pursue virtues within the marriage. It is apparent, then, that love is not a feeling and not an idea. Love makes demands of us, rather than we making demands of our spouse. Love is not a concept. It requires that we act personally, rather than intellectualize and imagine. Love is expressed more in the mundane acts of daily life than in the grand ideas and beliefs. Love is personal and requires that each person be present and willing to connect. Love is more synonymous with sacrifice than emotion.

What becomes apparent is that love is ascetic in its self-sacrificial orientation. Love is ascetic in the sense that calls us to deny our "natural" desire to use our spouse to meet our needs. "Love is above all a self-giving. "It is a sacrifice, whose archetype is Golgotha, involving losing one's life in order to gain it" (10). This ascetic orientation of love does not mean that we surrender our personal fulfillment within marriage and deprive ourselves of what is good, but realize our fulfillment as children of God through self-giving. Love calls us to surrender the fleshly in ourselves so that we may receive the divine. "The aim of asceticism is to transfigure our impersonal natural desires and needs into manifestations of the free personal will which brings into being the true life of love" (11). This asceticism within marriage does not mean that we simply give in or stop being who we are so our spouse can be happy. On the contrary, Christian asceticism might mean that we remain steadfast in our insistence or speak up about how we are in our marriage. It is not to be confused with pacifism, codependency, or enabling. Asceticism is not about being miserable, but about being filled with the joy of self-sacrificial love. "Within the tradition of the Church, asceticism is *philokalia*, love for the beauty of that uncompleted perfection which is personal fulfillment, the restoration of God's darkened image in man to its original beauty"(12).

As Orthodox we know that perfect love is divine love and the path towards acquiring this love is the path of acquiring the Holy Spirit (1 Cor 2:12-14; Gal 2:20). Love is not learned, but acquired. The process of acquiring the Holy Spirit is our journey of salvation. By learning to love our spouse, we learn to love God. We love God by loving our spouse.

He who wants to be an imitator of Christ, so that he too may be called a son of God, born of the Spirit, must above all bear courageously and patiently the afflictions he encounters, whether these be bodily illnesses, slander and vilification from men, or attacks from the unseen spirits. God in His providence allows souls to be tested by various afflictions of this kind, so that it may be revealed which of them truly loves Him (13).

Defining restraints

The patristic tradition, as well as contemporary psychology, has identified the restraints to perfect love. From an Orthodox perspective, if love is union with God, and the pursuit of love is the acquisition of the Holy Spirit then those things that separate us from God – sin, the passions, death, and the devil all represent restraints to perfect love. Our own self-centered, egocentric orientation, our fallen nature represent the biggest restraints to love. "When we speak of all the passions together, we call them 'the world.' So when Christians speak of renouncing the world, they mean renouncing the passions" (14).

For couples, therapy can articulate in what ways our fallenness is expressing itself within the marital relationship. Inasmuch as our passions, or fleshly desires, represent barriers to love, within marital counseling, each person's unique restraints are identified. Contemporary psychology has identified many of these expressions of fallen nature as they manifest themselves in relationships. Family-of-origin issues, gender roles, complicated grief, sexual abuse, mental illness, addictions, poor or inappropriate communication, infidelity, anger, or distorted cognitions, among other things, represent some of the specific restraints for couples. As Orthodox we are not immune to destructive effects of negative communication patterns, family-of-origin issues, destructive gender roles, mental illness, or any restraints to love. Orthodoxy serves to provide deep insight into human nature, sin and marriage. This knowledge is expressed within secular models of therapy. As Orthodox, we can make use of secular knowledge of these barriers to assist couples in moving beyond these barriers towards an intentional marriage.

Contemporary theories of therapy find their usefulness in identifying these barriers. Emotion-Focused Therapy, Attachment Theory, Integrative Couple Therapy, Narrative Therapy, or any other respected approach can be very effective in identifying restraints. Naming the barriers, or naming the demons, serves to render them impotent within the light of Christ, when the therapy has a clear direction. It is often the demons that are unnamed, but acutely experienced, that cause couples the most difficulty. While identifying barriers, or restraints, to loving is likely to diminish negative interactions between two people in the short term, it does not necessarily provide a direction for a marriage. Secular knowledge serves as a resource to identify barriers, passions, or sins when it is situated within divine call to love as Christ loves. Outside of this divine context of the Kingdom of God, identifying barriers can just as easily fuel conflict.

Therapy must be preoccupied with the personal call to love with perfect love.

The therapeutic process

Working with couples from within this framework means, initially, joining with a couple, defusing negative interactions by identifying them, and helping clients redefine the negative interactions within the marital injunction to love the other. The purpose of identifying perfect love as the goal of marriage is not to encourage couples to try harder. Perfect love cannot be obtained from our own efforts. Christian life cannot be reduced to some code of conduct and the purpose of therapy is not to get couples to live according to some abstract, divine principles of conduct. We cannot, through our own efforts, achieve perfect love. Lest we focus too much on our ascetic responsibility in the transformation of love within marriage, we must remember that Love is a gift from God. Love is made perfect within us (I John 4:17).

> The virtues are achieved by our personal effort and acquired by our own labor, but spiritual gifts are bestowed by God on those who struggle…To be in control of one's temper and anger belongs to a wondrous struggle and extreme effort, but to attain to their complete quiescence and obtain serenity of heart and perfect gentleness is the act of God alone and a transformation at His hand (15).

This process of learning to love, this divine mandate to become perfect, is essentially a mandate to do the impossible, because it is our fallen nature itself which represents the barrier to loving perfectly. Any progress towards perfect love is impossible through human effort alone. "Any…pursuit of taming his nature through his own powers is condemned by nature itself" (16). What is impossible for man alone becomes possible if we use our freedom to receive what God gives us. "Through the application of God's will and the practice of virtue, he demonstrates his attachment to Christ and keeps himself as a vessel capable of receiving the regenerative power and grace of God" (17).

This therapeutic process of exploring the restraints of love essentially is a process of coming to terms with our own fallenness and inability to love. To pursue perfect love is to become aware of my own inabilities. Couples often are acutely aware of the impossible nature of loving. This realization within therapy creates an environment of brokenness, repentance, and subsequently, transformation. "Repentance is the door to mercy, open to those who seek it diligently; by this door we enter into divine mercy, and by no other entrance can we find this mercy"(18). Within the mystery of marriage, this call to love becomes a call to take responsibility for our own inadequacies and to confess to each other (Js 5:16) where we have failed. This includes asking each other for forgiveness for specific failings to love, shifting how couples interact with each other. In addition, for Orthodox couples, this process finds its fulfillment as couples actively participate in the sacrament of confession.

If it were not for the divine mandate to love, the natural conclusion when faced with the impossible task of loving would be to abandon the process. However, the inescapable nature of a monogamous marriage provides the crucible for God's transforming grace to work. Couples therapy can best be summed up as a process of each person taking responsibility for his or her inability to love as he or she is called to love. Therapy oriented towards pursuing perfect love results in a movement towards mutual confession. This maintains a couple within the context to love and creates a process of mutual vulnerability and intimacy in addressing the sins or restraints of each person. Rather than attacking each other, couples work towards supporting each other in the mutual struggle with each person's own fallenness, fostering mutual vulnerability and intimacy.

Couples develop coping strategies together instead of criticizing each other. Once one person takes responsibility for his problem, it can then become the couple's problem as they learn to work together to support each other. Rather than criticizing, blaming, judging, mocking, or distancing, each person is called to love and to pray for the other in his/her struggle. By the grace of God, within the mystery of marriage, as we pursue patience and learn to pray for the sins of our spouse, we actively participate in our own transformation towards perfect love.

Conclusion

Without this orientation towards acquiring divine love within marriage therapy, the resources of contemporary psychology and couples counseling can be used to promote self-love. Identifying restraints can exacerbate the problems and sense of separation for a couple. Within the context of the journey towards acquiring perfect love, however, marriage therapy reorients a couple towards the Kingdom of God. Within this approach, the therapist shifts the conversation of a couple and situates the daily struggles of life in the context of this process of becoming Christlike, holding clients in their brokenness. We cannot solve our spouse's sins, but we can learn to love our spouse. The therapist holds couples as they shift their way of being together from warring partners to broken lovers. Couples therapy is the safe environment where the two learn to be vulnerable and learn that there is deep joy and transformation in that place. As one client reported, "I don't know how it works, but I hate it, and it makes us feel better to be together." Such is his simple honesty as he describes our hearts. "I hate it and it heals me and I want to be healed." "The more the spouses are united in Christ, the more their common cup, the measure of their life, is filled with the wine of Cana and becomes miraculous"(19).

As I think ahead to the next ten, twenty, or thirty or more years in my marriage, considering the self-sacrificial and ascetical nature of love, rather than resign myself to marriage as a laborious process of suffering, I anticipate the joy of personal transformation, because we know that Jesus saves the best wine for last.

Endnotes

1. John Chryssavgis, *The Sacrament of Marriage: an Orthodox Perspective,* (Studia Liturgia, 19, 1, 1989), p. 17-27.
2. Stephanos Charalambides, *Marriage in the Orthodox Church*, (One in Christ, 15,3 1979), p. 204-233.
3. Paul Evdokimov, *The Sacrament of Love* (Crestwood, NY: St. Vladimir's Seminary Press, 1985), p. 122.
4. George Berthold, trand., *Maximos Confessor: Selected Writings*, (New York: Paulist Press, 1985), p. 87.
5. Johanna Manley, trans., *Kassiana: Letters in Divine and Christian Love: From the Collected Writings of Nikolia Velimirovich,* (Seattle, WA: St. Nectarios Press, 1995), p.45.
6. Christos Yannaras, *Freedom of Morality,* (Crestwood, NY: St. Vladimir's Seminary Press, 1984), p. 111.
7. Allen Jenkins, *Invitations to Responsibility,* (Adelaide, South Australia: Dulwich Centre Publications, 1990).
8. E. E. Goulaeff, *My Life in Christ: Extracts from the Diary of St. John of Kronstadt,* (Jordanville, NY: Holy Trinity Monastery, 1994), p. 343.
9. Ibid, p. 95.
10. John Chryssavgis, *Love, Sexuality, and the Sacrament of Marriage,* (Brookline, MA: Holy Cross Orthodox Press, 1996), p. 4.
11. Christos Yannaras, *Freedom of Morality,* (Crestwood, NY: St. Vladimir's Seminary Press, 1984), p. 110.
12. Ibid, p. 111.
13. G.E.H. Palmer and others, trnas., *The Philokalia: The Complete Text Compiled by St. Nikodemos of the Holy Mountain and St. Makarios of Corinth*, Vol 3, (London: Faber and Faber, 1984), p. 342.
14. Isaac of Syria, quoted in Dee Pennock, *Who is God? Who am I? Who are you?* (Couth Canaan, PA: Early Church Publications, 1973), p. 29.
15. C. J. de Catanzaro, trans., *St. Symeon the New Theologian: The Discourses*, (New York: Paulist Press, 1980), p. 219.
16. Christos Yannaras, *Freedom of Morality,* (Crestwood, NY: St. Vladimir's Seminary Press, 1984), p. 114.
17. George Mantzaridis, *The Deification of Man*, (Crestwood, NY: St. Vladimir's Seminary Press, 1984), p. 61.
18. Isaac of Syria, quoted in Dee Pennock, *Who is God? Who am I? Who are you?* (Couth Canaan, PA: Early Church Publications, 1973), p. 108.
19. Paul Evdokimov, *The Sacrament of Love,* (Crestwood, NY: St Vladimir's Seminary Press, 1985), p. 123.

Chapter 8

EKKLESIA: FOSTERING THE RELATIONAL HEART OF COMMUNITY

Nicholas T. Graff

"Sainted Unmercenaries and Wonder Workers, regard our infirmities; freely you have received, freely share with us."
– Apolitikion of the feast of Saints Cosmas and Damian

It has been said that the mark of a good homily is that "it brings comfort to those who are in distress, and distress to those who are comfortable." I hope that my reflections find opportunity to do both. It really should go without saying that, as Orthodox Christians and members of the faith community, clergy and laity, we have an unfailing and unquestioning fidelity to the dogma, and the Holy Traditions of our Church. However, I believe that we have an equally strong obligation to question their application, as they relate to the *here and now* reality of the Church. Relevant application of universal Christian truths to a people who live in an age that is being increasingly defined as "post-Christian," seems to me a ridiculously obvious *strategic plan,* yet one that I find is often being tragically missed.

It behooves us to spend a little time discussing Church. We are all familiar with the grand and triumphant ecclesiology of our Orthodox Church. The iconic understanding of the Church as the Body of Christ, is a very powerful, biblical and well-developed theological reality. The Eucharistic community, the faithful people of God, the faith community, seem to bring this discussion into a more understandable, relational reality. For our purposes here, let it suffice to say that, although there are clear and dogmatic absolutes concerning the Church, the fact remains that we each, on a very human level, develop our own unique ecclesiology. For our discussion, it is not so much "what the Church is," but rather, how does it relate in itself, both vertically and horizontally.

I grew up in Baltimore which is famous for its row-houses, with their trademark marble front steps. But one would need a much more intimate experience with Baltimore to know what lies behind those endless rows of connected homes. Behind the homes are the alleys, those long veins of utility, where all the true work and play of the neighborhood takes place. Outsiders see the pristine facade of the front, its ornamentation, gilding and marble stoops. The very intent of the homeowner is to present the front of the house in such pristine fashion that one would be hard-pressed to know that a human being lives there, while real life, in all its honest utility, beauty and ugliness, takes place in an intimacy that is never permitted to be seen "out front."

From the uncoordinated clashing colors on the clotheslines to the stench and clang of the garbage truck, the cacophony of the bell of the icecream man's truck, to the children's chaotic play and women's conversations yelled down three houses over, the banging of men working on their cars, all give way to the reality of our lives in Baltimore. The front had to be managed and kept free from any obvious signs of humanity.

These alleys were my playground. On any given Saturday morning, there would be numerous activities and games being played. The older kids, the girls, the boys, the runts, the sissies, the little guys, the jocks, and any combination of the above would be engaged in games of stickball, football, dodge ball, tag, you're it, you've got cooties, hide and seek. Yelling, screaming, laughing, crying! Bruised knees, bruised egos! Plotting, scheming, coalitions formed, betrayals. Best friends made, enemies destroyed, re-alliances drawn. The incrowds, the cool kids, the nerds, the fags. The Greek kids, the xeni, the black kid, the spaz, the sped (special ed), the tard, the kid who didn't have a dad, the kid who didn't have shoes. It was in the alleys of Baltimore where the real living took place. In the mists of all this mix of the vile and the beautiful, the hurt and the fun, the chaos and the order of the games, there was one universally accepted phenomenon, and that was what we called "Safe Base."

"Safe Base," was this collectively agreed-upon place where, if you could get there, you were off-limits and safe. Sometimes it was a trash can lid or a torn-up box, and sometimes it was a hijacked shopping cart. It didn't really matter. The only thing that mattered was that we all agreed what "Safe Base" was, and what "Safe Base" meant. "Safe Base" was absolute, unquestioned, and guarded supreme by the entire collective. "Safe Base" was the place where, if you can get there, nothing bad can happen to you. No one can touch you. No one can hurt you. You cannot be tagged out, you cannot be given cooties. If the fag, the spaz, the sped, the black kid, could make it to "Safe Base," no one could beat him up. No matter what the peril, all you had to do is make it to "Safe Base," and you were safe, without question, and without qualification. No one dared challenge this rule, and no one violated its supreme sanctity.

If Christ indeed intended to leave a Church, he intended that Church to be "Safe Base." The church must be "Safe Base," and I, as a pastor, feel myself to be the citadel of that sanctity. If we are to foster the relational heart of the community, with the Church as the fiduciary agent of this relationship, we need foster the Church as a sanctuary and sanctified institution. The Church must be the place where, if we can make it there, we will find respite from the perils and dangers of the world. "We are in the world, but we are not of the world," our Lord tells us. This says to me, that although we are in a mundane place, we must be in it, in a different way, a unique way – *His way*. And, His way is unconditional and sacrificial Love.

The Church, as the Body of Christ, should be first and foremost the incarnation of the loving arms of Christ, used to welcome and embrace, to hold and to comfort, to soothe and to make feel safe, the broken-hearted children of God. We, the priests and all those who share in the healing ministries of the Church, become like the myrrh-bearing women, anointing and tending to His broken, yet wholly sublime Body.

Relationships must be founded on three fundamental principles: mutuality, fidelity, and trust. Whether it's a young couple coming for premarital counseling, or a family who is in crisis, the footings of mutuality, fidelity, and trust are foundational. These same principles are equally foundational to our discussion.

MUTUALITY

Fostering the relational heart of the community

To foster a relational heart, there must be established a context in which shared standards, goals and language exists. Mutuality is the fundamental environment in which any relationship can grow and develop. The Church must constantly seek mutual ground in which to make herself available to the culture in which she finds herself. There are those who feel strongly that the chasm between Orthodox Christians and the modern world is so wide that any suggestion of such a meeting would somehow lessen the Triumphant Church. Others appear to "speak for the mind of the Fathers," as the self-proclaimed protectors of Orthodoxy, feeling that it is our obligation to protect Orthodoxy from a defiling contact with the world.

I recall Bishop Gerasimos of Abydou (of blessed memory), who would often refer to audiences as *Esis oi Orthodoxoi*

("You, the Orthodox"). The didactic irony, that the speaker was a respected Hierarch of the Church, a professor, learned theologian, (and a sainted and holy man), was rarely lost on the audience.

May I suggest that we Orthodox must begin to avoid the arrogant folly of any attempt to speak the collective mind of the Fathers as if we had some unilateral privilege to hear a single voice which no one else can hear (there is a clinical diagnoses for this). Or, even worse, that Orthodox Christian theology is something meant to set us above and beyond – out of reach by the other. Instead, may we once again appreciate the eclectic and vastly diverse minds and teachings of the Fathers, most beautifully expressed in the Cappadocians. I refer you to one of the most magnificent expressions of this patristic ideal, Saint Basil's parable of the bumblebee.

> Let our use of books and learning in every case mirror the "icon" of the honeybee. For such does not visit every flower in the same manner, neither does the honeybee attempt to fly off bearing the burden of the entire flower. Rather, once it derives that which is needful from the flower, it leaves the rest behind and takes flight.
>
> So, too, if we are wise, once we derive from learning what resonates with truth, we too shall leave the rest behind and take flight. For is it not so that when we take a rose we avoid the thorns? So, too, let us approach diverse writings, harvesting the fruits that they offer for our objectives, while protecting ourselves from the damaging elements that may lie within them. In all our studies, let us take with us and take within us only what builds us up, and what leads us in the fulfillment of our mission…(1)

Another obstacle to a relational mutuality in fostering the heart of the community is the notion that one can speak on behalf of the collective consciousness of the Church. This is pernicious. And, it can be said that the Church is often neither collective nor conscious. It certainly becomes a problematic posture if any mutual foundation is to be sought with a post-modern world.

Parenthetically, the pre-modern age, generally framed from the beginning of recorded history, up to the dawn of the nineteenth century, is very loosely defined as an age where universal truths were sought in theology. A volcano erupted, wiping out half the village, leaving the survivors to seek answers, solace, resolve, vengeance, and assurance that this will never happen again, in the gods. Touting the failure of theology to give the answers to the big questions gives way to the Modern Age, generally framed from the late 1800s to the late 1900s, and is defined as an age where the universal truths were sought in the physical sciences. Discounting answers in the unseen, the big "out there," modern solutions were sought in the physical, the small and the "in here."

It is said that the seeds of post-modernity were sown in the ashes of Auschwitz and the other concentration camps of Nazi Germany. So there is no wonder that the post-modern world has simply placed the entire notion of universal truth in parentheses. The post-modern world, rather, says that truth can only be sought, and sought only in dialogue. Orthodoxy, with its foundational tradition of being dialogical in its very nature, is supremely postured to offer itself to the contemporary world by engaging in the contemporary conversations. If our offering of Orthodox Christianity is the open, eclectic, embracing, broad-minded, enthusiastic, relational, integrating Orthodoxy expressed in St. Basil's parable of the bumblebee, one can only be elated by the possibilities made available. In this light, Orthodoxy finds a vastly superior mutuality in the relational heart of the contemporary community. And thus, we can feel confident in the challenge offered by Archbishop Demetrios, to offer Orthodox Christianity to contemporary America.

If, on the other hand, we cling to antiquated typologies,

we will find little mutuality, and thus limit our opportunity to foster the relational heart. Such, for example, is the fundamentalist brand of Orthodoxy, which in type and form, and with great irony, idealizes and fossilizes the culture of the late and decaying Ottoman State. Where is the mutuality between a post-modern world and a culture that has yet to reconcile itself with electricity? Is it possible that the same Church culture that produced the Cappadocians now defines its value in τρίχες, both literally and figuratively?

Mutuality, and the vast and fertile possibilities it offers the great Church of Christ to foster a relational heart with a cultural community as compatible as our contemporary society, should be celebrated and embraced with enthusiasm. Society, more then ever before in its history, is open to dialogue, thus, it is open to Orthodoxy.

FIDELITY

Fostering the relational heart of the community

Outside of a total commitment to absolute fidelity and faithfulness, any relationship is bound to failure. There are clear lines which we hold as non-negotiable in our relationships, and there are others which are in constant negotiation. These lines must be agreed upon, and once agreed upon, held inviolate. To do otherwise would certainly lead to divorce.

The expectation of fidelity of the faithful to the sacred Dogma, Holy Traditions, and Canons of the Church are clear and non-negotiable. Fidelity is one of those fragile things which cannot be sustained by one partner. It takes a mutual and shared commitment. Fidelity is also particular in-as-much as you can't do it "just a little bit." Fidelity is an all or nothing, 100% commitment by all parties involved. In fostering the relational heart of the community, this sacred value cannot be reduced to "a pray, pay and obey" comedic shtick. But rather, fidelity, in fostering the relational heart, is our shared faithfulness to the most broken and marginalized of God's people. We must assure the broken-hearted that the Church will stand with them. I do not recall a group that Christ discounted, or a person that he rejected. He engaged faithfully with all who came to Him, and dealt with them in charity. He implored them to "sin no more," *only after he healed them*. Christ abandoned no one.

If the Church is to maintain credibility in the contemporary conversation of fostering relational hearts, issues of misogyny, sexism, racism, elitism, ethnocentricity, anti-Semitism, homophobia, clericalism, and parochialism (just to name a few) must become a part of the dialogue if the value of faithfulness and fidelity is to be established and held with any remote legitimacy.

The same Church that reacted so decisively and clearly to the Iconoclasm of the eighth century and condemned those who dared to violate the images of the sacred written by human hands in paint and tempera, must find that same resolve to defend the sacred images of the divine written by the very hand of God, in flesh and spirit. The iconoclasts of the twenty-first century are much more vile and dangerous then the iconoclasts of antiquity. Where are the defenders of the image of God today?

Several of these cancers erode the relational heart.

Misogyny: The very icon of fallen humanity, sin, and its subsequent result, death, is placed on the lap of womankind. From Eve to the historical and methodical slander of the person of Mary Magdalene, to the marginalizing of the apostolic women, to the vile and humiliating traditions surrounding women's unique biological menstrual functions, it becomes apparent that much dialogue is needed to foster the relational heart of over half the community. It seems to me that the Church does best with virgins and prostitutes, but, has a very hard time with the rest of the female population. An associated iconoclasm is sexism. Let it suffice to say that the Church is the only institution that is legally permitted to impose such restrictions on women. Such treatment would be deemed illegal, and certainly unethical, in any other setting. Isn't it strange?

Elitism: The sin of elitism also hinders the relational heart. At a recent national Church leadership meeting, a member rose to make a now all too familiar speech, about the perils of "our children leaving the Orthodox Church." He spoke about the fact that when we were young, we didn't have country clubs and private social clubs to go to, we only had the Church. "Now," he said, "our children all belong to country clubs, and they don't need the church." Excuse me? Do we really think that the average Joe out there belongs to a country club? Have our Sees begun to resemble the court of Louis XVI? Have we gotten so far out of touch with the average soul? I am reminded of the cartoon of Marie Antoinette being led to the guillotine. The caption, with her lifting her hand to the crowd, just before her head is lowered, reads: "Ok, ok, I give up, you can have ice cream with your cake." Elitism takes many forms, none of which facilitate fidelity in fostering the relational heart. This socio-economic elitism is just the tip of the iceberg.

Homophobia. Let it suffice to say, without regard to this explosive issue itself, as experienced by the Episcopal Church, I for one applaud them for having an open, honest, **transparent**, public dialogue. Good for them. It is interesting to note that this controversy is framed, not by the ordination of a gay bishop, but rather, the ordination of an **openly** gay bishop. Might it be that this hypocrisy is not exclusive to the Episcopal Church?

Chrestos Yannaras, in his book entitled *Elements of Faith*, in the opening lines of Chapter 7, writes:

> "In the Tradition of the undivided Church and its historical
> continuity in Orthodoxy, we learn the truth about man by
> studying the revelation of the truth about God. Therefore,

> since a descriptive anthropology is not enough for us, we
> look rather for an interpretation of the fact of human exis-
> tence, the illumination of those aspects of human beings
> which remain inaccessible to objective explanation... God
> is affirmed as a personal Existence, and man is created in
> the image of God."

The Orthodox Church has a most grand and sublime anthropology. It begins with God, and man as His image.
This magnificently sublime understanding is next lifted to
yet a more grand expression of our understanding of man
(in potential), in Saint Athanasios' famous credo of incarnational theology: "God became man, so man can become
God." What does this mean? And how has this foundation of
Christian anthropology been developed over the last 1,500
years, post-Cappadocians? Has it been developed at all?

Might it be suggested that, although the Church has an
exulted anthropology, she also has a problematically under-
developed anthropology? There seems to be a gaping hole,
right in the mid-section; one that we seem to ignore, like
the proverbial elephant in the room. It is no wonder that the
pressing conversations that seem to define the post-Christian
era are issues that fall right into that void. Issues of race,
gender, sexuality, gender identification, reproductive rights,
the right to die, all seem to be lost in that abyss of the pelvic
mid-section. Can a standard for fidelity be negotiated in the
relational heart, without first coming to a clear consensus of
what that human heart is? Is it qualified?

TRUST

Fostering the relational heart of the community

The most foundational quality of all relationship is that of
trust. Without it, there is nothing on which we can build. It
would be like building a house on the surface of the ocean:
every brick would sink, and the whole notion lost to the folly

and absurdity of the attempt. Any attempt to foster the relational heart of the community of God's faithful is equally doomed outside of an environment of trust. Trust does not come easily, but rather is in a constant state of test. We are called to "put our trust in the Lord." And, ultimately, that trust is all we have. There is only one way in which to establish trust, and that is through vulnerability.

To make oneself vulnerable to another, to expose ones wounds, to say, "I hurt here," is the path to trust. The paradox is not lost in the fact that wholeness can only be sought through the exposure of the broken, and health, through exposure of the disease. It can be said that healing presumes an environment of trust, both on the part of the one seeking the healing and the healing practitioner. This environment of trust is only established and fostered in an atmosphere in which all parties feel it safe to be vulnerable.

Following is a framework of this reality in the context of our three healing disciplines: the Medical, the Psychological, and the Religious.

Healing/trust/vulnerability: the medical paradigm
Let us consider the example of a forty-six-year-old executive, who wakes up one morning and notices a very small red spot on the front of his pajama bottom. His initial alarm soon is relieved by a myriad of alternate substances that could produce red. He finds solace. He tries to forget about it. A few weeks later, it happens again. He then notices dark flushes in his urine. Slowly, even his pool of resourceful denial is beginning to run shallow. There is something wrong. He agrees that it may be time for his annual checkup. In fact, it may be a little overdue. Checking his records, he finds that his last annual physical was about nine years ago. He gives his doctor a call and sets up an appointment. "Nothing specific..." he tells the doctor, "just a checkup." Scene 2 of Act 1 of this ballet begins to unfold. This act could be subtitled: "if you

can't find it, it's not there" ...and the games continue.

This dance is anticipated by any first-year medical resident. It reflects a primal rule that begins from the very first moment we can process fear, pain and discomfort, and becomes more and more sophisticated as we gain more and more experience. If "It hurts here" is met with salt in the wound often enough, we will be hard-pressed to expose our wounds again. The physician knows that his therapeutic relationship with his patient is founded on trust.

From the time we tearfully show our boo-boos to our mommies, who kiss them and make it all better, we hold all those to whom we expose our wounds to the same standard of compassion, gentleness and, effective healing. In order to be healed, the one seeking the healing must trust, and trust is established by laying open the wounds. The same cycle of healing/trust/vulnerability is equally applicable to the physician and healing practitioner. Again, with broad strokes, let us consider the effect of our litigious society on healing professions. What resources are being wasted? How many medical decisions are being made in a framework set by fear of malpractice suits, rather then sound medicine? I know medical professionals who hire full-time staff simply to "be present" in examining rooms in order to stave off any possible suggestion of misconduct.

The HIV/AIDS pandemic and recent SARS epidemic brought home clearly the daily reality of the medical professional being placed in very vulnerable situations. From the family doctor's office to the floors of the hospital to the bedside of the patient, the physician and other healing professionals are constantly exposed to the most dastardly pathogens. The surgeon spends his day literally up to his elbows in biohazards. Universal precautions accepted, it can be seen as no less than a miracle that our physicians are spared, given the vulnerable situations they must courageously place themselves in daily. The healing/trust/vulnerability cycle is apparent in the fostering of a healing environment of the physically broken. Effective medical healing is as much about good science as it is about fostering the relational heart.

Healing/trust/vulnerability: the psychotherapeutics paradigm

The relational cycle of healing/trust/vulnerability becomes obvious and equally foundational within the paradigm of psychotherapy. Clichés like "the presenting problem is never the problem," lend credence to the fact that we have a long journey together before we establish an environment in which healing takes place. In the psychotherapeutic model, the trusting and safe environment of the therapeutic setting itself becomes a primary instrument of healing. This often becomes a long process in which the client and the therapist enter into a relational interaction in which small, oftentimes minuscule increments of trust are earned by the therapist. Like the snail, the client cautiously, tentatively, comes out of his or her shell. This process may take weeks, months or years, and is often seen as the most monumental hurdle in the process of working towards mental and emotional health.

A young woman, working wife and mother of teenage children, suddenly begins to have paralyzing anxiety attacks every time her teenage daughter goes out in the evening. They began seemingly out of nowhere one Friday night when the fifteen-year-old stayed out two hours past her usual curfew of 11 pm. That evening, as the stress of the night unfolded, the mother experienced her first panic attack. They soon become so severe she thought she was going to have a heart attack. This sent her to her family doctor, who ruled out heart problems. In taking her history, the doctor suggested that she was having panic attacks, and helped her discern that these attacks always seemed to come on when she was worried about her only daughter. Referral to a psychologist was made.

In therapy, the woman presents her anxiety and fears about

her daughter, and the poor choices she is making. She is horrified that her daughter may be sexually active. Sessions go by, and the woman does not deviate from her presenting problem: her daughter. Although her panic attacks and anxiety continue and they are consistently being attributed to her concern for her daughter, much of the therapeutic time is used to address the woman's interest in the therapist's opinion of the dangers of teen sex.

The cycle of healing/trust/vulnerability is in full swing. The women is not about to lay open the wounds of her own adolescence and traumatic sexual history, until she establishes clearly that she will not be hurt or betrayed again. The therapist knows all so well that he or she must allow the ballet to unfold naturally, with some direction, but ever cautious not to go too far too fast.

The clinicians role in this cycle which lends way to a healing, therapeutic environment is one that also renders him or her vulnerable. The psychotherapist by definition is one who is willing to place one foot in the reality of the broken other, while keeping one foot firmly in his or her own reality. This in an attempt to establish a healing empathy with the patient. Small amounts of the therapist's own psyche must be doled out over the course of the therapeutic relationship, or the client will not be able to relate. Without this, the therapist is perceived as something other than human, and any attempt to foster the relational heart is thwarted. This, however, is often a slippery slope. Exposure to such broken souls on a daily basis certainly puts the therapist in vulnerable emotional places. It is in these places of pain and hurt that we meet with our patients, and together work towards a place of trust and health. The practitioner must be in constant touch with his or her own vulnerabilities and issues.

Counter-transference must be evaluated and processed internally and externally when deemed proper. What young psychotherapist will ever forget the time of seeing three persons with major depressive disorders on a Friday afternoon, and later found himself in bed with the sheets pulled up over his eyes until the following Monday morning, having been taken to the dark place himself. The lesson of scheduling is one hard-learned, as is the fact that we are changed by each patient, who takes a piece of us along with them. Empathy, sympathy, care, healing, trust, compassion – all have a price to be paid, and the currency is always our own vulnerability.

Healing/trust/vulnerability: the religious paradigm

In our discussion of Ekklesia, fostering the relational heart of the community, no greater obstacle faces us than a breakdown of the Christ-appointed cycle of healing/trust/vulnerability. Is it possible in the contemporary Church for hurting souls to point to their wounds and say, " I hurt here," and not expect salt to be poured on the wound? Has there been a waning in miraculous healing in the Church over the centuries? Has anyone asked why? When you think of your Church community, does it denote a safe place where you are confident that you can expose your most painful vulnerability, and find nothing but compassion and support?

It becomes painfully obvious that some serious self reflection is due, if the healing ministry of the Church is to be viable.

> "The pool of healing cured
> only one person each year.
> The temple of the Unmercenaries
> cures the whole multitude of the ailing,
> because the riches of the Saints
> are unfailing and inexhaustible.
> O Christ, by their intercessions,
> have mercy on us."

This Aposticha of the Vespers of our Patron Saints, the Unmercenary Physicians, Sts. Cosmas and Damian, has clear implications that the healing ministry of the Church is to be prolific. Where the pool of the old dispensation healed but one person each year, the unfailing and inexhaustible efforts of the saints is to cure multitudes.

It seems that this cycle of healing/trust/vulnerability is quite apparent in the healing ministry of Christ. I find it important to see the association and proximity of Christ's own healing ministry, as it relates to His own states of vulnerability. It soon becomes apparent that Jesus had a price to pay for his healing ministry. To point out a few from each Gospel:

• In Matthew 9:27-34, Christ opens the eyes of the blind man, and the response is: "He casts out demons by the prince of demons."

• In Mark 3:1-5, He heals the man with the withered hand, and in 3:6 "The Pharisees went out, and immediately held counsel with the Herodians against him, how to destroy him."

• In Luke 4:40-41, He heals many; Luke 4:42: "He departs to a lonely place."

• In Luke 18:35-43, He heals the blind man on the road to Jericho, and in 19:47 "The chief priests and the scribes and the principal men of the people sought to destroy him..."

• In John 5:1-17, the healing of the paralytic at the pool by the Sheep's Gate, and in 5:18 "This is why the Jews sought to kill him..."

Ultimately this thesis is most fully expressed in John 11:1-45, the raising of Lazarus from the dead, which is immediately followed by the fateful words of the high priest in John 11:45-53, "...you do not understand that it is expedient for you that one man should die for the people, and that the whole Nation should not perish ... so, from that day on they took counsel how to put him to death."

There seems to be a near cause and effect between Christ's healing ministry and His becoming increasingly vulnerable even to death. It seems that his ultimate healing, the raising of Lazarus, gives way directly to His ultimate sacrifice, the Cross. It becomes clear that Christ does not shy away from any fear of criticism, obstacle, or negative ramification when it comes to his healing ministry. Whether it is the plotting of the elite authorities, banishment by the village folk, or His own going into "a lonely place," Christ pays a price with each healing, even to the Cross.

Healing/trust/vulnerability seems to be an inescapable process in any setting in which true healing is to take place. How then can we expect to escape this truth in the healing ministry of the Church in its contemporary setting? It is obscene folly to delude ourselves that the relational heart of community can be fostered outside of an atmosphere where the broken hearted can feel it safe to expose the pain. Is the Church that safe haven? Do we model for our faithful that the Church is that "safe base," that unique place where their exposed wounds will never be met with salt?

Can priest-healers be vulnerable to one another? Can they expose their wounds to their Hierarchs? Can Hierarchs be vulnerable to one another? Does the leadership model for the faithful that the Church is a "safe base," a place where mutual trust can be founded surely on mutual vulnerability?

In fostering the relational heart of the community, we must first be able to say, "I hurt here, I am broken in this way," and be assured that my relational other, my community, will not throw salt on the wounds. The disconnect and the breakdown of the healing ministry of the Church, and the disconnect and breakdown of the healing/trust/vulnerability process are painfully intertwined.

In our competitive world, one is not afforded an opportunity to be vulnerable. The world seeks our vulnerability in order to seek our demise. Our weak point, our Achilles' heel, will be exploited and used against us, that is certain. Shouldn't it be different in the Church community? Can we even discuss the fostering of the relational heart of the community outside of a serious foundation of trust that can only be built on footings of mutual vulnerabilities, exposed, shared, and met with compassion and understanding?

Conclusion

Mutuality, fidelity and trust are the three fundamental values on which the relational heart of the community of God's faithful can be fostered. It is my hope that I have raised some questions this morning that will give rise to further reflection. In any discussion of the relational heart, it is the questions that count most. I find questions of vastly more value then answers, and I find people with questions vastly more interesting then people with answers. People with too many answers tend to be bullies or bores.

So, as I conclude my comments on Ekklesia, fostering the relational heart of the community, let me conclude with the prayer of another fellow who asked Jesus for a miracle: "I believe, O Lord, help me in my unbelief."

Notes

(1) Cf. Christou, Sakkos, Psevtongas & Zisis, trans. Kyprianos Bouboutsis, *Greek Fathers of the Church,* Vol. 7, (Thessaloniki, Greece: Gregorios o Palamas Editions, 1973).

RESPONSE TO FR. NICHOLAS GRAFF

GEORGE CHRISTAKIS

Jesus Christ the same yesterday,
today and yes, forever (Heb 13:8)

Father Nicholas characterizes our Orthodox Church quite starkly. Both disappointment and frustration are expressed, as he questions the application of Christ's universal Truths to today's world of inner city misery, crime, squalor, disease and the hopelessness he has witnessed. He states, challengingly, that the Church is not what it is, but what it does. He decries the dark and dirty places the poor call "homes" which he has witnessed growing up in Baltimore. The same was to be seen in upper and lower east side of Manhattan.

Father Nicholas, I know what you have seen, and I know a bit how you rightly feel, as I visited the homes of Latinos in the East Side of Spanish Harlem in New York City, and impoverished Kenyan families in the mud huts of Chavogere. The venues differ, but the poverty, dirt, disease, violence and smells are the same the world over. We are fortunate and privileged that our experiences brought us closer to the realities of which Christ spoke. For He visited, counseled and healed the poor, the hungry, the insane, the prostitutes, the epileptics and the lepers.

It was good of you to share your boyhood recollections of the "safe base" concept developed by the youth of Baltimore, where, if you could run fast enough to get to a particular place, the "toughies" couldn't get at you. The Orthodox Church is, in fact, the "safe base" for all of humanity who need and want to be there. The "safe base" is also the hospitals, homes for the elderly, and medical and spiritual services that Saint Basil developed together to bring to Christ, our supreme physician and healer, those and who are "...the betrayed, beaten, broken, hemorrhaging and suffering Body of the crucified Christ."

Fr. Nicholas describes a tripartite basis for successful relations between the Church and her people: mutuality, fidelity and trust." Mutuality implies things and concepts held in common, such as our Faith, our Creed. Mutuality can also mean mutual respect for one another, the sharing of equivalent standards, the development of a good attitude towards one another and the avoidance of personal offenses so that communication in love and in the Holy Spirit is facilitated among laity, priests and hierarchs. And without fidelity to Christ, to whom we are responsible and owe obedience, we will surely fail; for as He said: "Without me you can do nothing" (John 15:5). Furthermore we foster the relational heart of the community when we merit the trust of the people we serve.

Father Nicholas makes the point that while Orthodox Christians have an "unfailing and unquestionable fidelity to the dogma, and Holy Traditions of our Church" he believes that there should be an equally strong obligation to question the applications of the dogmas and Holy Traditions within the context of the contemporary Church. He recognizes that while there are "clear and dogmatic absolutes concerning the Church, the fact remains that we each, on a very human level, develop our own unique ecclesiology." If there are "clear and dogmatic absolutes", and if personal "ecclesiology" includes the ability of Orthodox Christians to interpret the Holy Scriptures as they like, then we have just defined the basic concepts of the Protestant Church.

The term "ecclesiology" as it refers to the Orthodox Church embraces the foundation, history, nature and scope of the Orthodox Church and he doctrines. It includes its origins and founding basis, administrative structures, commandments, Canons, rules and regulations, Holy Traditions, Liturgical practices, categories of clergy, and roles of laity.

The statement of Peter in Matthew 16:18, identifies and establishes Jesus Christ as the founder of his Church as revealed to Peter by the Father. This is confirmed by the Lord when He states: "And I tell you, you are Peter, and in this rock (the confession of Peter that Christ is the son of the Living God), I will build my Church. The Acts of the Apostles establishes the utility of local and regional Councils and synods to deal with the many vital issues emerging from the increasing number of persons desiring to become Christians. Paul became the inexhaustible "chosen vessel" who would bring Christianity to both Jews, Greeks and others.

Considering the 2000-year-history of Christ's Church and the current complex social, political and military status around the world, how does the Mutuality-Fidelity-Trust model compare with the Repentance-Confession model utilized by the Church since it origin? Most of the personal and sinful behaviors to which we humans are vulnerable and subject to, are exemplified in the Holy Scriptures. And the methods and manners in which sins are forgiven and diseases cured were accomplished by the Apostles through the Holy Spirit. Our Lord expects us, as His followers, to be vulnerable by confessing our sins to a priest, and "go and sin no more." It is essential that we acknowledge that the release of sins comes through the Mysteries of Repentance and Confession, and the prayers of absolutions given by a priest, and no other way. For this is the way described in Holy Scriptures (John 21:19). Jesus said to them "Peace be unto you. As the Father has sent me, even so I send you."

Jesus then breathed on them and said, "Receive the Holy Spirit. If you forgive the sins of any, they are forgiven; if you retain the sins of any, they are retained." And if we fall repeatedly, hope of our salvation never fails, even at the last breath we take as evidenced by the thief on the cross: "Lord, remember me when you come into your Kingdom."

Father Nicholas writes: "There are those who feel strongly that the chasm between Orthodox Christians and the modern world is so wide that any suggestion of such a meeting would somehow lessen the Triumphant Church." He continues: "Others appear to 'speak for the mind of the Fathers' as the self-proclaimed protectors of Orthodoxy, feeling that it is our obligation to protect Orthodoxy from a defiling contact with the world." But our contemporary Orthodox Church is experiencing a blessed defilement through its contact with the impoverished and malnourished families in central and eastern Africa through the programs of the Orthodox Christian Mission Center. And Greek Orthodox priests and hierarchs in Albania and Serbia are bringing new hope to fellow Orthodox ravaged by war.

Specific issues that Fr. Nicholas feels the Church needs to address are cited among them, the "cancers" of misogyny, elitism and homophobia. "The very icon of fallen humanity, sin and its subsequent result, death, is placed n the lap of womankind." Cited are Eve, the "slandered" Mary Magdalene and the "marginalization" of apostolic women. Yet it was a group of women who had the courage to run to Christ's tomb while the Apostles were hiding after the Lord's crucifixion. It was Jesus' mother Mary the Theotokos (God-bearer), and the myrrhbearing women who stayed close to Jesus as He was suffering on the Cross, and only the young Apostle John was there to fulfill the request of the dying Jesus that John should bring His mother to his home. And how can we consider the apostolic women "marginalized" when there are many thousands of women recognized by the Orthodox Church, and many Jewish women in the Old Testament that were prophets and played heroic roles alongside their husbands.

Concerning "elitism," most of us would think it relates mostly to describe the "country club" segment of society. But Mr. Webster defined elitism as a class of persons in a position to exercise a major share of authority or influence within the larger group (Webster's Encyclopedic Dictionary). Fr. Nicholas writes, "Elitism takes many forms, none of which facilitate fidelity in fostering the relational heart." Yet a very wealthy person who may appear elitist (wears $1000 suits), may quietly contribute large sums of money to support major Church projects directed towards fostering the relational heart of thousands of impoverished persons in developing countries. And according to the definition cited above, elitist persons can be capable of influencing Church policies and issues, many of which Father Nicholas and I agree should be held inviolate.

Concerning male and female homosexuality, Saint Paul makes it very clear: Do you not know that the unrighteous will not inherit the Kingdom of God? Do not be deceived; neither the immoral, nor idolaters, nor adulterers, nor homosexuals... will inherit the Kingdom of God.

In Romans 1:27, the chosen vessel of Christ documents the spiritual pathogenesis (how a passion and sin develops) of homosexuality:

> "For the wrath of God is revealed from heaven against all ungodliness and wickedness of men, who by their wickedness suppress the truth and though they know God, they did not honor Him as God or give thanks to Him, but they became futile in their thinking and their senseless minds were darkened... therefore God gave them up in the lusts of their hearts to impurity, to the dishonoring of their bodies amongs themselves, because they exchanged the truth about God for a lie and worshipped and served the creature

rather than the Creator, who is blessed forever! Amen. For this reason God gave them up to dishonorable prisons. Their women exchanged natural relations for unnatural, and the men likewise gave up natural relations with women and were consumed with passion for one another, men committing shameless acts with men and receiving in their own persons the due penalty for their error."

Father Nicholas, you state that our Church is archaic and have doubts that the Church is ready for whatever the twenty-first century may bring. The twenty-first century brought "September 11." And our Church and Her leader, Archbishop Demetrios, quickly and effectively, through prayer, visitations and spiritual support of the brave men and women who struggled to save lives, deserved and received much merited praise for his leadership during this frightful tragedy. He made Orthodox proud by his prayers, tears and manifest love at the site of that catastrophe. Much of our nation witnessed the deep concern of a Church many may never before have realized existed.

In analyzing the improvements our Church may need, we must not forget that the Greek Orthodox Church is among the youngest of the Orthodox Christian Churches in the United States. Courageous Russian monks and saints crossed the Bering Strait in very small boats to bring Holy Orthodoxy to America in the eighteenth century. From Alaska they entered the regions that were to become the states of Washington, Oregon and California, and established the first Orthodox Churches in North America. By contrast, the first Greek Orthodox Church was established in Galveston, Texas in 1862. In 1864 a second Greek community began in New Orleans, and by 1922, there were 141 Greek Orthodox Church that also served Russians, Slavs and Syrians; however, it was not until 1921 that a Greek Orthodox Archdiocese was established in New York City.

We are indeed a young Church. And in terms of other nations, the USA is a young country. In concluding, may I offer another view of the Orthodox Church in the year 2003. More churches now use English in the Liturgy. More missionary teams from the Orthodox Christian Mission Center are leaving for different countries. Our Archbishop of the Greek Orthodox Archdiocese in New York City is respected and loved for his dedication to Christ, his compassion, his theological wisdom, and for his strong yet humble demeanor. Not a few converts are finding their way into the Orthodox church. Medical supplies and equipment have been sent to Serbia from Orthodox Christian Churches. Miraculously, many new Orthodox Christian monasteries have been established in villages, towns, cities, mountainsides and deserts across America. The past 3 decades have witnessed a tidal wave of Orthodox publications translated into English from Greek, Russian and Serbian authors such as St. Theophan the Recluse, Bishop Vladimirovich, and his friend Justin Popovich, the Metropolitan Augustine Kantiotes of Florina, the biographies of contemporary Elders: Paisios of Mount Athos, Porphyrios of Oropos, Elder George of Drama. And in our lifetimes, we have the biography of Father Arseny, priest of the Soviet prison camps, Bishop Luke the Physician and other numerous to cite here. Are these advances consistent with a moribund Church, or one that gives new hope to our country, and indeed to a world which seems to be playing the overture to the Apocalypse?

RESPONSE TO FR. NICHOLAS GRAFF

FR. GEORGE MORELLI

Fr. Nicholas Graff has touched on the seemingly complex contradiction of the Church as the Body of Christ. She is both transcendent (glorious and resurrected) and existentially wounded, with the concomitant pain and suffering of the broken and fragmented. Inasmuch as we have to work out our own salvation in this existential world, it behooves us to heal our wounds. With Christ as the model, the "One and True Healer of souls and bodies." Fr. Nicholas suggests three modes of healing: mutuality, fidelity and trust.

Examination of his conception of each of these "environs," as he calls them, indicate how central they are to "Orthodoxy." Mutuality defined as "shared standards and language," fidelity defined by our "commitment to the dogma, holy traditions, and canons of the Holy Church" and trust, described as a "ballet involving complex moves including vulnerability."

These environs and the issues they raise require not a paper but an entire program. Fr. Nicholas, in discussing mutuality, questions whether the antiquated cultural typologies and forms of Orthodoxy are able to find a compatible language (to foster healing) in contemporary America. This excellent question cries out for developing an answer. Such an answer, however, would be hard fought. First there would have to be agreement on which cultural typologies and forms of Orthodoxy are "antiquated" versus essential; then only could we move on to discussion of what is essential Orthodox con-

255

temporary American language. This alone might be a theme for a Conference and surely a major issue for some future pan-Orthodox ecumenical council.

A similar perspective would have to be addressed when examining fidelity. Our clear lines are indeed non-negotiable. The relation between these clear lines and existential issues that make up the contemporary world is where problems ensue. For example, clearly the Orthodox Church condemns abortion as intrinsically wrong. Life begins at conception. This is basic incarnational theology. Now let's take an issue I discussed at length with Fr. John Breck on several occasions. Fr. John raised the question that the moment of conception may not be as clear-cut as previously thought. In the case of twins, for example, a single fertilized egg begins a splitting process (one, two, four, eight, etc). According to the traditional view, this would be a single human person. However, up to several hours later the single ball of cells that make up this person (in cases of twin development) itself splits in two, each of which continues development into two individual persons. Although conception of a single person occurred at fertilization, "individuation" can occur later in time.

This type of unexpected finding challenges us to the arduous task of incorporating this information into Orthodox theology and its ethical and moral consequences. Fr. Nicholas invites us to quite a challenge. The issues he suggests, of "misogyny, sexism, racism, elitism, anti-Semitism, homophobia, etc." are equally complex. I believe along with Fr. Nicholas that, as Christians anointed by the Holy Spirit at our baptism, we are required to take on this task.

Trust, states Fr. Nicholas, is equally important. He views it as the greatest value necessary for healing and indicates that one must first become vulnerable in order to trust. Trust and vulnerability are the most psychological of environs fostering the healing of the relational heart of the community. One challenge for Orthodoxy will be to relate theological moral issues such as free will with psychobiological determination. It behooves us at this point to find out what scientific research psychology suggests about these processes. Psychological researchers have focused both on the developmental basis of trust and the fostering of trust in later life. To cite one example, Malatesta and Wilson (1988), based on discrete-emotions analysis of attachment, have suggested avoidant behavior revolves around a fear/anger axis. The efficacy of cognitive-behavioral interventions in treating fear (anxiety) and anger have been well-established (O'Leary and Wilson, 1987). Interventions from cognitive restructuring to gradu-ated exposure have been used in such treatment. Thus the healing ministry in the contemporary church has this tool, used in mutuality and with fidelity to foster the relational heart of the community. I do caution, however, that scien-tific psychology should not be trivialized by pop psychology or psychology that is actually armchair philosophy. Some time ago, Bandura (1969) warned clinicians and researchers "Theoretical models of dubious validity (e.g. Adler, Freud, Jung, Rogers) persist largely because they are not stated in refutable form … psychodynamic explanations in terms of symptom-underlying disorder become superfluous." The in-tegrity of Christ's healing ministry, therefore, should not be contaminated by such approaches. Let us use, as Fr. Nicholas so aptly states, true mutuality, true faith and my caveat of true psychology in the spirit of St. Paul's letter to the Philippians (4:8): "Finally, brethren, whatever is true, whatever is honor-able, whatever is just, whatever is pure, whatever is lovely, whatever is gracious, if there is any excellence, if there is anything worthy of praise, think about these things."

Inasmuch as the questions raised by Fr. Nicholas cut to the core of the Orthodox faith in terms of how it is to be prac-ticed in the modern world, it behooves all to heed his warn-ing that we should be quick to question and slow to answer. Sincere, Spirit-inspired questioning can lead us to maintain the faith given to us by Christ and avoid contamination of our faith and practice by secularist and 'politically-correct' misconceptions. Indeed this is the challenge.

References

Albert Bandura, *Principles of Behavior Modification*, (New York: Holt, Rinehart and Winston, 1969).

Nicholas Graff, *Ekklesia: Fostering the Relational Heart of the Community.* (Paper presented at the meeting of the Orthodox Christian Association of Medicine, Psychology and Religion, Brookline, MA, November, 2003).

C. Z. Malatesta and A. Wilson, "Emotion/cognition interaction in personality development: A discrete emotions, functionalist analysis." (*British Journal of Social Psychology,* 27, 19988), pp. 91-112.

K. Daniel O'Leary and G. T. Wilson, *Behavior Therapy: Application and Outcome* (Englewood Cliffs, NJ: Holt, Rinehart and Winston, 1987).

CONTRIBUTORS

Stephen Muse, PhD, M.Div., directs the Pastoral Counselor Training program at the Pastoral Institute, Inc. in Columbus, Georgia. He is adjunct faculty with Columbus State University and helps train military chaplains in pastoral counseling and marriage and family therapy. Dr. Muse served as editor of *The Pastoral Forum* from 1993-2000 and is past president of OCAMPR. Previous books include *Beside Still Waters: Resources for Shepherds in the Market Place* (Smyth & Helwys, 2000).

John Demakis, MD served as the National Director of the VA's Health Services Research and Development Service and is currently Professor of medicine at the Loyola University Stritch School of medicine of Chicago.

Peter Bistolarides, MD, MDiv (cand.), is a board certified general surgeon and recently ordained to the deaconate in the G.O. Church. Prior to beginning his theological studies, he was corporate medical director for a national health services company based in Ann Arbor, Michigan.

Paul Kymissis, MD, is Clinical Professor of Psychiatry, Behavioral Sciences and Pediatrics at New York Medical College and Chief of Psychiatry at Children's Village.

Jeff Rediger, MD, M.Div. is medical director at McLean Hospital Southeast, and an instructor in the Department of Psychiatry at Harvard Medical School.

Fr. Stephen Plumlee, PhD, MDiv, is a Orthodox priest attached to the Church of the Holy Spirit in Venice, Florida. He maintains a full-time practice in psychoanalytic psychotherapy with a specialty in Imago couples therapy.

Demetra Velisarios Jaquet, M.Div. (D.Min cand) is a Pastoral Counselor and Spiritual Director at Pastoral Counseling for Denver, Denver, Colorado and Adjunct Faculty in Religious Studies at Regis University, School for Professional Studies, Denver.

Fr. George Morelli, PhD is Assistant Pastor of St. George's Antiochian Church, San Diego and Director of Holy Cross Center for Cognitive Therapy. He has taught at St. Vladimir's Seminary, Rutgers University and Kean University (NJ).

Jamie Moran, PhD is a psychotherapist and senior lecturer in counseling and psychology at Roehampton Institute, London. He was a psychotherapist in private practice and trainer at Regents College psychotherapy training institute. Dr. Moran is a sub chief in the Lakota Cante Tenze [Brave Hearts] warrior society.

John N. H. Perkins, BD. is a Jungian analyst in private practice and author of *The Forbidden Self: Symbolic Incest and the Journey Within* (Shambhala, 1993).

Philip Mamalakis, PhD. is Assistant Professor of Pastoral Care at Holy Cross Greek Orthodox School of Theology and a marriage and family therapist.

Fr. Niko Graff, D.Min. is Pastor of Saint John the Divine Greek Orthodox Church in Jacksonville, Florida and Executive Director of Saint Photios National Shrine, Saint Augustine, Florida. He currently serves as President of OCAMPR.

George Christakis, MD, MPH, MS (Nutrition) has served on several faculty and consulted internationally for the World Health Organization. He is currently Medical Director for Weight Watchers International and a consultant in epidemiology with Continental Insurance Company.

Made in the USA